WORKING CAPITAL
management

WORKING CAPITAL management

KRISH RANGARAJAN
ANIL MISRA

EXCEL BOOKS

ISBN: 81-7446-453-0

First Edition: New Delhi, 2005
Reprint: 2010, 2015

EXCEL BOOKS
Delhi: E-77, South Ext., Part-I, Delhi-110049
Noida: B-25/5&6, Sector-59, Noida-201301

+91-8130438484, +91-120-4974400

info@excelbooks.com/eb@excelbooks.com
internationalalliance@excelbooks.com

www.excelbooks.com

SALES OFFICES
2/8, Ansari Road, Darya Ganj, New Delhi-110 002
No. 10, Kalidasa Marg, Gandhi Nagar, Bengaluru-560 009
27/31 Joe Slovo (Field) Street, Durban, 4000, KZN, South Africa

Published by **Dr Rajan Chopra** for **Excel Books**, B-25/5&6, Sector-59, Noida-201 301
and printed by him at Excel Printers Pvt. Ltd., Plot No. 317, Sector-7, Phase-II, IMT Manesar, Gurgaon-122 050

Dedicated to the holy spirit of
my Mother
&
my family,
loving BB and PATs

Contents

Preface

This book grew out of our passion for the subject, which with mixes our experiences in the classroom teaching of Working Capital Management. Working Capital, though such a wonderful concept, was mostly treated in a stereotyped manner by a lot of books on financial management. Thus was born the idea of bringing out a specific book to focus on the nuances of Working Capital.

Management of Working Capital has become crucial for every firm, given the increasing pressure on the operating cycles. This book is an attempt to put forth the concepts in a practical, lucid, simple and succinct manner. It has dealt with the topic of working Capital Finance extensively, a topic that involves the issue of guidelines from the Reserve Bank of India from time to time.

The book is divided into six chapters which extensively deal with the elements of Working Capital Management. It will be more useful for Post Graduate courses like M.Com, MBA, MFM, MFA, etc., and also to those pursuing different professional courses like CA, ICWA, CFA etc. Practising Managers may also refer to this book for conceptual clarity. We will be incorporating case studies in our upcoming new edition, shortly.

It would have been impossible to prepare this book without aid and support from my young but adequately exposed co-author, Dr. Anil Misra. The book would not have come about without the constant motivation from my senior faculty colleague, Dr. Ravi Shanker, Chairperson, Graduate Studies Division at IIFT, to whom I'm highly indebted. I'm grateful to my *Guru*, Dr. P K Mishra, who brought me to academics and enriched in his *Gurukul*.

I'm thankful to our Director, Mr. Prabir Sengupta, IAS (Retd), who inculcated the urge to always do something better. I would like to place my appreciation on record for the immense support of Dr. (Mrs) Satinder Bhatia, Chairperson Research, Dr. (Mrs.) Vijaya Katti, Chairperson MDP, all my colleagues at IIFT and the other faculty fraternity with whom I am associated with and also would like to thank Mrs. Saroj Bala for secretarial support, and Mr. Anurag Jain, Publisher of Excel Books, and his team.

I hope to receive constructive suggestions for incorporation in the next edition of this book. Finally,. I record my gratitude to my family members and friends for their support extended to me. I'm highly indebted to all my students whom I have taught, particularly for stimulating and sharpening my thinking on the subject.

KRISH RANGARAJAN

About the Authors

Dr. Krish Rangarajan is Professor at IIFT. He holds Masters in Commerce with Management Specialisation and remained first class through out his academic career. He holds University Rank for the top performance in his Masters Degree. He has completed doctoral degree and has many research papers and articles to his credit. He has guided six doctoral theses and actively involved in the research of Global business Strategy. He is an Accredited Management Teacher (AMT) conferred by All India Management Association and member of several professional bodies including AIMM (Australia). His expertise includes Business Strategy and Strategic Planning. His areas of interest are Organizational Restructuring, Corporate and Business Level Strategies and Cluster Development. He has written more than ten cases which were published and also carried out case analysis of various MNCs.

He has almost two decades of experience in teaching and consultancy which includes four years of industry experience at middle level with MNC, three years in overseas university and one & a half decade of post graduate teaching. He has widely traveled including UK, US and Asia Pacific on various academic assignments. He has lectured on Strategic Issues of the industry on various national and international forums and Associations like SIMA, KNITMA, Textile Committee and Management Development Forum. He has been faculty for more than 10 MDPs conducted for the textiles and clothing sector. He has conducted a research study entitled, "Implications of EU and US GSP Rules of Origin on the Exports of Indian Textiles and Clothing Industry" for the Commonwealth Secretariat, UK. He has coordinated with SMEs at various levels on strategic issues. He also writes regularly on issues regarding the sector on National Dailies and Refreed Journals. He has conducted several seminars/workshops in Textile Clusters like Tirupur, Coimbatore, Madurai, Noida & Karur. He is also serving as National Expert for UNIDO, Austria for their Innovation in Textiles Industry Project.

Dr. Anil Misra is Assistant Professor, Finance & Accounts, at IIFT. He is an MBA and Ph.D in Finance and carries about 8 years of experience in research and training in the area of finance. His areas of research are corporate finance and corporate valuation. His training interests include total cost management, value creation techniques for shareholders' wealth maximisation besides the basic finance for non finance managers and advanced financial management for working finance executives. He is actively associated with both academics and industry in the area of finance.

CHAPTER I

Introduction to Working Capital Management

Learning Objectives

- ❑ Understand the principles underlying the management of working capital.
- ❑ Evaluate the impact of financing of current assets on the risk return profile of the firm.
- ❑ Decide the appropriate level of working capital using the hedging principle.

Chapter Organization

- The chapter is foundational in nature. It begins with the fundamentals of working capital management.
- Thereafter, the risk return trade off in the financing of working capital requirements has been dealt with elaborately.
- The last section illustrates the efficacy of hedging principle in financial planning.

CHAPTER 1

Introduction to Working Capital Management

Traditionally, working capital has been defined as the firm's investment in current assets. Current assets are comprised of all assets that the firm expects to convert into cash within the year, including cash, marketable securities, accounts receivable and inventories. Managing the firm's working capital, however, has come to mean more than simply managing the firm's investment in current assets. In fact, a more descriptive title for this chapter might be Net Working Capital Management, where net working capital refers to the difference in the firm's current assets and its current liabilities:

Net working capital = current assets – current liabilities

Thus, in managing the firm's net working capital we are concerned with managing the firm's liquidity. This entails considering two related problems:

1. Managing the firm's investment in current assets,
2. Managing the firm's use of short-term or current liabilities.

This chapter provides the basic principles underlying the analysis of both the aforesaid problems. The enunciated principles are then applied in subsequent chapters.

Managing Current Assets

A firm invests in inventories because of the expected benefits derived from holding inventory. Likewise, the firm acquires fixed assets because of the future cash flows those assets are expected to generate. In this chapter, our interest in the firm's investment decisions relates to their effect on the firm's net working capital or liquidity. Other things remaining the same, the greater the firm's investment in current assets, the greater is its liquidity.

As a means of increasing its liquidity, the firm may choose to invest additional funds in cash and/or marketable securities. Such action involves a trade-off, however, since such assets earn little or no return. The firm thus, finds that it can reduce its risk of illiquidity only by reducing its overall return on invested funds and vice-versa.

The Risk Return Trade-off from Investing in Current Assets

The risk-return trade-off involved in managing the firm's liquidity via investing in marketable securities is illustrated in the following example.

Firms A and B are identical in every respect but one: Firm B has invested Rs 10,000 in marketable securities, which has been financed with "common Equity"

That is, the firm sold shares of common stock and raised Rs 10,000. The balance sheets and net incomes of the two firms are shown in Table 1.1. Note that firm A has a current ratio of 2.5 (reflecting net working capital of Rs 30,000) and earns a 10 per cent return on its total assets, while firm

B, with its larger investment in marketable securities, has a current ratio of 3 and has net working capital of Rs 40,000. Since the marketable securities earn a return of only 6 per cent before taxes (3 per cent after taxes with a 50 per cent tax rate), firm B earns only 9.6 per cent on its total investment. Thus, investing in current assets, particularly in marketable securities, does have a favourable effect on the firm's liquidity, but also has an unfavourable effect on the rate of return it earned on invested funds. The risk-return trade-off involved in holding more cash and marketable securities is one of added liquidity versus reduced profitability.

Table 1.1: The effects of investing in Current Assets on liquidity and profitability

Balance Sheets

	Firm A	Firm B
Cash	Rs 1,000	Rs 1,000
Marketable Securities		10,000
Accounts receivable	19,000	19,000
Inventories	30,000	30,000
Current assets	Rs 50,000	Rs 60,000
Net fixed assets	100,000	100,000
Total	Rs 150,000	Rs 160,000
Current liabilities	Rs 20,000	Rs 20,000
Long-term debt	30,000	30,000
Common equity	100,000	110,000
Total	Rs 150,000	Rs 160,000
Net income	Rs 15,000	Rs 15,300
Current ratio (Current assets / current liabilities)	$\frac{\text{Rs } 50{,}000}{\text{Rs } 20{,}000} = 2.5$ times	$\frac{\text{Rs } 60{,}000}{\text{Rs } 20{,}000} = 3$ times
Net working capital (current assets-current liabilities)	Rs 30,000	Rs 40,000
Return on total assets (Net income/total assets)	$\frac{\text{Rs}15{,}000}{\text{Rs}150{,}000} = 10\%$ -	$\frac{\text{Rs}15{,}300}{\text{Rs}160{,}000} = 9.6\%$

During the year, firm B held Rs 10,000 in marketable securities with a 6 per cent return or Rs 600 for the year. After paying taxes at a rate of 50 per cent, the firm earned Rs 300 return on this investment.

Managing the Firm's Current Liabilities

The second and final determinant of the firm's networking capital relates to its use of current versus long-term debt. Here too, the firm faces a risk-return trade-off. Other things remaining the same, the greater its reliance upon short-term debt or current liabilities in financing its asset investments, the lower will be its liquidity. On the other hand, the use of current liabilities offers some very real advantages to the user, in that they can be less costly than long-term financing and they provide the firm with a flexible means of financing its fluctuating needs for assets. To demonstrate the risk-return associated with the use of current liabilities as a source of financing, we now discuss the advantages and disadvantages associated with their use. This shall be followed by an example to demonstrate the risk-return trade-off associated with the use of current versus long-term liabilities.

Advantages of Current Liabilities

Flexibility

Current liabilities offer the firm a flexible source of financing. They can be used to match the timing of a firm's needs for short-term financing. If for example, a firm needs funds for a three-month period during each year to finance a seasonal expansion in inventories, then a three-month loan can provide substantial cost savings over a long-term loan (even if the interest rate on short-term financing should be higher). This results from the fact that the use of long-term debt in this situation involves borrowing for the entire year rather than for the three-month period when the funds are needed; this increases the level of interest cost the firm has to bear. This brings us to the second advantage, generally associated with the use of short-term financing.

Interest Cost

In general, interest rates on short-term debt are lower than on long-term debt for a given borrower. This relationship is usually referred to as the term structure of interest rates. For a given firm, the term structure might appear as follows:

LOAN MATURITY	INTEREST RATE
3 months	9.00%
6 months	9.00%
1 year	9.80%
3 years	10.20%
5 years	10.90%
10 years	11.40%
30 years	12.80%

Note that this term structure reflects the rates of interest applicable to a given borrower at a particular point in time; thus, it would not describe the rates of interest available to another borrower or even those applicable to the same borrower at a different point in time.

Disadvantages of Current Liabilities

The use of current liabilities or short-term debt as opposed to long-term debt subjects the firm to a greater risk of illiquidity. That is, short-term debt due to its very nature must be repaid or rolled over more often, and so it enhances the possibility that the firm's financial condition might deteriorate to a point where the needed funds might not be available.

A second disadvantage of short-term debt is the uncertainty of interest costs from year to year. For example, where a firm borrows during a six-month period each year to finance a seasonal expansion in current assets, it might incur a different rate of interest each year. This rate reflects the current rate of interest at the time of the loan, as well as the lender's perception of the firm's riskiness. If long-term debt were used, then the interest cost would be known for the entire period of the loan agreement.

The Risk Return Trade-off from Using Current Liabilities

Consider the risk-return characteristics of firm X and Y, whose balance sheets and income statements are given in Table 1.2. Both firms had the same seasonal needs for financing throughout the past year. In December, they each required Rs 40,000 to finance a seasonal expansion in accounts receivable. In addition, during the four-month period beginning with August and extending through November both firms needed Rs 20,000 to support a seasonal build up in inventories. Firm X financed its seasonal financing requirements using Rs 40,000 in long-term debt carrying an annual interest rate of 10 per cent. Firm Y, on the other hand, satisfied its seasonal financing needs using short-term borrowing on which it paid 9 per cent interest. Since firm Y borrowed only when it needed the funds and did so at the lower rate of interest on short-term debt, its interest expense for the year was only Rs 900, whereas firm X incurred Rs 4000 in annual interest expense.

The end result of the two firms' financing policies is evidenced in their current ratio, net working capital and return on total assets which appear at the bottom of Table 1.2. Firm X, using long-term rather than short-term debt, has a current ratio of 3 times and Rs 40,000 in net working capital, whereas firm Y's current ratio is only one, which represents zero net working capital. However, owing to its lower interest on account of short term financing, the return on total assets of firm Y is 10.8%, which is higher than 10% return for firm X.

The dangers of such a policy are readily apparent in the experiment of firms that have been forced into bankruptcy. Nitel, a telecom venture of PTI and Govt. of M.P. was unable to meet its current obligations and went into technical insolvency before it was taken over by the RPG Group in the early 1990s. Interest expense calculations are found in the footnotes to Table 1.2.

Table 1.2

Balance Sheets

	Firm X	Firm Y
Current assets	Rs 60,000	Rs 60,000
Net Fixed assets	140,000	140,000
Total	Rs 200,000	Rs 200,000
Accounts payable	Rs 20,000	Rs 20,000
Notes payable	—	40,000
Current liabilities	Rs 20,000	Rs 60,000
Long-term debt	40,000	—
Common equity	140,000	140,000
Total	Rs 200,000	Rs 200,000

Income Statements

Net operating income	Rs 44,000	Rs 44,000
Less: Interest expenses	4,000	900
Earnings before taxes	40,000	43,100
Less: Taxes (50%)	20,000	21,550
Net income	Rs 20,000	Rs 21,550

$$\text{Current ratio } \frac{\text{current assets}}{\text{current liabilities}} \quad \frac{\text{Rs } 60{,}000}{\text{Rs } 20{,}000} = 3 \text{ times}, \quad \frac{\text{Rs } 60{,}000}{\text{Rs } 60{,}000} = 1 \text{ time}$$

Net working capital Rs 40,000 Rs 0

[Current assets-Current Liabilities]

$$\text{Return on total assets } \frac{\text{net income}}{\text{total assets}} \quad \frac{\text{Rs } 20{,}000}{\text{Rs } 200{,}000} = 10\%, \quad \frac{\text{Rs } 21{,}550}{\text{Rs } 200{,}000} = 10.8\%$$

Firm X paid interest during the entire year on Rs 40,000 in long-term debt at a rate of 10 per cent. Its interest expense for the year was 10% × Rs 40,000 = Rs 4,000.

Firm Y paid interest on Rs 40,000 for one month and on Rs 20,000 for four months at 9 per cent interest during the year. Thus firm Y's interest expense for the year equals Rs 40,000 × .09 × 4/12, or Rs 300 + Rs 600 = Rs 900.

Thus, a firm can reduce its risk of liquidity through the use of long-term debt at the expense of a reduction of its return on invested funds. Once again we see that the risk-return trade-off involves an increased risk of illiquidity versus increased profitability.

Appropriate Level of Working Capital

Introduction to Working Capital Management

Managing the firm's net working capital position (that is, its liquidity) has been shown to involve simultaneous and interrelated decisions regarding the firm's investment in current assets and its use of current liabilities. Fortunately, a guiding principle exists that can be used as a benchmark for the firm's working capital policies: this is the hedging principle, or principle of self-liquidating debt. This principle is a guide to the maintenance of a level of liquidity sufficient for the firm to meet its maturing obligations on time.

Hedging Principle

The hedging principle involves matching the cash flow generating characteristics of an asset with the maturity of the source of financing used to finance its acquisition. For example, a seasonal expansion in inventories, according to the hedging principle, should be financed with a short-term loan or current liability. The rationale underlying the rule is straightforward: Funds are needed for a limited period of time, and when that time has passed, the cash needed to repay the loan will be generated by the sale of the extra inventory items. Obtaining the needed funds from a long-term source (longer than one year) would mean that the firm would still have the funds after the inventories (they helped finance) had been sold. In this case the firm would have "excess" liquidity, which they either hold in cash or invest in low-yielding marketable securities until the seasonal increase in inventories occurs again and the funds are needed. This would result in an overall lowering of firm's profits, as we saw earlier in the example presented in Table 1.2.

Consider a second example in which a firm purchases a new conveyor belt system, which is expected to produce cash savings to the firm by eliminating the need for two labourers and, consequently, their salaries. This amounts to an annual savings of Rs 14,000. While the conveyor belt costs Rs 1,50,000 to install and will last 20 years, if the firm chooses this asset with a one-year note, then it will not be able to repay the loan from the cash flow generated by the asset. Hence, in accordance with the hedging principle, the firm should finance the asset with a source of financing that more nearly matches the expected life and cash flow generating characteristics of the asset. In this case a 15 to 20-year loan would be more appropriate than a one-year loan.

Permanent and Temporary Assets

The notion of maturity matching in the hedging principle can be most easily understood when we think in terms of the distinction between permanent and temporary investments in assets as opposed to the more traditional fixed and current asset categories. A permanent investment in an asset is one that the firm expects to hold for a period longer than one year. Note that we are referring to the period of time the firm plans to hold an investment and not the useful life of the asset. For example, permanent investments are made in the firm's minimum level of current assets, as in its fixed assets. Temporary asset investments, on the other hand, are comprised of current assets that will be liquidated, and not replaced, within the current year. Thus, some part of the firm's current assets is permanent and the remainder is temporary. For example, seasonal increase in the level of inventories is a temporary investment, as the build-up in inventories will be eliminated when it is no longer needed, e.g., retail stocks to cater to seasonal upsurge in demand, as seen during Diwali or Christmas.

Spontaneous, Temporary, and Permanent Sources of Financing

Since total assets must always equal the sum of spontaneous, temporary, and permanent sources of financing, the hedging provides the financial manager with the basis for determining the sources of financing to use at any point in time.

Now, what constitutes a temporary, permanent, and spontaneous source of financing? Temporary sources of financing consist of current liabilities. Specifically, short-term notes payable constitute the most common example of a temporary source of financing. Examples of notes payable include unsecured bank loans such as temporary clean over drafts, commercial paper, and loans secured by accounts receivable and inventories. Permanent sources of financing include intermediate term loans, long-term debt, preferred stock, and common equity.

Spontaneous sources of financing consist of trade credit and other accounts payable that arise spontaneously in the firm's day-to-day operations. For example, as the firm acquires materials for its inventories, trade credit is often made available spontaneously or on demand from the firm's suppliers. Trade credit appears on the firm's balance sheet as accounts payable, and the size of the accounts payable balance varies directly with the firm's purchases of inventory items. In turn, inventory purchases are related to the firm's anticipated sales. Thus, a part of the financing needed by the firm is spontaneously provided in the form of trade credit.

In addition to trade credit, wages and salaries payable, accrued interest, and accrued taxes also provide the firm with valuable sources of spontaneous financing. These expenses accrue throughout the period until they are paid. For example, if a firm with a wage expense of Rs 10,000 a week pays its employees monthly, then its employees effectively provide financing equal Rs 10,000 by the first week following payday Rs 20,000 by the end of the second week, and so forth. Since these expenses generally arise in direct conjunction with the firm's ongoing operations, they too are referred to as spontaneous.

Study Questions

1. Define and contrast the terms 'working capital' and 'net working capital'.

2. Discuss the risk-return relationship involved in the firm's asset investment decisions as it pertains to working capital management.

3. What advantages and disadvantages are generally associated with the use of short-term debt? Discuss.

4. Explain what is meant by the statement "The use of current liabilities as opposed to long-term debt subjects the firm to a greater risk of illiquidity."

5. Define the hedging principle. How can this principle be used in the management of working capital?

   a. Permanent asset investments

   b. Temporary asset investments

   c. Permanent source of financing

   d. Temporary source of financing

   e. Spontaneous source of financing

Self-Test Problems

ST-1. (Using Marketable Securities to increase Liquidity). The balance sheet for the Simplex Mfg. Co. is presented below for the year ended December 31, 1995:

SIMPLEX MFG. CO. Balance Sheet December 31, 1995

Cash	Rs 10,000		
Accounts receivable	50,000		
Inventories	40,000		
Total current assets		Rs 100,000	
Net fixed assets		Rs 100,000	
Total			Rs 200,000
Current liabilities		Rs 60,000	
Long-term liabilities		Rs 40,000	
Common equity		Rs 100,000	
Total			Rs 200,000

During 1995, the firm earned net income after taxes of Rs 20,000 based on net sales of Rs 400,000.

a. Calculate Simplex's current ratio, net working capital position, and return on total assets ratio (net income/total assets) using the above information.

b. The vice-president for finance at Simplex is considering a plan for enhancing the firm's liquidity. The plan involves raising Rs 20,000 in common equity and investing in marketable securities that will earn 8 per cent before taxes and 4.8 per cent after taxes. Calculate Simplex's current ratio, net working capital, and return on total asset ratio after the plan has been implemented, (Hint: net income will now become Rs 20,000 plus .048 times Rs 20,000, or Rs 20,960).

c. Will the plan proposed in part (b) enhance the firm's liquidity? Explain.

d. What effect does the plan proposed in (b) above have on the firm's profitability? Explain.

ST-2. (Using Long-Term Debt to Increase Liquidity). On April 30, 1998, the Jamax Sales Company had the following balance sheet and income statement for the year just ended:

JAMAX SALES COMPANY Balance Sheet March 31, 2004

Cash	Rs 10,000		
Accounts receivable	50,000		
Inventories	40,000		
Total current assets		Rs 100,000	
Net fixed assets		Rs 100,000	
Total			Rs 200,000
Current liabilities		Rs 60,000	
Long-term liabilities		Rs 40,000	
Common equity		Rs 100,000	
Total			Rs 200,000

Balance sheet contd.

Partial Income Statement for the year ended March 31, 2004

Net operating income	Rs 72,800
Less: Interest expense	12,800
Earnings before taxes	Rs 60,000
Less: Taxes (50%)	30,000
Net income	Rs 30,000

- The short-term notes are outstanding during the latter half of the firm's fiscal year in response to the firm's seasonal need for funds.

- Total interest expense for the year consists of 14 per cent interest on the firm's Rs 40,000 note for a six-month period (1.4 × Rs 40,000 × ½), plus 10 per cent of the firm's Rs 100,000 long-term note for a full year (.10 × Rs 100,000), or Rs 10,000. Thus total interest expense for the year is Rs 2800 plus Rs 10,000 or Rs 12,800.

a. Calculate JAMAX's current ratio, net working capital, and return on total assets.

b. The financial controller of JAMAX was recently advised by the firm's investment banks that its current ratio was considered below par. In fact, a current ratio of 2.00 was considered to be a sign of a healthy liquidity position. In response to this news, the financial controller devised a plan wherein the firm would issue Rs 40,000 in 13 per cent long-term debt and pay off its short-term notes payable. This long-term note would be outstanding all year long, and when the funds were not needed to finance the firm's seasonal asset needs, they would be invested in marketable securities earning 8 per cent before taxes. If the plan had been in effect last year, other things being the same, what would have been the firm's current ratio, net working capital, and return on total assets ratio? (Hint: The firm's net income with the change would have been Rs 29,600.)

c. Did JAMAX's liquidity rise to the desired level (based on the desired current ratio of 2.0)?

d. How was the firm's profitability in relation to total investment affected by the change in financial policy?

Study Problems

1. *(Managing Firm's Liquidity)* On September 30, 2000, the balance sheet and income statement for Lifelong Mfg. Company appeared as follows:

LIFELONG MFG. COMPANY Balance Sheet September 30, 2000

Current assets	Rs 500,000
Net fixed assets	500,000
Total	Rs 1,000,000
Accounts payable	100,000
Notes payable (17%)	400,000
Total	Rs 500,000

LIFELONG MFG. COMPANY Balance Sheet September 30, 2000 (contd.)

Long-term debt (12%)	100,000
Common equity	400,000
Total	Rs 1,000,000

- Short-term notes are used to finance a three-month seasonal expansion in Lifelong's assets needs. This period is the same for every year and extends from July through September with the note due on October 1.

LIFELONG MFG. COMPANY Income Statement for the year ended September 30, 2000

Net operating income	Rs 195,666
Less: interest expense	(29,000)
Earnings before taxes	166,666
Less: Taxes (40%)	(66,666)
Net income	Rs 100,000

Interest expense was calculated as follows:

Notes payable (.17 × Rs 400,000 × ¼ year)	Rs 17,000
Long-term debt (.12 × Rs 100,000 × 1 year)	12,000
	Rs 29,000

a. Calculate the current ratio, net working capital, return on total assets, and return on common equity ratio for Lifelong.

b. Assume that you have just been hired as vice-president, finance of the firm. One of your first duties is to assess the firm's liquidity position. Based upon your analysis, you plan to issue Rs 400,000 in common stock and use the proceeds to retire the firm's notes payable. Recalculate the ratios from part (a) above and assess the change in the firm's liquidity.

c. Given your actions in part (b) above, assume now that in the future you will finance your three-month seasonal need for Rs 400,000 due to increased inventories and receivables. In addition, you estimate that during the nine-month period in which you do not need the funds, they can be invested in marketable securities to earn a rate of 10 per cent. Recalculate the financial ratios from part (a) for 2001 where all revenues and non-finance expenses are expected to be the same as in 2000. Analyse the results of your plan.

2. *(Managing Firm's Liquidity)* Re-analyse part (c) of problem 1 assuming that a three-month short-term note is used as opposed to the bonds. This carries a rate of 15 per cent per annum.

3. *(The Hedging Principle)* Kerlosker & Co. estimates that its current assets are about 25 per cent of sales. The firm's current balance sheet is presented below:

Kerlosker & Co. Balance Sheet December 31, 2000 (crores of Rupees.)

Current assets	Rs 2.0	Trade credit and	
Fixed assets	2.8	Accounts payable	Rs .8
		Long-term debt	1.0
Total	Rs 4.8	Common equity	3.0
		Total	Rs 4.8

Kerlosker & Co. pays out all of its net income in cash dividends to its stockholders. Trade credits and accounts payable equal 10 per cent of the firm's sales.

a. Based on the following five-year sales forecast, prepare five end-of-year pro forma balance sheets that indicate "additional financing needed" for each year as a balancing account. Fixed assets are expected to increase by Rs 0.2 crore each year.

Year	Predicted sales (Rs In crore)
2001	10
2002	11
2003	13
2004	14
2005	15

b. Develop a financing plan for Kerlosker & Co. using your answer to part (a) above that is consistent with the following goals:

1. A minimum current ratio of 2.0 and a maximum of 3.0.

2. A debt to total assets ratio of 35-45 per cent. You may issue new common stock to raise equity funds.

Self-Test Solutions

1.a. Current Ratio $= \dfrac{\text{Current Assets}}{\text{Current Liabilities}}$

$$= \frac{\text{Rs } 100{,}000}{\text{Rs } 60{,}000} = 1.67$$

Net working capital = Current assets – Current Liabilities

= Rs 100,000 – Rs 60,000 = Rs 40,000

Return on Total Assets $= \dfrac{\text{Net Income}}{\text{Total Assets}}$

$$= \frac{\text{Rs } 20{,}000}{\text{Rs } 200{,}000} = 10\%$$

b. Current Ratio $= \dfrac{\text{Rs } 120{,}000}{\text{Rs } 60{,}000} = 2$

Net Working Capital = Rs 120,000 – Rs 60,000 = Rs 60,000

Return on Total Assets $= \dfrac{\text{Rs } 20{,}960}{\text{Rs } 220{,}000} = 9.52\%$

c. Yes, the firm's liquidity position as measured by the current ratio and the amount of net working capital has definitely improved. However, as we see in the answer to part (b), the firm's profitability has been adversely affected.

d. Simplex's return on total assets declined from 10 to 9.52 per cent as a result of the new financing plan. This occurred because it was earning 10 per cent after tax on its Rs 200,000 investment and it invested Rs 20,000 in marketable securities earning only 4.8 per cent after taxes. The result was a decline in firm's profitability in relation to assets.

2.a. Return on Total Assets $= \dfrac{\text{Net Income}}{\text{Total Assets}}$

$$= \frac{\text{Rs } 30{,}000}{\text{Rs } 300{,}000} = 10\%$$

b. Current Ratio $= \dfrac{\text{Rs } 100{,}000}{\text{Rs } 30{,}000} = 3.33$

Net Working Capital = Rs 100,000 - Rs 30,000 = Rs 70,000

Return on Total Assets $= \dfrac{\text{Rs } 29{,}600}{\text{Rs } 300{,}000} = 9.87\%$

c. Yes, the current ratio of 3.33 is now well above the 2.0 standard when the funds are needed. Furthermore, if we include Rs 40,000 in marketable securities in current assets, the current ratio rises to 4.67 (Rs 100,000 + Rs 40,000 / Rs 30,000 = 4.67) during those times when the funds are seasonally idle.

d. The firm's profitability declined slightly because the firm used a permanent source of financing to replace a more flexible short-term source. The firm actually saves interest expense through the plan during the six-month period when the funds are needed (13 per cent on long-term funds versus 14 per cent on short-term notes); however, during the six month when the funds are not needed, the firm can only earn a before-tax return of 8 per cent while the funds cost 13 per cent.

In this case, the added liquidity of the plan appears to overshadow the modest loss in expected profitability.

Appendix

A Numerical Illustration of the Hedging Principle

In this appendix, an example problem is analysed wherein all necessary computations are explained in detail. Two factors will become apparent in our analysis: First, the pattern of projected asset needs for a firm will not follow the smooth curves. This more erratic pattern of asset financing needs is more in keeping with realistic financial planning problems. Second, strict adherence to the hedging principle in every planning period will involve careful analysis and foresight.

The hedging principal can be applied to the financial planning problem using the five-step procedure. Note that each step in the procedure is stated both verbally and algebraically. The solution procedure or algorithm presented here is rather rudimentary. More sophisticated solutions to the problem of financial planning are readily available that use various forms of mathematical programming techniques.

The financial planning problem faced by the Simplex Mfg. Co., as presented in Table A-1 is used to demonstrate the application of the hedging principle. Each step involved in applying the hedging strategy is discussed in detail below.

STEP 1: Predicting the firm's needs for current, fixed, and total assets over the planning horizon.

The forecast of these asset categories will involve use of the financial forecasting methodology. The per cent of sales method of forecasting is widely used for this purpose.

STEP 2: Distinguish between the firm's permanent and temporary assets for each period in the planning horizon.

To identify what part of the firm's total assets for a given period are permanent, the analyst must look forward over the planning horizon to determine that quarter in which the firm's total asset needs drop to their lowest level. This minimum level of total assets equals the firm's permanent assets.

SETP 3: Project spontaneous financing for each period within the planning horizon.

SETP 4: Estimate the firm's need for permanent financing. This step can be accomplished by locating those calendar quarters in which temporary asset investments are zero. In these quarters, total assets equal permanent assets. Thus, for these quarters the firm's permanent plus spontaneous financing sources must equal total assets. Since we have already projected total assets in step 1 and spontaneous financing in step 3, we can easily solve the need for permanent sources of financing. Note that this procedure works only for those calendar quarters in which temporary assets and thus temporary sources of financing are zero. For the intervening quarters where temporary financing is non-zero, we simply set permanent financing equal to the level estimated for the most recent past quarter.

STEP 5: Estimating the firm's temporary financing needs for each period in the planning horizon.

Each period's estimate of temporary financing needs is found by subtracting the sum of permanent plus spontaneous financing from total assets (or simply total financing needed).

This completes the development of financial plan which indicates the appropriate use of spontaneous, short-term (temporary), and permanent financing in accordance with the hedging principle. As we have seen, following this principle involves classifying the firm's projected needs for assets into permanent and temporary categories and then matching permanent assets with permanent plus spontaneous sources of financing and temporary assets with temporary financing sources.

A word of caution: The development of a financing plan that adheres strictly to the hedging principle may be more complicated than discussed here. In addition, as we noted the firm may not wish to follow the hedging principle strictly.

A key element in the application of the hedging principle that can greatly complicate the analysis is spontaneous sources of financing. Were it not for this type of financing, it would be a simple matter to match permanent assets and financing sources as well as temporary assets and temporary financing sources. However spontaneous financing sources, which are something of a hybrid in that they are used continuously by the firm but are short-term forms of financing, can end up financing both permanent and temporary asset needs. In the simplex example, the projected level of spontaneous financing followed a simple growth trend that mirrored the firm's overall growth in assets. A somewhat realistic pattern for spontaneous financing might follow the pattern of change in the level of current assets. For example, a principal source of spontaneous financing consists of accounts payable, which vary closely with the firm's inventories. Thus, as the firm's inventories expand temporarily with increased seasonal demand for its product, its accounts payable also expands. Similarly, when inventories contract, accounts payable are extinguished, and this important source of spontaneous financing disappears. Note that spontaneous financing has been used to partially finance a seasonal and temporary need for funds.

Study Problems

1. The projected assets for the Indian Pharma Company are tabulated below. The firm's projected levels of spontaneous financing also are included. Complete the financing plan, using the hedging principle. All figures are in crores of Rupees.

Year	Quarter	(1) Fixed Assets	(2) Current Assets	(3) Total Assets	(4) Permanent Assets	(5) Temporary Assets	(6) Spontaneous Financing	(7) Permanent Financing	(8) Temporary Financing	(9) Total Financing
2000	I	Rs 100	Rs 80	Rs 180	Rs 180	Rs 0	Rs 30			
	II	100	100	200	194	6	30			
	III	102	110	212	194	18	30			
	IV	102	105	207	194	13	30			
2001	I	104	90	194	194	0	30			
	II	104	110	214	210	4	30			
	III	106	115	221	210	11	30			
	IV	106	112	218	210	8	30			
2002	I	108	102	210	210	0	30			

2. The current balance sheet for the Zora Manufacturing Company appears as follows:

Zora Mfg. Co. Balance Sheet March 31, 2001 (Rs in crore)

Current assets	Rs 100	Account payable and	
Fixed assets	100	Accrued expenses	Rs 25
		Notes payable	25
Total	Rs 200	Long-term debt	50
		Common equity	100
		Total	Rs 200

Estimated current and fixed asset investment for the firm are presented for each quarter of the coming 2 years as follows:

(All figures in Rs crore)

Quarter Ended	Fixed assets	Current assets	Total assets	Permanent assets
6/30/99	100	105	205	205
9/30/99	100	106	206	205
12/31/99	101	108	209	205
3/31/00	101	104	205	205
6/30/00	102	105	207	207
9/30/00	102	107	209	209
12/31/00	103	109	212	209
3/31/00	103	106	209	209
6/30/01	104	107	211	211
9/30/01	104	109	213	212
12/31/01	105	110	215	212
3/31/02	105	107	212	212

The firm wants to develop a financial plan that will accommodate its total needs for funds. Furthermore, Zora believes that a minimum issue of Rs 2 crore is required to justify the issuance of long-term debt or common stock.

a. Develop a financing plan for Zora, using the hedging concept, where accounts payable and accrued expenses are expected to equal 25 per cent of current assets and the firm expects quarterly earnings, after taxes, of Rs 1 crore. The firm also plans to pay cash dividends equal to the full Rs 1 crore each quarter.

b. Modify your plan in part (a) above to include compliance with the following objectives for each quarter in the planning period:

   1. A 40-60 per cent debt ratio (total liabilities/total assets).

   2. A current ratio of 1.5 or higher.

c. If short-term debt will cost Zora 6 per cent and long-term debt 8 per cent, what is the total of your plan in part (b) above to Zora over the three-year period? (Hint: Assume that short-term debt financing is retired at the end of each quarter and that any long-term debt issued during the planing period remains outstanding over the entire planning horizon).

Summary

Traditionally, working capital has been defined as the firm's investment in current assets. Managing working capital entails considering two related problems of managing the firm's investment in current assets and managing the firm's use of short-term or current liabilities.

Investing in current assets does have a favourable effect on firm's liquidity, but also has an unfavourable effect on the firm's rate of return earned on invested funds. Financing of current assets also involves a risk-return trade off. Other things remaining the same, the greater the reliance upon short-term debt or current liabilities in financing its asset investments, the lower will be its liquidity. On the other hand, the use of current liabilities offers some very real advantages to the user, in that, they can be less costly than long-term financing and they provide the firm with a flexible means of financing its fluctuating needs for assets.

Managing the firm's net working capital position (that is, its liquidity) has been shown to involve simultaneous and interrelated decisions regarding the firm's investment in current assets and its use of current liabilities. Fortunately, a guiding principle exists that can be used as a benchmark for the firm's working capital policies: this is the hedging principle, or principle of self-liquidating debt. This principle is a guide to the maintenance of a level of liquidity sufficient for the firm to meet its maturing obligations on time.

CHAPTER II

Short-Term Financing

Learning Objectives

- Understand the estimation of the effective cost of short-term credit.
- Develop a detailed understanding of different sources of secured and unsecured short-term credits and the terms and conditions of their availability.
- Evaluate a lease vs buying situation that is faced by a typical firm.

Chapter Organization

- The chapter focuses on the liabilities side of the firm's Balance-Sheet. All the prominent sources of short-term financing available to a firm have been dealt with in detail in the chapter. The chapter begins with the determination of effective cost of credit (short-term), which is frequently used as an input in the subsequent sections of the chapter.
- Thereafter, all possible sources of short-term financing, both secured and unsecured, have been taken up. The terms of their availability and conditions applicable for their access have been discussed in detail.
- The last section illustrates as to how the decision should be made in a situation where a firm is faced with the leasing vs borrowing alternatives.
- This chapter discusses sources of financing. By convention, all sources of financing that must be repaid within one year are considered to be short-term, those that must be repaid in one to five years are intermediate term, and all sources with maturities longer than five years are classified as long-term.

CHAPTER 2

Short-Term Financing

Two major issues involved in managing the firm's use of short-term financing are: (1) How much short-term financing should the firm use? and (2) What specific sources of short-term financing should be selected? The earlier chapter used the hedging principle of working capital management to answer the first of these two questions. Basically, that involved an attempt to match temporary needs for funds with short-term sources of financing and permanent needs with long-term sources.[1] The objective of this chapter will be to answer the second of the above questions:

How should the financial manager select a source of short-term credit?

In general, three basic factors should be considered in selecting a source of short-term credit: (1) the effective cost of credit, (2) the availability of

---

1. Temporary needs for funds arise in response to a temporary need for current assets. These include current assets that the firm does not plan to hold throughout the indefinite future. Permanent needs for funds arise in conjunction with a permanent need for certain assets. These assets consist of fixed assets plus the firm's minimum level of investment in current assets. Thus, when discussing working capital management, we abandoned the current-fixed assets classification in favour of the more useful concept of temporary and permanent assets.

credit in the amount needed and for the period of time when financing is required, and (3) the influence of the use of a particular credit source on the cost and availability of other sources. To begin with, we discuss the problem of estimating the cost of short-term credit followed by the second and third factors listed above.

Estimating the Cost of Short-Term Credit

Approximate Cost-of-Credit Formula

The procedure used in estimating the cost of short-term credit is a very simple one and relies on the basic interest equation.

Interest = principle × rate × time ....(2.1)

Where, interest is the amount of interest on a principal that is borrowed at some annual rate for a fraction of a year (represented by time). For example, a six-month loan for Rs 1000 at 8 per cent interest would require interest payments of Rs 40:

Interest = Rs 1000 × .08 × 1/2 = Rs 40

The problem faced in assessing the cost of a source of short-term financing generally involves estimating the annual effective rate (RATE) where the interest amount, the principal sum, and the time for which financing will be needed are known.

Thus, solving the basic interest equation for RATE produces

$$\text{Rate} = \frac{\text{Interest}}{\text{Principal} \times \text{Time}} \qquad \text{............................(2.2)}$$

Or $$\text{Rate} = \frac{\text{Interest}}{\text{Principal}} \times \frac{1}{\text{Time}}$$

Example: The SKC Corporation plans to borrow Rs 1000 for a 90-day period. At maturity, the firm will repay the principal amount plus Rs 30 interest. The effective annual rate of interest for the loan can be estimated using the RATE equation as follows:

$$\text{Rate} = \frac{\text{Rs } 30}{\text{Rs } 1000} \times \frac{1}{90/360}$$

$$= .03 \times \frac{360}{90} = .12, \text{ or } 12 \text{ per cent}$$

The effective annual cost of funds provided by the loan is therefore 12 per cent.

The Annual Percentage Rate Formula

Compound interest was not considered in the simple RATE calculation. To consider the influence of compounding, we can use the following equation:

$$\text{APR} = (1 + r/m)^m - 1 \qquad \text{.............................(2.3)}$$

Where APR is the annual percentage rate, r is the nominal rate of interest per year (12 per cent in the above example) and m is the number of compounding periods within a year (m = 1/TIME = 1/(90/360) = 4) in the example above. Thus, the effective rate of interest in the example problem, considering compounding, is

$$\text{APR} = (1 + .12 / 4)^4 - 1 = .126, \text{ or } 12.6 \text{ per cent}$$

The effect of compounding is to raise the effective cost of short-term credit. Since the differences between the two methods for periods less than one year are usually small, the simple interest version of RATE discussed above will be used.

Sources of Short-Term Credit

Short-term credit sources can be classified into two basic groups: unsecured and secured. Unsecured loans include all those sources that have as their security only the lender's faith in the ability of the borrower to repay the funds when due. There are three major sources of unsecured short-term credit: trade credit, unsecured bank loans, and commercial paper. Secured loans involve the pledge of specific assets as collateral in the event the borrower defaults in payment of principal or interest. The principal suppliers of secured credit include commercial banks, finance companies, and factors. The primary sources of collateral include accounts receivable and inventories.

Unsecured Sources: Trade Credit

Trade credit provides one of the most flexible sources of financing available to the firm. To arrange for credit, the firm only needs to place an order with one of its suppliers. The supplier checks the firm's credit and, if it is good, sends the merchandise. The purchasing firm then pays for the goods in accordance with the supplier's credit terms.

Credit Terms and Cash Discounts

Very often the credit terms offered with trade credit involve a cash discount for early payment. For example, a supplier might offer terms of 2/10, net 30, which means that a 2 per cent discount is offered for payment within 10 days or the full amount is due in 30 days. Thus, a 2 per cent penalty is involved for not paying within 10 days or for delaying payment from the tenth to the thirtieth day (that is, for 20 days). The effective annual cost of not taking the cash discount can be quite severe. Using a Re.1 invoice amount, the effective cost of passing up the discount period in the above case can be computed as:

$$\text{Rate} = \frac{\text{Rs } .02}{\text{Rs } .98} \times \frac{1}{20/360} = .3673, \text{ or } 36.73 \text{ per cent}$$

Note that the 2 per cent cash discount is the interest cost of extending the payment period an additional 20 days. Note also that the principal amount of the credit is Rs 98. This amount constitutes the full principal amount as on the tenth day of the credit period, after which time the cash discount is lost. The effective cost of passing up the 2 per cent discount for 20 days is quite expensive, 36.73 per cent. Furthermore, once the discount period has passed, there is no reason to pay before the final due date (the thirtieth day). Table 2.1 lists the effective annual cost of a number of alternative credit terms. Note that the cost of trade credit varies directly with the size of the cash discount and inversely with the length of time between the end of the discount period and the final due date.

Table 2.1: Effective rates of interest on Selected Trade Credit Terms

Credit Terms	Effective Rate
2/10, net 60	14.69%
2/10, net 90	9.18%
3/20, net 60	27.84%
6/10, net 90	28.72%

Stretching on Trade Credit

Firms utilising trade credit sometimes engage in stretching of their trade accounts. This practice involves not paying within the prescribed credit period. For example, a firm might purchase materials under credit terms of 3/10, net 60; however, when faced with a shortage of cash the firm might extend payment to the eightieth day. Continued violation of trade terms could eventually lead to a loss of credit. However, for short periods, and at infrequent intervals, stretching offers the firm a potentially useful source of short-term credit.

Advantages of Trade Credit

As a source of short-term financing, trade credit has a number of advantages. First, trade credit is easily and conveniently obtained as a normal part of the firm's operations. Second, no formal agreements are generally involved in extending credit. Furthermore, the amount of credit extended, expands and contracts with the needs of the firm; this is the reason for its earlier classification as a spontaneous source of financing.

Unsecured Sources: Bank Credit

Commercial banks provide unsecured short-term credit in two basic forms: lines of credit and transaction loans (notes payable). Maturities of both types of loans are usually one year or less, with rates of interest depending on the creditworthiness of the borrower and the level of interest rates in the economy as a whole.

Line of Credit

A line of credit is generally an informal agreement or understanding between the borrower and the bank. Under this type of agreement, there is no legal commitment on the part of the bank to provide the stated credit. In a revolving credit agreement, which is a variant of this form of financing, such a legal obligation is involved. The line of credit agreement generally covers a period of one year corresponding to the borrower's fiscal year. Thus, if the borrower is on a July 31 fiscal year, its lines of credit will be based on the same annual period.

Credit Terms

Lines of credit generally do not involve fixed rates of interest but state that credit will be extended at ½ per cent over prime or some other spread over the bank's prime rate.[2] Furthermore, the agreement usually does not spell out the specific use that will be made of the funds beyond some general statement, such as for working capital purposes.

Lines of credit usually require that the borrower maintains a minimum balance in the bank throughout the loan period. This compensating balance

2. The "prime rate of interest" represents the rate that a bank charges its most creditworthy borrowers.

(which can be stated as a per cent of the line of credit or the loan amount) increases the effective cost of the loan to the borrower unless a deposit balance equal to or greater than the required compensating balance is ordinarily maintained in the bank.

The effective cost of short-term bank credit can be estimated using the RATE equation. Consider the following example:

Example: M&M Beverage Company has a Rs 300,000 line of credit which requires a compensating balance equal to 10 per cent of the loan amount. The rate paid on the loan is 12 per cent per annum, Rs 200,000 is borrowed for a six-month period, and the firm does not, at present, have a deposit with the lending bank. The cost of the loan includes the interest expense and, in addition, the opportunity cost of maintaining an idle cash balance is equal to the 10 per cent compensating balance. To accommodate the cost of the compensating balance requirement, assume that the added funds will have to be borrowed and simply left idle in the firm's checking account. Thus, the amount actually borrowed will be larger than the needed Rs 200,000. In fact, the needed Rs 200,000 will comprise 90 per cent of the total borrowed funds due to the 10 per cent compensating balance requirement, hence 90B = Rs 200,000, such that B = Rs 222,222. Thus, interest is paid on Rs 222,222 loan (Rs 222,222 × .12 × ½ = Rs 13,333.32), of which only Rs 200,000 is available for use by the firm.[3] The effective annual cost of credit, therefore, is

$$\text{RATE} = \frac{\text{Rs}\,13{,}333.32}{\text{Rs}\,200{,}000} \times \frac{1}{18/360} = 13.33\ \text{per cent}$$

If the firm normally maintains at least Rs 200,000 (or 10 per cent of the needed funds) in a demand deposit with the leading bank, then the cost of the credit is

3. Although technically incorrect, the same answer could have been obtained by assuming a total loan of Rs 200,000 of which only 90 per cent of Rs 180,000 was available for use by the firm; that is,

$$\text{RATE} = \frac{\text{Rs}\,12{,}000}{\text{Rs}\,180{,}000} \times \frac{1}{18/360} = 13.33\text{per cent}$$

Interest is now calculated on the Rs 200,000 loan amount (Rs 12,000 = Rs 200,000 × .12 × ½).

$$\text{RATE} = \frac{\text{Rs}\,12{,}000}{\text{Rs}\,200{,}000} \times \frac{1}{18/360} = 12 \text{ per cent}$$

In the M&M Beverage Company example, the loan required the payment of principal (Rs 222,222) plus interest (Rs 13,333.32) at the end of the six-month loan period. Frequently, bank loans will be made on a discount basis. That is, the loan interest will be deducted from the loan amount before the funds are transferred to the borrower, extending the M&M Beverage company example to consider discounted interest involves reducing the loan proceeds (Rs 200,000) in the previous example by the amount of interest for the full six months (Rs 13,333.32). The effective rate of interest on the loan is now:

$$\text{RATE} = \frac{\text{Rs } 13{,}333.32}{\text{Rs}\,200{,}000 - \text{Rs}\,13{,}333{,}32} \times \frac{1}{18/360} = .1429, \text{or } 14.29 \text{ per cent}$$

The effect of discounting interest was to raise the cost of the loan from 13.33 per cent to 14.29 per cent. This results from the fact that the firm pays interest on the same amount of funds as before (Rs 222,222); however, this time they get the use of Rs 13,333.32 less, or Rs 200,000 - Rs 13,333.32 = Rs 186,666.68.[4]

Transaction Loans

Still another form of unsecured short-term bank credit can be obtained in the form of transaction loans. Here the loan is made for a specific purpose.

---

4. If M&M needs the use of a full Rs 200,000, then they will have to borrow more than Rs 222,222 to cover both the compensating balance requirement and the discounted interest. In fact, the firm will have to borrow some amount B such that

$$B - .10\,B - (.12 \times ½)\,B = \text{Rs } 200{,}000$$

$$.84\,B = \text{Rs } 200{,}000$$

$$B = \frac{\text{Rs } 200{,}000}{.84} = \text{Rs } 238{,}095$$

The cost of credit remains the same at 14.29 per cent, as we see below:

$$\text{RATE} = \frac{\text{Rs}\,14{,}285{,}70}{\text{Rs}\,238{,}095 - \text{Rs}\,23{,}810 - \text{Rs}\,14{,}285.70} \times \frac{1}{18/360} = .1429, \text{ or } 14.29 \text{ per cent}$$

This is the type of loan that most individuals associate with bank credit. The loan is obtained by signing a demand promissory note, usually backed by third-party guarantee, agreement of hypothecation of stocks held/ acquired with the loan funds, and agreement for non-diversion of sale proceeds, but no tangible security as collateral.

Unsecured transaction loans are very similar to a line of credit with regard to their cost, term to maturity, and compensating balance requirements. In both instances, commercial banks often require that the borrower clean up its short-term loans for a 30-45 day period during the year.

This means, very simply, that the borrower must be free of any bank debt for the stated period. The purpose of such a requirement is to ensure that the borrower is not using short-term bank credit to finance a part of its permanent needs for funds.

Unsecured Sources: Commercial Paper

Only the largest and most creditworthy companies are able to use commercial paper, which is simply a short-term promise to pay that is sold in the market for short-term debt securities.

Credit Terms

The maturity of this credit source is generally six months or less, although some issues carry 270-day maturities. The interest rate on commercial paper is generally slightly lower (one-half to one per cent) than the prime rate on commercial bank loans. Also, interest is usually discounted, although commercial paper is available at times that is interest bearing.

New issues of commercial paper are either directly placed (sold by the issuing firm directly to the investing public) or dealer placed. Dealer placement involves the use of a commercial paper dealer, who sells the issue for the issuing firm. Many of the major finance companies place their commercial paper directly. The volume of direct versus dealer placements is roughly four to one in favour of direct placements. Dealers are used primarily by industrial firms that make only infrequent use of the commercial paper market or those that, owing to their small size, would have difficulty placing the issue without the help of a dealer.

Commercial Paper as a Source of Short-term Credit

A number of advantages accrue to the user of commercial paper:

Using commercial paper for short-term financing, however, involves a very important risk. That is, the commercial paper market is highly impersonal and denies even the most creditworthy borrower any flexibility in terms of repayment. When bank credit is used, the borrower has someone with whom he can work out any temporary difficulties he might encounter in meeting a loan deadline. This flexibility simply does not exist for the user of commercial paper.

Estimating the Cost of Commercial Paper

The cost of commercial paper can be estimated using the simple effective cost of credit equation (RATE). The key points to remember are that commercial paper interest is usually discounted and that if a dealer is used to place the issue, a fee must be paid. Even if a dealer is not used, the issuing firm will incur costs associated with preparing and placing the issue, which also must be considered in estimating the cost of credit.

Example: The EPG Mfg. Company uses commercial paper regularly to support its needs for short-term financing. The firm plans to sell Rs 100 crore in 270-day-maturity paper on which it expects to have to pay discounted interest at an annual rate of 12 per cent per annum. In addition, EPG expects to incur a cost of Rs 100,000 on dealer placement fees and other expenses of issuing the paper. The effective cost of credit to EPG can be calculated as follows:

$$\text{RATE} = \frac{\text{Rs 9 crores}}{\text{Rs 100 crores - Rs 100,000 - Rs 9 crore}}$$

$$= .1320, \text{ or } 13.20 \text{ per cent}$$

where the interest cost is calculated as Rs 100 crore × .12 × 270/360 = Rs 9 crores. Thus, the effective cost of credit to EPG is 13.2 per cent.

Secured Sources: Accounts Receivable Loans

Secured sources of short-term credit have certain assets of the firm pledged as collateral to secure the loan. Thus, upon default of the loan agreement the lender has first claim to the pledged assets in addition to his claim as a general creditor of the firm. Hence the secured credit agreement offers an added margin of safety to the lender.

Generally a firm's receivables are among its most liquid assets. For this reason they are considered by many lenders to be prime collateral for a secured loan. Two basic procedures can be used in arranging for financing based on receivables: pledging and factoring.

Pledging Accounts Receivable

Under the pledging arrangement, the borrower simply pledges accounts receivable as collateral for a loan obtained from either a commercial bank or a finance company. The amount of the loan is stated as a per cent of the face value of the receivables pledged. If the firm provides the lender with a general line on its receivables, then all of the borrower's accounts are pledged as security for the loan. This method of pledging is simple and inexpensive. However, since the lender has no control over the quality of the receivables being pledged, he will set the maximum loan at a relatively low per cent of the total face value of the accounts, generally ranging downward from a maximum of around 75 per cent. In other words, the lender will retain a margin of 25% or more.

Still another approach to pledging involves the borrower's presenting specific invoices to the lender as collateral for a loan. This method is somewhat more expensive in that the lender must assess the creditworthiness of each individual account pledged; however, given this added knowledge he will be willing to increase the loan as a per cent of the face value of the invoices. In this case, the loan might reach as high as 85 or 90 per cent of the face value of the pledged receivables, i.e., a margin of only 10% to 15% will be retained.

Credit Terms Accounts receivable loans generally carry an interest rate 2 to 5 per cent higher than the bank's prime lending rate. Finance companies charge even a higher rate. In addition, the lender will usually charge a handling fee stated as a per cent of the face value of the receivables processed. This fee may be as much as 1 to 2 per cent of the face value.

Example: The A. B. Good Company sells electrical supplies to building contractors on terms of net 60. The firm's average monthly sales are Rs 100,000; thus, given the firm's two-month credit terms, its average receivables balance is Rs 200,000. The firm pledges all of its receivable to a local bank, which in turn advances up to 70 per cent of the face value of the receivables at 3 per cent over prime and with a 1 per cent processing charge on all receivables pledged. A. B. Good follows a practice of borrowing the maximum amount possible, and the current prime rate is 10 per cent.

The effective cost of using this source of financing for a full year is computed as follows:

$$\text{RATE} = \frac{\text{Rs } 18{,}200 + \text{Rs } 12{,}000}{\text{Rs } 140{,}000} \times \frac{1}{360/360} = 21.57 \text{ per cent}$$

Where the total cost of the loan consists of both the annual interest expense (.13 × .70 × Rs 200,000 = Rs 18,200) and the annual processing fee (.01 × Rs 100,000 × 12 months = Rs 12,000). The amount of credit extended is .70 × Rs 200,000 = Rs 140,000. Note that the processing charge applies to all receivables pledged. Thus, the A. B. Good Company pledges

Rs 100,000 each month, or Rs 1,200,000 during the year, on which a 1 per cent fee must be paid for a total annual charge of Rs 12,000.[5]

One added point should be made about the cost of loans secured by the pledge of accounts receivable. The lender, in addition to making advances or loans, may be providing certain credit services for the borrower. For example, the lender may provide billing and collection services. The value of these services should not be considered a part of the cost of credit. In the preceding example, A. B. Good Company may save credit department expenses of Rs 10,000 per year by pledging all its accounts and letting the lender provide those services. In this case, the cost of short-term credit is only 14.43%

$$\text{RATE} = \frac{\text{Rs } 18{,}200 + \text{Rs } 12{,}000 - \text{Rs } 10{,}000}{\text{Rs } 140{,}000} \times \frac{1}{360/360} = 14.43 \text{ per cent}$$

Advantages and Disadvantages of Pledging

The primary advantage of pledging as a source of short-term credit relates to the flexibility it provides the borrower. Financing is available on a continuous basis. As new accounts are credited through credit sales, they provide the collateral for the financing of new production. Furthermore, the lender may provide credit services that eliminate or at least reduce the need for similar services within the firm. The primary disadvantage associated with this method of financing is its cost, which can be relatively high compared with other sources of short-term credit, owing to the level of the interest rate charged on loans and the processing fee on pledged accounts.

---

5. If only one month's accounts are factored and those accounts are collected in 60 days, then the cost of credit can be calculated as follows:

$$\text{RATE} = \frac{\text{Rs } 1{,}516{,}67 + \text{Rs } 1{,}000}{\text{Rs } 70{,}000} \times \frac{1}{60/360} = .2157, \text{ or } 21.57 \text{ per cent}$$

Where interest equals Rs 100,000 × .70 × .13 × 1/6 = Rs 1,516,67 and the pledging fee equals .01 × Rs 100,000 = Rs 1000.

Factoring Accounts Receivable

Factoring receivables involves the outright sale of a firm's accounts to a factor. A factor is a financial institution that acquires the receivables of other firms. The factor may be a commercial finance company that engages solely in the factoring of receivables (known as an old-line factor) or it may be a commercial bank. The factor, in turn, bears the risk of collection and, for a fee, services the accounts. The fee is stated as a per cent of the face value of all receivables factored (usually from 1 to 3 per cent).

The factor typically does not make payment for factored accounts until the accounts have been collected or the credit terms have been met. Should the firm wish to receive immediate payment for its factored accounts, it can borrow from the factor, using the factored accounts as collateral. The maximum loan the firm can obtain is equal to the face value of its factored accounts less the interest on the loan. For example, if Rs 100,000 in receivables is factored which carry 60-day credit terms, a 2 per cent factor's fee, a 6 per cent reserve, and interest at 1 per cent per month on advances, then the maximum loan or advance the firm can receive is computed as follows:

Face amount of receivables factored		Rs 100,000
Less:	Fee (.02 × Rs 100,000)	(2,000)
	Reserve (.06 × Rs 100,000)	(6,000)
	Interest (.01 × Rs 92,000 × 2 months)	(1,840)
Maximum advance		Rs 90,160

Note that interest is discounted and calculated based upon a maximum amount of funds available for advance Rs 92,000 (Rs 100,000 - Rs 2000 - Rs 6000). Thus, the effective cost of credit can be calculated as follows:

$$\text{RATE} = \frac{\text{Rs } 1840 + \text{Rs } 2000}{\text{Rs } 90{,}160} \times \frac{1}{60/360} = 25.55 \text{ per cent}$$

Secured Sources: Inventory Loans

Inventory loans provide a second source of security for short-term secured credit. The amount of the loan that can be obtained depends on both the marketability and perishability of the inventory. Some items, such as raw materials (oil, lumber, and chemicals), serve as excellent sources of collateral, since they can easily be liquidated. Other items, such as work-in-process inventories, provide very poor collateral, owing to their lack of marketability.

There are several methods by which inventory can be used to secure short-term financing. These include a floating or blanket lien, chattel mortgage, field warehouse receipt and terminal warehouse receipt.

Floating Lien Agreement

Under a floating lien agreement, the borrower gives the lender a lien against all his inventories. This provides the simplest but least secure form of inventory collateral. The borrowing firm maintains full control of the inventories and continues to sell and replace them as it sees fit. Obviously, this total lack of control over the collateral greatly dilutes the value of this type of security to the lender. Correspondingly, loans made with floating liens on inventory as collateral are generally limited to a relatively modest fraction of the value of the inventories covered by the lien. In addition, floating liens usually include future as well as existing inventories.

Chattel Mortgage Agreements

The lender can increase his security interest by having specific items of inventory identified (by serial number or otherwise) in the security agreement. Such an arrangement is provided by a chattel mortgage. The borrower retains title of the inventory but cannot sell the items without the lender's consent. This type of agreement is very costly to implement, as specific items of inventory must be identified; thus, it is used only for major items of inventory such as machine tools or other capital assets.

Field Warehouse Financing Agreements

Increased lender control over inventories used as loan collateral can be obtained through the use of a field warehouse agreement. Here the inventories used as collateral are physically separated from the firm's other inventories and placed under the control of a third-party field warehousing firm. Note that the inventories are not removed from the borrower's premises, but they are placed under the control of a third party that is responsible for protecting the security interests of the lender. This arrangement is particularly useful where large bulky items are used as collateral. For example, a refinery might use a part of its inventory of fuel oil to secure a short-term bank loan. Under a warehousing agreement, the oil reserves would be set aside in specific tanks or storage vessels, which would be controlled (monitored) by a field warehousing concern.

The warehousing concern, upon receipt of the inventory, takes full control of the collateral. This means that the borrower is no longer allowed to use or sell the inventory items without the consent of the lender. The warehousing firm issues a warehouse receipt for the merchandise, which carries title to the goods, represented therein. The receipt may be negotiable, in which case title can be transferred through sale of the receipt, or non negotiable, whereby title remains with the lender. With a negotiable receipt arrangement, the warehouse concern will release the goods to whoever holds the receipt, whereas with a non negotiable receipt the goods may be released only on the written consent of the lender.

The cost of such a loan can be quite high, since the services of the field warehouse company must be paid for by the borrower.

Example: The M.M. Company follows a practice of obtaining short-term credit, based on its seasonal finished goods inventory. The firm builds up its inventories of outdoor furniture throughout the winter months for sale in spring and summer. Thus, for the two-month period ended March 31, it uses its fall and winter production of furniture as collateral for a short-term bank loan. The bank lends the company up to 70 per cent of the value of the inventory at 14 per cent interest plus a fixed fee of Rs 2000 to cover the costs of a field warehousing arrangement. During this period, the firm usually has about Rs 200,000 inventories, which it borrows against. The annual effective cost of the short-term credit is therefore

$$\text{RATE} = \frac{\text{Rs } 3267 + \text{Rs } 2000}{\text{Rs } 140000} \times \frac{1}{60/360} = 22.57 \text{ per cent}$$

where the financing cost consists of two months' interest Rs 140,000 × .14 × 60/360 = Rs 3267 plus the field warehousing fee of Rs 2000.

Terminal Warehouse Agreements

The terminal warehouse agreement differs from the field warehouse agreement just discussed in only one respect. Here, the inventories pledged as collateral are transported to a public warehouse that is physically removed from the borrower's premises. An added degree of safety or security is provided to the lender, as the inventory is totally removed from the borrower's control. Once again, the cost of this type of arrangement is increased by the necessity for paying the warehouse concern; in addition, the inventory must be transported to (and eventually from) the public warehouse.

The same warehouse receipt procedure described earlier for field warehouse loans is used. Again, the cost of this type of financing can be quite high.

Study Questions

1. What distinguishes short-term, intermediate-term, and long-term debt?

2. What factors should be considered in selecting a source of short-term credit? Discuss each.

3. How can the formula "interest = principal × rate × time" be used to estimate the effective cost of short-term credit?

4. How can we accommodate the effects of compounding in our calculation of the distinguishing characteristics of each?

5. There are three major sources of unsecured short-term credit; list and discuss the distinguishing characteristics of each.

6. What is meant by the following trade credit terms: 2/10, net 30? 4/20, net 60? 3/15, net 45?

7. Define the following:

    a. Line of credit

    b. Commercial paper

c. Compensating balance

d. Prime rate

8. List and discuss four advantages of the use of commercial paper (CP).

9. What "risk" is involved in the firm's use of commercial paper as a source of short-term credit? Discuss.

10. List and discuss the distinguishing features of the principal sources of secured credit based upon accounts receivable.

11. List and discuss the distinguishing features of the primary sources of secured credit based upon inventories.

Self-Test Problems

ST-1

(Analysing the Cost of Short-term Credit) The Samples Mfg. Co. provides speciality steel products to the oil industry. Although the firm's business is highly correlated with the cyclical swings in oil exploration activity, it also experiences some significant seasonality. It is this seasonality in its need for funds that the firm is currently concerned about. The firm needs Rs 500,000 for the two-month period July-August each year, and as a result the company's vice-president of finance is currently considering the following three sources of financing:

a. Establish a line of credit with the No Money Bank, Malgudi. The bank has agreed to provide samples with the needed Rs 500,000, carrying an interest rate of 14 per cent with interest discounted and a compensating balance of 20 per cent of the loan balance. Samples does not have an account with No Money Bank and would have to establish one to satisfy the compensating balance requirement.

b. Samples can forgo its trade discounts over the two months of July and August when the funding will be needed. The firm's discount terms are 3/15, net 30.

c. Finally, Samples could enter into a pledging arrangement with a local finance company. The finance company has agreed to extend Samples the needed Rs 500,000 if it pledges Rs 50,000 in receivables. The finance company has offered to advance Rs 500,000, with 12 per cent annual interest payable at the end of the two-month loan term. In addition, the finance company will charge a one-half of one per cent fee based on face value of pledged receivables to cover the cost of processing the company's accounts (this fee is paid at the end of the loan period).

Analyse the cost of each of the alternative sources of credit and select the best one. Note that a total of Rs 500,000 will be needed for a two-month period (July-August) each year.

ST-2

(Analysing the Cost of Short-term Credit) The Finance Manager of the Lights-a-Lot Mfg. Company is faced with the choice of three alternative bank loans. The firm wishes to select the one that minimises its cost of credit on a Rs 200,000 note which it plans to issue in the next ten days. Relevant information for the three loan configurations is found below:

a. An 18 per cent rate of interest with interest paid at year-end and no compensating balance requirement.

b. A 16 per cent rate of interest but carrying a 20 per cent compensating balance requirement. This loan also calls for interest to be paid at year-end.

c. A 14 per cent rate of interest which is discounted plus a 20 per cent compensating balance requirement.

Analyse the cost of each of these alternatives. You may assume that the firm would not normally maintain any bank balance that might be used to meet the 20 per cent compensating balance requirements of alternatives (b) and (c).

Study Problems

1. (Cost of Trade Credit) Calculate the effective cost of the following trade credit terms where payment is made on the net due date.

    a. 2/10, net 30

    b. 3/15, net 30

    c. 3/15, net 45

    d. 2/15, net 60

2. (Annual Percentage Rate) Compute the cost of the trade credit terms in problem 1 using the compounding formula or annual percentage rate.

3. (Cost of Short-term Financing) The Maran Construction Company needs to borrow Rs 100,000 to help finance the cost of a new Rs 150,000 hydraulic crane used in the firm's commercial construction business. The crane will pay for itself in one year and the firm is considering the following alternatives for financing its purchase:

    Alternative A - The firm's bank has agreed to lend the Rs 100,000 at a rate of 14 per cent. Interest would be discounted, and a 15 per cent compensating balance would be required. However, the compensating balance requirement would not be binding on Maran since the firm normally maintains a minimum demand deposit (checking account) balance of Rs 25,000 in the bank.

    Alternative B - The equipment dealer has agreed to finance the equipment with a one-year loan. The Rs 100,000 loan would require payment of principal and interest totaling Rs 116,300, at maturity.

    a. Which financing alternative should Maran select?

    b. If the bank's compensating balance requirement were to necessitate idle demand deposits equal to 20 per cent of the loan, what effect would this have on the cost of the bank loan alternative?

4. (Cost of Short-term Bank Loan) On July 1, 2001, the Bharat Forging Corporation arranged for a line of credit with the National Bank of Delhi. The terms of the agreement called for a Rs 100,000 maximum loan with interest set at 1 per cent over prime. In addition, the firm has to maintain a 20 per cent compensating balance in its demand deposit throughout the year. The prime rate is currently 12 per cent.

   a. If Bharat normally maintains a Rs 20,000 to Rs 30,000 balance in its checking account with NB of Delhi, what is the effective cost of credit through the line-of-credit agreement where the maximum loan amount is used for a full year?

   b. Recompute the effective cost of credit to Bharat if Bharat will have to borrow the compensating balance and they borrow the maximum possible under the loan agreement. Again, assume the full amount of the loan is outstanding for a whole year.

5. (Cost of Commercial Paper) Tri-State Enterprises plans to issue commercial paper for the first time in the firm's 35-year history. The firm plans to issue Rs 500,000 in 180-day maturity notes. The paper will carry a 10 1/4 per cent rate with discounted interest and will cost Tri-State Rs 12,000 (paid in advance) to issue.

   a. What is the effective cost of credit to Tri-State?

   b. What other factors should the company consider in analysing whether to issue the commercial paper?

6. (Cost of Accounts Receivable) Johnson Enterprises is involved in the manufacture and sale of electronic components used in small AM-FM radios. The firm needs Rs 300,000 to finance an anticipated expansion in receivables due to increased sales. Johnson's credit terms are net 60, and its average monthly credit sales are Rs 200,000. In general, the firm's customers pay within the credit period; thus the firm's average accounts receivable balance is Rs 400,000.

   Gurumurthy, Johnson's comptroller, approached the firm's bank with a request for a loan for Rs 300,000 using the firm's accounts receivable as collateral. The bank offered to make the loan at a rate of 2 per cent over prime plus 1 per cent processing charge on all receivables pledged (Rs 200,000 per month). Furthermore, the bank agreed to lend up to 75 per cent of the face value of the receivables pledged.

a. Estimate the cost of the receivables loan to Johnson where the firm borrows Rs 300,000. The prime rate is currently 11 per cent.

b. Gurumurthy also requested a line of credit for Rs 300,000 from the bank. The bank agreed to grant the necessary line of credit at a rate of 3 per cent over prime and required a 15 per cent compensating balance. Johnson currently maintains an average demand deposit of Rs 80,000. Estimate the cost of the line of credit to Johnson.

c. Which source of credit should Johnson select? Why?

7. (Cost of Factoring) MDM is considering the factoring of its receivables. The firm has credit sales of Rs 400,000 per month and has an average receivables balance of Rs 800,000 with 60-day credit terms. The factor has offered to extend credit equal to 90 per cent of the receivables factored less interest on the loan at a rate of 10½ per cent per month. The 10 per cent difference in the advance and the face value of all receivables factored consists of a 1 per cent factoring fee plus a 9 per cent reserve, which the factor maintains. It will sell them all, so that it can reduce its credit department costs by Rs 1500 a month.

a. What is the cost of borrowing the maximum amount of credit available to MDM through the factoring agreement?

b. What considerations other than cost should be accounted for by MDM in determining whether or not to enter the factoring agreement?

8. (Inventory Financing) In June of each year the Excel Publishing Company builds up its inventories for fall sales. The company has explored the possibility of a field warehouse security agreement as collateral for an inventory loan from its bank during the three months. During these months, inventories average Rs 400,000. The field warehouse arrangement will cost Excel a flat fee of Rs 2000 a month

on its entire inventory regardless of the amount the firm borrows. The bank has agreed to lend up to 70 per cent of the value of the inventory at a rate of 14 per cent.

a. If Excel borrows Rs 200,000 using the inventory loan for June through August, what is the effective cost of credit?

b. What is the effective cost of borrowing Rs 280,000 for the June through August period?

9. (Cost of Secured Short-term Credit) Satish and Co. needs Rs 500,000 for the three-month period ending September 30, 2000. The firm has explored two possible sources of credit.

   a. Satish has arranged with its bank for a Rs 500,000 loan secured by accounts receivable. The bank has agreed to advance 80 per cent of the value of its pledged receivables at a rate of 11 per cent plus a 1 per cent fee based on all receivables pledged. Satish's receivables average a total of Rs 1 crore year-round.

   b. An insurance company has agreed to lend Rs 500,000 at a rate of 9 per cent per annum, using a loan secured by Satish's inventory of salad oil. A field warehouse agreement would be used, which would cost Satish Rs 2000 a month.

   Which source of credit should Satish select? Explain.

10. (Cost of Short-term Financing) You plan to borrow Rs 20,000 from the bank to pay for inventories for a gift shop you have just opened. The bank offers to lend you the money at 10 per cent annual interest for the six months the funds will need.

    a. Calculate the effective rate of interest on the loan.

    b. In addition, the bank requires you to maintain a 15 per cent compensating balance in the bank. Since you are just opening your business, you do not have a demand deposit at the bank that can be used to meet the compensating balance requirement. This means that you will have to put 15 per cent of the loan amount from your own personal money (which you had planned to use to help finance the business) in a checking account. What is the cost of the loan now?

c. In addition to the compensating balance requirement in (b) above you are told that interest will be discounted. What is the effective rate of interest on the loan now?

11. (Cost of Factoring) A factor has agreed to lend the JVC Corporation working capital on the following terms. JVC's receivables average Rs 100,000 per month and have a 90-day average collection period (note that accounts receivable average Rs 300,000 due to the 90 day average collection period). The factor will charge 12 per cent interest on any advance (1 per cent per month paid in advance), will charge a 2 per cent processing fee on all receivables factored, and will maintain a 20 per cent reserve. If JVC undertakes the loan, it will reduce its own credit department expenses by Rs 2000 per month. What is the annual effective rate of interest to JVC on the factoring arrangement? Assume that the maximum advance is taken.

12. (Opportunity Cost of Decreasing Wages Payable) In June of this year the AMB Manufacturing Company negotiated a new union contract with its employees. One of the provisions of the new contract involved increasing the frequency of its wage payments from once a month to once every two weeks. AMB's biweekly payroll averages Rs 250,000 and the firm's opportunity cost of funds is 12 per cent per annum.

a. What is the annual cost of this new wage payment scheme to AMB?

b. What is the maximum percentage increase in wages that AMB would have been willing to accept in lieu of the increased frequency of wage payments?

Self-Test Solutions

1. Interest for two months = .14 × 2/12 × Rs 500,000

= Rs 11,667

Loans proceeds (for Rs 500,000 loan)

$$= \text{Rs } 500{,}000 - (.2 \times \text{Rs } 500{,}000 + \text{Rs } 11{,}667) = \text{Rs } 388{,}333$$

$$\text{RATE} = \frac{\text{Rs}\,11{,}667}{\text{Rs}\,388{,}333} \times \frac{12}{2}$$

$$= .030043 \times 6 = .18026, \text{ or } 18.026\%$$

Note that Samples would actually have to borrow more than the needed Rs 500,000 in order to cover the compensating balance requirement. However, as we demonstrated earlier, the effective cost of credit will not be affected by adjusting the loan amount for interest expense charges accordingly.

b. $\text{RATE} = \frac{.03}{.97} \times \frac{12}{2} = .18557$, or 18.557 per cent

c. Interest for two months $= .12 \times \frac{2}{12} \times \text{Rs}\,500{,}000 = \text{Rs}\,10{,}000$

Pledging Fee = .005 × Rs 750,000 = Rs 3750

$$\text{RATE} = \frac{\text{Rs}\,10{,}000 \times \text{Rs}\,3{,}750}{\text{Rs}\,500{,}000} \times \frac{12}{2}$$

$$= .0275 \times 6 = .165, \text{ or } 16.5 \text{ per cent}$$

2. a. $\text{RATE} = \frac{.18 \times \text{Rs}\,200{,}000}{\text{Rs}\,200{,}000} \times \frac{1}{1} = .18$, or 18 per cent

b. $\text{RATE} = \frac{.16 \times \text{Rs}\,200{,}000}{\text{Rs}\,200{,}000 - .20 \times \text{Rs}\,200{,}000} \times \frac{1}{1} = .20$, or 20 per cent

c. $\text{RATE} = \frac{.14 \times \text{Rs}\,200{,}000}{\text{Rs}\,200{,}000 - .14 \times \text{Rs}\,200{,}000 - .2 \times \text{Rs}\,200{,}000} \times \frac{1}{1}$

$$= .21212, \text{ or } 21.212 \text{ per cent}$$

Alternative (a) offers the lower cost service of financing, although it carries the highest stated rate of interest. The reason for this, of course, is that there is no compensating balance requirement or any discounting of interest, for this alternative.

Innovations for Recreations, a manufacturer of games and toys, had increased sales beyond expectations, following the launch of a couple of new products. These new products were viewed to be fad items and would not have "staying power" in the toys market. Company management recognised this and therefore did not plan a major plant expansion. However, in keeping with industry trends, it was starting to relax its credit terms. The need for additional investment in receivables coupled with the need to increase raw materials purchases was putting a severe financial strain on the firm. After investigation, the firm established that it could raise short-term temporary funds from three sources: an unsecured line of credit with a bank, accounts receivable financing through a commercial lending firm, and factoring of accounts receivable. It selected one of these alternatives, caught up on its slow payments on accounts payable, and staved off a potential bankruptcy.

Short-term financing includes any debt that was originally scheduled for repayment within one year. Major sources of short-term credit are trade credit, unsecured and secured loans, and commercial paper. These sources of short-term funds are discussed in the next section.

Trade Credit

A firm buying goods and services on credit enters an amount, equal to the cost of the goods and services, on its balance sheet as accounts payable. Account payable of trade credit is the liability assumed by the firm in buying goods on credit. Since the items purchased have not been paid for at purchase time, trade credit is a short-term financing vehicle. A recent balance sheet for an MNC will show that accounts payable constitutes approximately 44 per cent of total current liabilities. This shows the importance of managing the short-term obligations of a firm and the importance of trade credit in short-term financing. In this section, we consider types of trade credit, factors that influence credit terms, various types of credit terms, and when to use trade credit.

Types of Trade Credit

Three types of trade credit arrangements are usually encountered in business: open account, promissory notes, and trade acceptances.

Open Account. Under this arrangement, the buyer requests a line of credit from the seller. After investigating the buyer's creditworthiness, the seller may approve or disapprove credit. If credit is approved, along with a certain credit limit, the buyer can place orders for materials. Upon shipping the goods, the seller sends an invoice to the buyer. The invoice describes the goods, quantity shipped, selling price per unit, total amount due, and the terms of the sale. The buyer does not have to sign a special credit agreement each time a purchase is made. Rather, once credit is approved, the buyer is free to buy as much and as often as desired, provided that the approved credit limit is not exceeded. This credit arrangement is called an open account.

Promissory Note. Another method of extending credit is for the seller to have the buyer sign a promissory note. This promissory note provides the seller with tangible evidence that the buyer is acknowledging his indebtedness. Its use is appropriate when inventory turnover is slow and the seller helps finance the buyer's inventory. This is commonly used in the distribution of large ticket, slow-turnover items such as furs, diamonds, and expensive jewellery.

Trade Acceptance. Trade acceptance is similar to a promissory note in that the buyer formally acknowledges his indebtedness to the seller. Under this method of trade credit, the seller prepares a draft on the buyer. The draft obligates the buyer to pay the designated amount at a future time. The buyer accepts the draft and names a bank where the draft will be paid on its due date. Simultaneously with the buyer's acceptance of the draft, the seller releases the merchandise to the buyer. The draft also becomes a trade acceptance as soon as the buyer accepts it. When the trade acceptance matures, the seller presents it at the buyer's designated bank for collection.

In this section, we have considered three types of trade credit arrangements. The most prevalent is the open account.

Factors that Influence Credit Terms

The credit terms or terms of sale specify the credit arrangements with which the buyer must conform. Credit terms also affect the extent to which trade credit is utilised for short-term financing. Four factors influence credit terms and ultimately trade credit as short-term financing. These factors are merchandise characteristics, status of buyer, status of seller and industry practice.

Merchandise Characteristics. The terms of sale are influenced by seasonality, perishability, obsolescence, cost, and demand patterns of merchandise sold on credit. One general rule to remember is that very rarely is the credit period longer than the inventory turnover period. If the buyer is turning over his inventory every 20 days, then it is not desirable to extend him credit for 30 days – he will have free use of the sale proceeds for the 10 days before paying the invoice. Perishable items have shorter credit periods, whereas big-ticket or expensive, low-turnover items have much longer credit periods. The credit period may be 5 days in selling bread and 5 months in selling diamond-studded watches. Seasonal merchandise may have longer credit periods during off-season sales. A bathing suit manufacturer may offer extended terms in December to move his inventory of bathing suits.

Status of Buyer. A financially strong buyer can generally negotiate terms of sale in his favour. A major detergent manufacturer pays at the end of the credit period and still takes the discount. Smaller chemical firms who supply the chemical feed stocks for making detergents are in no position to enforce the nominally stated credit terms for fear of losing sales.

Status of Seller. Financially weak sellers cannot afford to extend trade credit and generally prefer to sell for cash. A seller in an industry faced with excess capacity or slack demand is liable to extend liberal credit terms to attract sales. For example, in the steel industry, some firms have been known to discount the "book" or list price of their products by offering extended credit terms.

Industry Practice. Credit terms are influenced by industry trade credit practices also. Industry trade credit managers meet occasionally on a professional basis and are knowledgeable about prevailing industry trade practices. The desire to deviate to any extent from industry practices is stimulated by the financial strength of the buyer and the seller. The average firm in the industry can be expected to conform to industry norms for trade credit.

Types of Credit Terms

There are various types of credit terms. These credit terms involve a credit discount, a discount period, and a credit period. For example, terms of 2/10, net 30 mean that a 2 per cent discount can be taken on the amount invoiced provided the payment is made within the discount period of 10 days. The full amount of the invoice is payable no later than the last day of the credit period, or within 30 days. Some variations on this basic term of sale will now be discussed.

Credit Period Only. When a credit period is specified but no cash discount is given, the terms will be, for example, "net 30."

EOM. EOM stands for 'End of Month', and appended to a credit term, means that the credit period starts from the first day of the next month. Terms of "net 20, EOM" on an invoice received on September 19 mean that the invoiced amount is due by October 20.

Cash Discount and EOM. On occasion, the credit terms will include a cash discount as well as a credit period starting at the end of the month. For example, terms of '2/10, net 30, EOM' mean that irrespective of when the invoice was received, the credit period and cash discount period begin on the first of the following month. On an invoice received on September 19 with terms or 1/10, net 20, EOM means that the buyer can take a cash discount anytime until October 10, and the credit period extends through October 20.

ROG. Another credit arrangement might specify 'ROG', or 'receipt of goods'. Terms of '2/10, net 30, ROG' mean that the credit period does not begin until the day the goods are received. On the day that the goods are received, this credit term becomes identical to '2/10, net 30'. This credit term is frequently used when the seller sells throughout a large geographical area. This credit term puts distant buyers on an equal footing with buyers located closer to the seller's shipping warehouses.

Datings. Occasionally, buyers will try to stimulate off-season sales by seasonal dating. Seasonal dating is a credit arrangement in which the credit period is extended into the selling season for the goods being sold. For example, a manufacturer of lawn chairs may make the invoice due on April 15 irrespective of whether the chairs were sold last November or this March. The seller has a better estimate of demand under seasonal dating. In addition, inventory is carried by the buyer, not the seller. From the buyer's viewpoint, the merchandise does not have to be paid until the start of the selling season. An additional benefit is that given high rates of inflation, the buyer is able to buy goods more cheaply than he would some months later.

COD and CBD. 'COD' and 'CBD' stand for 'cash on delivery of goods' and 'cash before delivery' respectively. Since the goods are paid for before or at delivery time, no trade credit is associated with these terms. Buyers may impose these terms if they feel that the seller is not financially creditworthy, or if the supplied items are premium goods, i.e., there is very strong demand for them, in a Seller's market.

When to use Trade Credit

As indicated previously, the use of trade credit is a way of life in the industrial sector of the economy. Once a firm has established its credit credentials, it finds the process of buying on an open account a relatively smooth operation. For a firm with increasing sale volume, trade credit provides "spontaneous" or automatic financing for part of the increases in working capital requirements. The decision on when trade credit should be used is governed by the explicit and implicit costs of trade credit.

Evaluating Explicit Trade Credit Costs

First of all, if credit terms do not involve a cash discount, the invoice should not be paid until the end of credit period. If terms are "net 30," then the buyer should wait until the end of the 30-day credit period before paying the invoice. If credit terms involve a cash discount, then the buyer needs to calculate the opportunity cost of not taking the cash discount. The annualised cost of not taking the discount or the cash discount is given by:

Credit discount cost = 360 × credit discount/Credit period - discount period

The equation gives a very good approximation of the actual cash discount cost. For example, if the buyer borrows on a credit line to pay within the discount period, it needs to borrow only the invoice net amount. The actual cash discount rate is obtained by dividing the cash discount cost in the above equation by the invoice net amount expressed as a fraction of the invoice face amount.

Table 2.2: Credit Terms and Cash Discount Costs

Credit Terms	Cash Discount Cost (per cent)
1/10, net 20	36
1/10, net 30	18
1/10, net 50	9
2/10, net 20	72
2/10, net 30	36
3/10, net 20	108
3/10, net 30	54
1/15, net 20	72
1/15, net 30	24
2/15, net 30	48
2/15, net 50	21

Some popular credit terms and the associated cash discount costs are given in Table 2.2. Assume that a firm can borrow on a credit line at an annual rate of 10 per cent. It buys merchandise on credit with terms of 1/10, net 50. Since the opportunity cost of not taking the cash discount is 9 per cent and is less than the cost of borrowing on the credit line, the firm should forego the cash discount and pay the full invoice amount at the end of the credit period. If terms are, for example, 2/10, net 30, the firm should take the cash discount.

Evaluating Implicit Trade Credit Costs

Trade credit may also involve implicit costs. Terms of "net 60" or "5/10, net 40" may appear very attractive from a financing viewpoint. An important determinant of whether these terms are attractive is to see whether quality and price of goods being bought is competitive. On occasion, the seller may use liberalised trade credit as an inducement to buyers. In these cases, it is worthwhile to take advantage of extended credit terms or high credit discounts. However, if they are associated with higher prices, lower quality goods, or poorer delivery service, then perhaps the buyer ought to forego them in favour of buying from a reputed supplier of good quality goods, albeit on more traditional terms.

Spot Quiz on Trade Credit

1. The transaction of buying on an open account is completed when the buyer signs a promissory note. T ❑ F ❑

2. Low turnover goods require smaller credit periods. T ❑ F ❑

3. Financially strong sellers may provide extended credit terms to gain market share. T ❑ F ❑

4. The opportunity cost of not taking the cash discount for credit terms of 2/10, net 30 EOM cannot be calculated without knowing the invoice date. T ❑ F ❑

5. Immediately paying an invoice amount with credit terms of "net 30" represents good financial management. T ❑ F ❑

Unsecured Loans

Loans from banks are an important source of financing for businesses. These loans are typically of a "self-liquidating" nature. Borrowing occurs when the firm has seasonally high financing needs. The loans are liquidated as borrowing requirements decrease. Unsecured loans are most frequently associated with inventory and accounts receivable financing. A publisher such as Excel will have high accounts receivable financing requirements in the fall. In early summer, a publisher will have excess cash on hand. It may meet its seasonally high accounts receivable financing requirements by borrowing on a short-term basis from a bank. In this section we consider the dimensions of unsecured loans, types of unsecured loans, compensating balances, and interest rates on unsecured loans.

Dimensions of Unsecured Loans

Banks are a very important source of short and intermediate-term financing for firms. It has been estimated that approximately two-thirds of the bank loans to firms are short-term. One-third of all bank loans are term loans. These loans are availed by firms ranging in size from tiny Fast Food corners next to the college campus to the multi-crore giants of industry. The size of these loans varies from a few thousand rupees to crores of rupees for a large firm.

The loans being discussed here are unsecured loans. That is, the lending bank does not require any collateral from the firm before disbursing the loan. Since the loans are unsecured, banks investigate the creditworthiness of the borrowing firm very thoroughly. The banks insist on protective provisions as conditions for loans. Typical provisions include maintenance of certain financial ratios, exclusively as regards all banking transactions, daily or weekly stock statement, continuity of key personnel, annual "cleanups," i.e., adjusting the loan account and compensating balances. The bank may require that the borrower maintain a minimum current ratio of, say, 2.2:1. If the current ratio falls below the minimum required level, the bank can 'call up', i.e. 'recall'. The loan, by simply serving a demand notice. Alternatively, it can activate previously obtained standing instructions to debit the borrower's account without any prior need to refer. This would, in any case, be perfectly legitimate even without any documents, given the banker's 'right to set-off', and debit the borrower's credit balance in any account(s) maintained at the bank. In India, public sector banks play a key role in such short-term financing, whose operations are conducted under the guidelines received from time to time from the Reserve Bank of India, The various guidelines and provisions are discussed separately.

Types of Unsecured Loans

Short-term unsecured loans have an original maturity date of one year or less. Certain types of unsecured loans may be renewed and extended beyond one year. Three principal types of short-term unsecured loans are line of credit, revolving credit agreement, and transaction loans.

Line of Credit. A line of credit signifies an arrangement between the bank and the client firm and represents the maximum amount of credit that the bank is willing to make available to the firm. A line of credit of Rs 300,000 means that the client firm can borrow up to Rs 300,000 from the bank. Normally, at least in theory, lines of credit are established for a period of one year. At the end of the one-year period, the bank's commercial lending officer and the client firm's financial manager review the firm's financial performance and its short-term borrowing needs for the coming year. Based on the firm's performance and needs, the line of credit may be renewed and the maximum credit limit may be adjusted upward or downward. Thus, a well-conducted account adhering to good financial decline in line with the terms of credit, may theoretically continue indefinitely.

The cash budget summarises the firm's expected cash inflows and outflows. If cash inflows are greater than outflows, the firm has a positive net cash flow figure. If the net cash flow figure is negative, the firm needs to borrow to make up the difference between its expected cash outflows and its inflows. Firms typically have seasonal variations in cash inflows and outflows. Short-term borrowings on a line of credit are designed to provide temporary financing to bridge the gap between cash inflows and outflows. By looking at a cash budget, one can determine whether borrowing needs are temporary or permanent. If borrowing needs are temporary, then sometimes during the cash budget period, the firm will show that on a cumulative basis, needed cash flows are positive. The maximum line of credit requirement is equal to the largest negative net cash flow figure on a cumulative basis.

Banks expect that borrowings on line of credit are to meet temporary financing requirements. This purpose is accomplished by requiring the borrower to "annually cleanup" the line of credit for a period of 30 to 60 days. During the cleanup period, as mentioned previously, there should not be a debit balance in the line of credit account. This requirement assures the bank that line of credit borrowings are being used for the purpose for which they were sanctioned, i.e., to meet temporary financing requirements—banks rightly being highly sensitive about proper end-use of loaned funds.

The line of credit provides the firm with considerable flexibility in financial planning. The funds are borrowed only when needed. When the firm has positive net cash flows, the surplus cash can be applied to reducing the balance on the line of credit, and, concomitantly, eliminating the interest burden. It should, however, be remembered that when a bank approves a line of credit, it is not guaranteeing that the funds will be made available on demand. However, most banks will honour line of credit arrangements for a firm that has not violated the credit provisions and whose credit worthiness has not deteriorated.

Revolving Credit Agreement. A revolving credit agreement is similar to a line of credit except that the bank makes a formal, legally binding commitment to extend credit to the client firm up to the agreed-upon credit limit. The client firm has to pay a commitment charge for the privilege of having funds made available on demand. Commitment charges could be either a lump sum payment due at the time the loan agreement is reached or could be based on the unused portion of the revolving credit. Assume that a company has received approval for a Rs 1 crore revolving credit loan. The bank may require a 0.5 per cent commitment fee of Rs 50,000. Alternatively, the commitment fee could be 1 per cent of the average unused balance on the revolving credit. For example, if the firm's borrowings average Rs 70,00,000, and its average unused balance is Rs 30,00,000, it will be required to pay a commitment fee of Rs 30,000.

Transaction Loans. A firm that seeks to borrow funds for some special purpose for a short time may not find a line of credit or revolving credit an appropriate source of funds. In this situation, the firm will find it convenient to take out a transaction loan. A transaction loan typically is of a very short duration—between 30 and 90 days. The bank is careful to assure itself that the borrower will have the funds available in a short time period for repayment of the loan.

Compensating Balances

Banks require client firms with a line of credit or a revolving credit arrangement to maintain a current account or demand deposit balance that is related either to the credit limit or to the amount borrowed. The required balances are called compensating balances and under some circumstances have the effect of raising the interest rate on the loan. The usual practice is for banks to require that 10 to 20 per cent of the funds borrowed on a line of credit be kept as a demand deposit balance. The rationale behind this provision is twofold: not only does this arrangement represent the borrower's stake in the business, spreading the risk, but it is also given the bank recourse to pre-empt this amount should the firm fail to adjust the outstanding on time. In other words, it is a cash margin retained by the bank on the loan, a sort of partial (and very tangible security).

Assume that a firm borrows Rs 2 crore on a line of credit and the lending bank requires a 15 per cent credit balance; 15 per cent of this Rs 2 crore loan, or Rs 30,00,000, will have to be kept in the firm's current account at the bank to meet the compensating balance requirement. Whether this compensating balance effectively raises the interest rate on the loan is dependent on whether the firm has a need to maintain a cash balance of Rs 30,00,000. Assume that the interest rate on the loan is 8 per cent. The firm wants to maintain a minimum balance of Rs 37,00,000 in its unit account. In this case, meeting the compensating balance requirement does not increase the interest rate on the credit line.

Next, assume that the firm has no need to maintain any unit account balance at the lending bank. By maintaining a compensating balance of 15 per cent of the loan, it is effectively getting to use only 100 - 15 = 85 per cent of the loan. However, the interest rate is applicable on 100 per cent of the loan. Therefore, the effective interest is higher than 8 per cent and is given by effective interest rate.

RATE = stated interest rate / 1 - compensating balance fraction

= 8 % / 1 - 0.15 = 9.4 %

The effective interest rate is 9.4 per cent.

Firms borrowing on a line of credit can try to reduce the effective interest rate by shifting some of their cash maintenance needs to the bank where they have their line of credit. The effective interest rate can also be lowered by securing a line of credit at the bank where the firm conducts the majority of its cash receipts and disbursements transactions. However, as per extant RBI guidelines, firms normally cannot avail loans from two separate banks, which amounts to double-financing—a serious offence in the eyes of Indian bankers. The answer to reducing the effective interest burden would be to make accounts receivable more efficient, and channelise all collections through/into the account maintained with the lending bank.

Interest Rates on Unsecured Loans

Interest rates on unsecured loans are negotiated between the bank and the client firm. In general, though the interest rate is related to the client's creditworthiness, the most creditworthy clients pay the prime rate. The prime rate is the lowest rate applicable to business loans. The lower the credit worthiness of the firm, the higher the interest rate the bank is going to charge on unsecured loans. The Interest Rates applicable to a firm are determined by the bank's risk classes and loan pricing matrix.

Risk Classes. Banks typically classify credit applicants into a series of risk classes. They may also use Credit Rating Agencies ratings to substantiate the creditworthiness of the applicants. Selected risk categories may be maintained as follows:

Class 1. Highest rated. Long-term debt is AAA rated. Stable Cash flows, interest coverage.

Class 2. High quality. Long-term debt is rated AA. Good interest coverage.

Class 3. Upper-medium quality. Debt is rated A. Interest coverage, though good, may be impaired under adverse economic conditions.

Class 4. Medium quality. Debt is rated BBB. Adequate interest coverage. Access to alternative financial markets limited except during favourable economic periods.

Class 5. Lower-medium quality with debt rated at BB or B. Interest coverage is acceptable but is subject to severe fluctuations.

Class 9. Collections of loans is questionable. Not enough collateral to cover existing debt.

Class 10. Debt is not collectible.

Loan Pricing Matrix. Once a credit applicant has been assigned a risk class, the interest rate applicable will be established from using a loan-pricing matrix. The loan-pricing matrix of a bank is shown in Table 2.3. According to this loan pricing matrix, a firm in risk class 3 that borrows on a Line of Credit would be paying the prime rate plus 0.7 per cent as interest rate on its loan. A firm in risk class 4, seeking an unsecured transaction loan for 60 days, would incur an interest rate of prime plus 1.5 per cent.

The assignment to risk classes is based strictly on conservative financial considerations. On occasion, the bank may feel that the need to develop the market for the bank's commercial lending practices requires that marketing considerations be given precedence over financial considerations. A risk class 2 firm may find that a bank, eager to expand its borrowing business, is willing to assign the firm to risk class 1. However, very rarely if ever will a bank be willing to treat a risk class 9 or 10 firm as a risk class 5 firm.

Table 2.3: Commercial Loan Pricing Matrixa[a]

Type of Loan	Risk Class				
	1	2	3	4	5
Unsecured, for up to 90 days	P	P	P + 1.50	P + 1.50	P + 2.25
Secured, for up to 90 days	P	P	P + 1.00	P + 1.00	P + 1.50
Unsecured, for 90 days to 1 year	P	P + 0.25	P + 1.75	P + 1.75	P + 2.50
Secured, for 90 days to 1 year	P	P + 0.25	P + 1.50	P + 1.50	P + 2.25

[a] P stands for the prime lending rate at the time loan is issued. Interest rates are in per cent.

Spot Quiz on Unsecured Loans

1. Unsecured loans generally do not impose any restrictive provisions on the borrower. T ❑ F ❑

2. A line of credit and a revolving credit agreement are identical except that the former involves a firm loan commitment on the lending bank's behalf. T ❑ F ❑

3. The "annual cleanup" is a short-term loan feature and is designed to ensure that the loan is used only for seasonal financing requirements. T ❑ F ❑

4. A contractor who has almost finished construction on a new home, has sold it, and will receive payment when construction is completed. He needs Rs 5,000 to finish construction and should obtain a transaction loan. T ❑ F ❑

5. Compensating balances are designed to either raise the interest rate or to shift the borrower's banking business to the lending bank. T ❑ F ❑

6. Using Table 2.3, and with a prime rate of 8 per cent, a risk class 5 borrower would pay 9.50 per cent on a line of credit loan. T ❑ F ❑

Secured Loans

Given a preference between a secured and unsecured loan, most firms would prefer to obtain an unsecured short-term loan. The primary reason is that the record-keeping costs of a secured loan can be fairly high. For a financially strong firm, one from risk classes 1 through 4, obtaining an unsecured loan is not much of a problem. However, for a firm that is not considered to be financially strong or for a relatively small firm, it becomes difficult to obtain an unsecured loan. These firms find that banks require collateral for a loan. A collateral is an asset that is used as a security to guarantee payment of principal and interest on a loan. If the collateral is sufficiently liquid, even a risk class 10 firm would have no problem in getting a loan. Government bonds and other marketable stocks and bonds make excellent collateral. In case of default, these assets can be quickly liquidated and the bank can recover its loan and delinquent interest. Other collateral items are land, buildings, equipments, accounts receivable, and inventories. Typically, land, buildings, and equipments are used to secure term and long-term borrowing. Short-term loans are typically secured by receivables and inventories. In this section, we shall discuss funds raised by pledging receivables, factoring, and inventory financing.

Pledging Accounts Receivable

After cash and marketable securities, accounts receivable are considered to be the most liquid assets on a firm's balance sheet. Other things being equal, a financial institution such as a bank or finance company will readily sanction a loan secured by accounts receivable. The lender will evaluate the quality of the receivables to be pledged, and the average size of the account pledged, i.e. the level of turnover over a period of time. Once these have been established, the pledging procedure can be implemented. These steps are explained in the following paragraphs.

Quality of Receivables Pledged. The lending institution evaluates thoroughly the quality of the receivables the borrower wants to pledge. If, on an average, the receivables appear to be of very high quality with almost a 100 per cent probability of payment, the lender may loan up to 90 per cent of the face amount of the receivables pledged. If the receivables appear to be of relatively low quality, the lender may be willing to lend only 25 per cent of the face value of the receivables. The higher the receivable quality, the higher their loan value.

Although a lender may be willing to lend anywhere from 25 to 90 per cent of the face value of the receivables pledged, he retains the right to reject any receivable that he does not wish to accept as a pledge. In addition, the lender holds the borrower liable for any accounts that become delinquent or default after they have been pledged.

Size of Accounts. Pledging receivables involves a considerable amount of record keeping for the lender. These record-keeping costs remain relatively constant irrespective of the rupee amount of the account being pledged. Smaller-size accounts cost the banks more per rupee of loan to service, than larger-size accounts. A firm with a lot of small-size accounts receivable will find it difficult to raise funds by pledging receivables at a reasonable cost. A firm may be able to negotiate a "floating lien" loan with a lending institution. With a floating lien, the lender does not maintain records on individual accounts. Rather, a general lien is assigned to all receivables. Since the lender is not tracking individual accounts under a floating lien, the chances of fraud by the borrower are higher than with specific pledging of accounts. As a precaution against exposing itself to undue risk, a lender will rarely lend more than 25 per cent of the face amount of receivables subject to a floating lien.

Pledging Procedure. Once the loan value of receivables has been established, the borrower sends to the lender a list of accounts, billing dates, and amounts involved. Assume that the lender has agreed to lend 80 per cent of the face value of receivables pledged. The borrower sends to the lender a schedule of accounts totaling Rs 1 crore. The borrower is now eligible to borrow any amount up to 80 per cent of Rs 1 crore, i.e., Rs 80,00,000, upon signing a promissory note.

Pledging of receivables can be either on a notification or non-notification basis. On a notification basis, the borrower notifies its accounts that payments on the receivables are to be made directly to the lender. On a non-notification basis the account is not informed of the financial arrangements between borrower and lender. The account remits payments to the borrower, who forwards it to the lender. The lender then checks the payment against the schedule provided by the borrower and reduces the borrower's loan balance by a corresponding amount. When pledging receivables is on a non-notification basis, the lender relies on the borrower to forward account payments to him. Should the borrower keep the checks, the lender would be ultimately holding (and financing) "receivables" that have already been paid! To prevent fraud of this nature, non-notification pledging allows the lender to randomly audit the borrower's books to see that payments on all pledged accounts are being forwarded to the lender.

The lender will also adjust the rupee value of accounts pledged for any discrepancies between the amount invoiced and the amount paid. These discrepancies are caused by the account taking a cash discount for early payment, taking credit for merchandise returned or adjusting for other invoice errors.

Interest Rates. Interest rates with pledged receivables financing are 2 to 4 per cent higher than the prime-lending rate. The lending institution may also charge a processing fee, which may equal 1 to 3 per cent of the average annual loan. Commercial finance companies charge rates that are higher than the rates charged by banks. The total effective interest with this type of receivables financing will vary from 10 to 20 per cent. This high interest rate does not imply that secured loans are more expensive than unsecured loans. The rates are high because the borrower is risky and does not have access to normal sources of unsecured loans.

Factoring Receivables

Factoring receivables is different from pledging receivables in that the receivable are sold to the factor or financial institution. In this section we examine the services provided by a factor and the mechanics of factoring.

Services Provided. A factor is a bank or other financial institution that buys the receivables of other firms. A factor provides two or three services: (1) credit checking, (2) lending, and perhaps (3) risk bearing. A factor acts as the credit-checking arm of the firm. Typically, when the firm receives the sale and is willing to buy the receivable the firm proceeds with filling the order. If the factor does not approve the sale and will not factor the receivable, the selling firm has to decide whether to reject the sale order or whether to fill it and carry the receivable itself. Factors have highly skilled credit checking departments. A small firm may choose to go with the factor's decision each time and simply not maintain its own credit department.

The factor also lends money in advance of the account payment. If the sale has been made on terms of net 30, the seller can obtain a loan immediately from the factor. The mechanics are explained later.

The factor may or may not perform a risk-bearing function. If the factoring is with recourse, the factor does not bear risk of default on the account. In factoring with recourse, bad-debt losses are charged against a reserve set up by the selling firm. In factoring without recourse, the factor absorbs bad-debt losses and does perform a risk-bearing function. The risk of bad-debt losses is transferred from the selling firm to the factor in factoring without recourse. The majority of factoring arrangements involve factoring without recourse.

Mechanics of Factoring. The services to be performed by the factor are detailed in a formal agreement. Most factoring agreements allow the selling firm the following options: (1) It can borrow an amount equal to the receivables factored less reserves and expenses; and (2) it can receive payment at the end of the credit period or earlier if the accounts pay before the end of the credit period. Most factoring agreements are on a notification basis. That is, the account is notified to send his payment directly to the factor. However, the account is generally not informed that his receivable has been sold to a factor.

Assume that the selling firm supplies goods worth Rs 20,000. It stamps the invoice notifying the buyer to pay directly to the factor. The factor charges 3 per cent of the invoice amount for credit checking and risk bearing. If the selling firm wants to borrow, the interest rate is 1 per cent per month. Furthermore, if the selling firm borrows on its account, it will need to pay 5 per cent of the invoice amount into a reserve fund. The reserve account is set up to adjust for damaged goods, returned goods, and cash discounts. Assuming that the firm sold goods on terms of net 30 and is borrowing funds, how much will it receive from factoring the Rs 20,000 receivable? The calculations are

Amount of receivable pledged		Rs 20,000
Less: Factoring commission (3%)	Rs 600	
Interest (1% for 30 days)	200	
Reserve (5%)	1000	
Total deductions		1,800
Amount of loan received		Rs 18,200

The firm will receive Rs 18,200. In addition, if the account pays the invoice amount without dispute then the selling firm is also paid the Rs 1,000 reserve amount. In this example, the interest rate was applied to the invoice amount. Frequently, factoring agreements call for applying the interest rate to the invoice amount less the factoring commission and reserve amount. In practice, these types of details are negotiated between the factor and the selling firm.

Factoring Costs. Factoring costs tend to be high. As shown in the preceding example, interest and factoring commissions equal 4 per cent of the invoice amount. Part of this high cost is accounted for by the amount of record keeping involved in factoring. However, it should be borne in mind that these costs include credit checking and risk-bearing services which, in the absence of factoring, would have to be borne by the selling firm.

Other Considerations. As with pledging receivables, factoring provides continuous financing. Once the financial relationship and satisfactory comfort levels between the factor and the selling firm has been established, the factor may allow the selling firm to occasionally overdraw its account during peak financing periods. For smaller firms, the costs of credit checking, controlling bad-debt expenses, and collecting may be higher than factoring costs. Finally, with the advent of high speed, large memory, low-cost computers, the record-keeping costs are coming down along with factoring costs.

Inventory Financing

Inventories are also used frequently as collateral for short-term loans. Inventory characteristics determine their loan value. Inventory financing may occur through a floating lien, trust receipts. These topics are discussed in the following paragraphs.

Inventory Characteristics. The extent to which inventory can be utilised as collateral for short-term loans is dependent upon its three major characteristics: perishability, marketability, and price stability. An item that is highly perishable will not command much collateral value; in case of default, the lender may simply be left with high-cost garbage as collateral. On the other hand, nonperishable items can be readily used as collateral. Inventory financing statistics reveal that approximately one-fifth of all inventory financing involves canned foods as collateral. Lumber, coal, grains, and vegetable oils are other products frequently used as collateral.

A second requirement for inventory used as collateral is that it be readily marketable. An inventory of lithographs and serigraphs by Krishna Reddy and Wilbur Streech will be nonperishable and may have high price stability, but they may not have marketability. A lending institution generally has no ambitions of going into the art gallery business and would most probably pass up the opportunity to provide a loan secured by valuable but slow moving inventory.

The final requirement for inventory to possess collateral value is that it have price stability. If the borrower defaults and the lender has to liquidate the collateral, the lender needs to be assured that the potential for recovering the loan amount is present. Such is not the case with inventory items whose market prices tend to fluctuate wildly over time. In general, if the price of the inventory is very unstable, its loan value will be relatively low.

Floating Lien. Under a floating lien the borrower pledges his entire inventory without any specific identification of inventory items. The lien is, in general, difficult to monitor. For example, the borrower can sell the liened inventory. Because of the vague nature of the collateral value of a floating lien, it is more often used as a subsidiary to another major collateral. This type of arrangement is usually referred to as hypothecation of stocks, in Indian banking parlance.

Trust Receipts. Under this short-term financing arrangement, the borrower acknowledges that he holds merchandise in trust for the lender. Examples of trust receipts financing are automobile dealers, farm equipment dealers, and television and appliance retailers. For example, an automobile dealer orders cars and pays for them through a bank loan. The automobile dealer also issues a trust receipt to their bank, indicating that he is holding the cars on trust for the bank. When a car is sold, the funds from the proceeds are sent to the bank to reduce the dealer's indebtedness.

The requirements for trust receipts financing call for specific identification of inventory goods. Cars, for example, have to be identified by their engine and chassis serial numbers to ascertain that all inventoried items listed as unsold are physically present on the premises.

Terminal Warehouse Receipts. With trust receipts financing, there is always the risk that the borrower will liquidate the inventory without transmitting funds to the lender. This problem is overcome through terminal warehouse receipts financing, which involves an independent third party. The inventory in question is stored in a bonded, public, or terminal warehouse. The warehouse issues a receipt describing the borrower's goods inventoried in the warehouse. The warehouse releases the goods only on the authorization of the lender. As a result, the lender is in a position to exercise considerable control and can be assured that inventoried items are released only after the borrower has met certain loan performance standards.

Field Warehouse Receipts. The procedure outlined in the preceding paragraph involves inventories in a public warehouse, but field warehouse receipts financing involves securing the inventory on the borrower's premises. Suppose that a lumber and paper products company has an inventory of plywood boards that it pledges to a bank as collateral. It is not economically and physically realistic to move this collateral into a public warehouse. Consequently, a field warehouse company sets up a temporary fence around the plywood boards on the borrower's premises, designates the area a field warehouse, inventories the goods, and sends a copy of the inventory to the lender. The field Warehouse Company will not release any goods in its possession without the lender's authority. This type of financing is called 'Factory-type pledge' in Indian banking parlance, and banks normally take precaution of posting a godown keeper and/or a godown chowkidar (at borrower's cost) for security considerations, and to release stocks only on written permission from the branch manager or other senior branch official.

The borrowing firm manufactures plywood boards and places them in the field warehouse. As construction firms place orders for the plywood boards, the lumber company forwards the orders to the lending bank which, in turn, directs the field warehouse company godown keeper to release appropriate amounts of goods from its custody. As the lumber company receives payment, it turns them over to the lender to credit its loan account.

Financing Costs. Inventory financing costs generally tend to be high. In the case of warehouse receipts financing, they tend to be especially high. Inventory financing is not a feasible alternative for firms with small inventories. Inventory financing is desirable from the viewpoint that debt raising capacity increases as financing requirements due to rising inventory levels increase. Also, it is reputed that pilferage and physical damage to the inventory is minimised with warehouse receipt financing.

Spot Quiz on Secured Loans

1. A secured loan requires that the borrower identify a specific collateral item for a loan. T ❑ F ❑
2. A firm with a conservative approach to granting credit to its buyers, should be able to borrow up to a high percentage of the face amount of its accounts receivable. T ❑ F ❑
3. Smaller-size accounts receivable result in lower cost per loan rupee than larger-size receivables. T ❑ F ❑
4. Interest rates are higher for secured loans than for unsecured loans for firms in a high-risk class. T ❑ F ❑
5. High perishability and low marketability increase the loan value of inventories. T ❑ F ❑
6. Floating liens are not significantly meaningful as collateral devices. T ❑ F ❑
7. A corrupt field warehouse company can negate the collateral value of warehouse inventories. T ❑ F ❑

Commercial Paper

Large, financially strong corporations can borrow on a short-term unsecured basis by issuing commercial paper. Commercial paper refers to short-term unsecured promissory notes issued by firms and purchased by other firms, banks, insurance companies, and other financial institutions.

Characteristics of Commercial Paper

Commercial paper can be issued only by large, financially strong firms. Small firms, even if they are financially strong, will not find a market for their commercial paper. The original maturity of commercial paper can vary from 30 days to 180 days. The interest rate on commercial paper is about 0.5 per cent *lower* than the prime rate. Commercial paper allows the issuer to raise short-term funds quickly and at comparatively low rates. It allows the buyers to invest their excess cash in safe, highly liquid, marketable securities. One of the disadvantages of commercial paper is that it can be sold most readily only during periods when firms have cash surpluses. During periods of high economic activity and tight money supply, the competition for funds in the commercial paper market tends to become spirited. As a result, the differential between the prime rate and the commercial paper rate diminishes during tight money periods.

Whereas banks are legally prevented from extending credit over a certain amount to a client, such limitations do not apply to raising funds by issuing commercial paper. Large finance companies would not be able to meet their borrowing needs by dealing with banks. They have to issue commercial paper for short-term borrowing. One disadvantage in using commercial paper is that it cannot be repaid before maturing, whereas a short-term bank loan can be repaid before it matures.

Issuing Commercial Paper

Commercial paper can be issued either directly by the seller or through a dealer. Large firms with large amounts of commercial paper outstanding will sell their paper directly to investors. The interest rate on directly placed paper is lower than paper sold through dealers. Small industrial firms find it easier to sell their paper through dealers. Dealers will handle the commercial paper of a firm only if they feel the firm is financially sound.

Unsecured bank loans and commercial paper are similar as they both provide short-term financing. Each has its advantages and disadvantages. A firm that has easy access to the commercial market should still maintain a cordial banking relationship. During tight money periods, the firm may find that it is easier to deal with a bank rather than a temporarily restricted paper market.

Spot Quiz on Commercial Paper

1. A firm that is turned down by a bank for a loan will find the borrowing easier in the commercial paper market. T ❑ F ❑

2. Commercial paper interest rates are low because they are safe, liquid investments for buyers. T ❑ F ❑

Questions

1. What is meant by trade credit? What types of trade credit arrangements exist? Explain briefly.

2. What type of trade credit arrangement is most suitable for the following situations:

   a. A school supplies manufacturer needs to finance seasonally high inventory levels.

   b. A tool and die shop in Noida receives an order from an automobile manufacturer and needs to increase inventories.

   c. A retailer has submitted the winning bid on the merchandise of a clothing store that is going out of business.

   Explain your answers.

3. Sometimes trade credit is used because it has been extended. Other times firms make a conscious effort to utilise trade credit. What factors would influence a firm's decision to utilise trade credit?

4. Explain the credit terms you would use in the following situations:

   a. Accepted industry terms are 2/10, net 30 and you are trying to increase sales by offering more attractive credit terms.

   b. A new company has won a multi-crore contract from the government and wants to buy raw materials from you on credit. Its inventory turnover is expected to be approximately 10.

5. What types of unsecured loans would be available to a firm? What are the relative merits of each one?

6. What are compensating balances? Why do banks require firms to maintain one?

7. If you were a president of a small bank, would you utilise the risk classes and loan pricing matrix mentioned in this chapter? Why or why not?

8. What factors influence the loan value of receivables to be pledged?

9. What are the important differences in the functions being performed by a lender with receivables as collateral and a factor of receivables?

10. Explain or describe the following terms:

    a. Inventory financing

    b. Trust receipt financing

    c. Warehouse receipts

11. Explain the differences, if any, between the following pairs of words or phrases:

    a. Pledging and factoring.

    b. Terminal warehouse receipts and field warehouse receipts.

    c. Commercial paper and unsecured loans.

    d. Implicit costs and explicit costs.

12. If rates on commercial paper are lower than the prime rate, should a large, risk class one firm raise short-term funds strictly by issuing commercial paper? Explain your answer.

Problems

1. Calculate the opportunity cost of not taking the cash discount under each of the following credit terms:

    a. 1.5/10, net 30.

    b. 1.5/10, net 30, EOM, invoice received May 15.

    c. 3/10, net 60, ROG, shipped May 15, received June 18.

    d. 10/60, net 61.

2. Rockbottom Corporation has a Rs 5 crore line of credit with a bank. The bank requires Rockbottom to maintain 20 per cent of borrowings on the credit line as compensating balance. The interest rate on borrowings on the line of credit is 8.5 per cent.

   a. Rockbottom needs Rs 3 crore to pay for increased inventories. How much would it have to borrow to obtain the necessary Rs 3 crore?

   b. What is the effective interest rate on the line of credit borrowing?

3. United Breweries has a Rs 3 crore line of credit with a bank. UB is expected to maintain a certain compensating balance for any borrowing on the credit line. The interest rate on the line of credit is 9 per cent. For the year, UB's borrowing has averaged Rs 2.5 crore of which Rs 50,00,000 was maintained as a compensating balance.

   a. What are the compensating balance requirements?

   b. What is the effective interest rate that UB paid on its credit line borrowing?

   c. Is there any other way to verify the answer for part (b) above? Explain.

4. Essel Corporation is seeking to raise short-term funds by factoring receivables. It has talked with two factors and is trying to decide which factor to use. Factor A charges 3.5 per cent factoring commission on gross invoices. Interest rate is 1 per cent per month on the gross invoice amount. Factor A requires that 5 per cent of the gross invoice amount be placed in a reserve until the account has paid. Factoring would be with recourse. Factor B charges 4.0 per cent factoring commission on the gross invoice amount and 1.0 per cent per month interest on the invoice amount less factoring commissions and reserve (which is 5 per cent of the invoice amount). Factoring is without recourse.

   a. Assume that Essel wants to immediately factor Rs 1,00,000 in receivables and borrow the maximum amount allowed. What is the amount of the loan it will receive from factor A and Factor B? You may assume that the receivables to be factored will average a collection period of one month.

b. Essel wishes to enter into a continuous long-term factoring arrangement with either factor A or factor B. What does it need to consider before selecting A or B? Should Essel give its business to A or B? Support your answer with illustrations/examples.

5. Funskool has recently started manufacturing a new toy called "Minerva." It does absolutely nothing at all and is rapidly becoming a fad item on campuses across the nation. The sudden surge in sales and inventory requirement surprised Funskool. The efforts to increase sales resulted in creating cash shortages. As a result the company has delayed payments on its payables. Although the credit terms allowed Funskool to call for payment in 30 days, the present level of payables shows 60 days of payables outstanding. The company is seeking a way to become current on its payables. It would prefer not to do so by using permanent financing, since it knows that the surge in sales is temporary. Funskool balance sheet is as follows:

Funskool Cooperative

Balance Sheet (in Rs)

Cash	Rs 200	Accounts payable	Rs 2,200
Receivables	800	Notes payable	400
Inventory	3,000	Accruals	300
Current assets	Rs 4,000	Current liabilities	Rs 2,900
Building	1,200	Long-term debt	1,700
Net plant	1,800	Net worth	2,400
Total assets	Rs 7,000	Total claims	Rs 7,000

What types of financing alternatives are available to Funskool? Which alternative or alternatives should it use to become current on its payables? Support your answer. (The answer to this problem should be descriptive rather than quantitative).

6. HMT Ltd. is seeking to raise Rs 50 crore on a short-term financing basis. It has three alternatives available:

a. It could forego cash discounts on credit terms of 1/10, net 30. The increase in payable outstanding would be sufficient to provide it with the required financing.

b. It could borrow any amount up to Rs 100 crore on a line of credit at 8.5 per cent. The compensating balance requirement is 20 per cent.

c. It could issue commercial paper at 8 per cent. The dealer would charge a handling fee of Rs 50,000 per year on Rs 5 crores paper issue.

Evaluate the advantages and disadvantages of each issue. Which is the best source of financing from a cost basis? What type of financing plan would you recommend for HMT and why?

Answers to Spot Quizzes

Trade Credit

1. No promissory note is involved. T ❑ F ☑
2. Lower turnover goods generally require extended credit periods. T ❑ F ☑
3. This is a viable strategy gaining market share. T ☑ F ❑
4. It is still 36 per cent. T ❑ F ☑
5. An invoice should be paid on the due date. T ❑ F ☑

Unsecured Loans

1. Unsecured loans typically involve protective provisions. T ❑ F ☑
2. The revolving credit agreement has the commitment. T ❑ F ☑
3. It is designed to ensure that the financing need is short term. T ☑ F ❑
4. The transaction loan is appropriate here. T ☑ F ❑
5. Either way the bank is seeking to increase its return on the loan. T ☑ F ❑
6. It would be 10.25 or 10.50 per cent. T ❑ F ☑

Secured Loans

1. A loan can be secured with a general lien. T ☐ F ☑
2. Its receivables would include few doubtful accounts. T ☑ F ☐
3. They result in higher cost per loan dollar. T ☐ F ☑
4. They are higher for unsecured loans. T ☐ F ☑
5. They reduce the loan value. T ☐ F ☑
6. They are difficult to monitor. T ☑ F ☐
7. By releasing inappropriate amount of goods. T ☑ F ☐

Commercial Paper

1. The commercial paper market is limited to strong firms. T ☐ F ☑
2. Investors buy them as short-term investments. T ☑ F ☐

Intermediate-term and Lease Financing

More than 900 years ago, during the reign of William the Conqueror, the Manor of Aldenham was leased from the Abbot of St. Albans by the Abbot of Westminster for a period of 20 years at an annual rent of 100 shillings.[6] This lease is an example of a financial lease and is no different in concept from the leases being written now. Leases are viewed by businesses as an alternative to borrowing and buying. For example, a company that wishes to acquire data processing capabilities can do so either by borrowing the funds to buy a computer or by leasing it. If the computer is bought, its purchase may be financed by an intermediate-term loan. An intermediate-term loan is one repaid within 1 to 10 years. Intermediate-term loans are popularly called term loans.

6. See Happy Pierce, "Leasing and the Lessee,: Management, vol. 57 (December 1975), p. 33.

Term loans and leases have a number of factors in common. First, both term loans and leases are liabilities. A term loan generally has an explicit interest rate and has to be repaid according to a fixed schedule. A lease may have an explicit or an implied interest rate. It too involves requirements for periodic payments. Second, both term loans and leases provide intermediate-term financing. Third, in evaluating term loans and leases, one considers the loan and lease requirements and the interest rates. The question of whether the use of the equipment should be acquired has already been decided during the capital budgeting stage. These similarities between term loans and leases lead financial managers to consider them as alternative methods for intermediate-term financing. In this chapter, discussion on term loans is followed by a consideration of lease financing.

Intermediate-Term Loans

A short-term loan is one having a maturity of less than one year. Loans maturing within 1 to 10 years are considered to be intermediate-term or term loans. Sources for term loans are banks, and financial institutions. Some of the more important characteristics of term loans are discussed in the following paragraphs.

Characteristics of Term Loans

Term loans are different from other types of loans in a variety of ways including maturity, repayment schedule, collateral, costs, and provisions.

Maturity. As stated previously, the maturity for a term loan varies from 1 to 10 years. The 10-year limit is somewhat arbitrary in classifying a loan as a term loan. However, in recent years financial institutions are becoming less reluctant to issue term loans with maturities up to 10 years. The classification of loans with maturities of up to 10 years as term loans is becoming very common. The maturity of a term loan is dependent upon the financial institution lending the funds. Banks are generally reluctant to issue term loans with maturities in excess of 5 to 6 years. On the other hand, financial institutions frequently underwrite term loans with maturities of 10 years.

Short-term loans are generally repaid as the firm generates excess cash flows. Long-term loans are generally repaid in full at maturity. Term loans are typically repaid according to a specified schedule. The most typical situation requires fixed payments, which include both principal and interest, on a monthly, semiannual, quarterly, or annual basis. The size of the periodic payment is such that when the last payment is made, the loan is fully paid and the lender is provided his required return. The repayment of term loans is discussed in the following section.

The particular procedure of making equal payments periodically to repay a loan is called loan amortisation. For example, a company borrows Rs 800,000 for 10 years and makes year-end equal payments of Rs 124,655.25 every year for 10 years. At the end of the tenth year, the loan will have been fully repaid and will have provided the lender a 9 per cent interest rate. On rare occasions, the loan amortisation is such that only a portion of the loan is repaid, leaving a large or "balloon" final payment. For example, the lender and borrower by mutual agreement may amortise only Rs 600,000 of the Rs 800,000 loan. In this case, the 10 annual payments would be Rs 111,491.44 each. The borrower would also have to repay the unamortised Rs 200,000 portion of the loan at the end of the tenth year. Both of these examples are explained in the next section.

Collateral. Financial institutions underwriting term loans generally require collateral on the loans. Since these loans are used for specific purposes such as purchase of computers, machinery, and so forth, the loans can be readily secured by the new equipment being purchased. Occasionally, stocks bonds, real estate, and other assets are also used as collateral for term loans, especially those of amounts of 5 lacs and above.

Costs. The interest rate on a term loan is usually higher than the interest rate on short-term loans. Term loans rates also reflect the credit worthiness of the borrower and the liquidity and marketability of the collateral used to secure the loan. For a financially sound borrower, the term loan rate will be about 0.5 per cent higher than the prime lending rate.

Interest rates on term loans can either remain fixed for the duration of the loan or vary with changes in the prime rate. If the term loan has a variable "ceiling" rates. For example, a term loan agreement may provide that the interest on the unamortised portion of the loan will be at a prime plus 0.5 per cent rate but in no case will be higher than 10 per cent or lower than 7 per cent. In this case, the 7 and 10 per cent rates are the floor and ceiling rates, respectively.

In addition to interest expense, term loans may entail other costs. The lending institution may charge a moderate loan commitment fee. Occasionally, the lending institution may require that warrants or options to buy common stock at specified prices be provided by the borrower. This allows the lender to participate in the anticipated growth of the borrower's business. Insurance companies providing term loans prefer to use this device to gain additional returns.

Provisions. Financial institutions making term loans need to assure themselves that the borrower continues to have the potential to make interest and principal payments at the scheduled intervals. This need to secure their financial position leads term lenders to incorporate a variety of provisions in the lending agreement. These provisions are designed to provide the lender with timely financial information about the borrower and to impose certain restrictions on the borrower. For example, the lending arrangement may require the borrower to maintain a minimum current ratio. If the borrower's current ratio falls below the minimum level, then, at its option, the lender may require immediate payment of the unamortised portion of the term loan.

Another provision regulates the amount of new long-term debt that the borrower can acquire. This provision typically requires that the borrower must secure the lender's approval before the borrower can issue any new long-term debt or sign leases. This provision allows the lender to exercise control over the borrower's indebtedness and to keep the borrower from becoming too indebted.

Another common term loan provision requires the borrower to provide the lender with periodic balance sheets, income statements, cash budgets and sources, and uses of funds statements. This allows the lender to monitor the borrower's financial condition and to take or suggest corrective actions when needed.

Finally, the term loan agreement may also require the borrower not to make changes in its executive ranks without the lender's permission. The lender may also require sufficient life insurance on the borrower's key managerial personnel. These provisions are designed to protect the lender from losses resulting from unforeseen changes in the borrower's important personnel.

Repaying Term Loans

Term loans are generally repaid on a periodic, systematic basis. Term lenders prefer this procedure because it enhances the borrower's capability to repay the loan. A large lump-sum loan repayment at maturity may place a heavy financial burden on the borrower, whereas with small periodic payments the borrower is not unduly financially burdened. A second reason for amortising loans has to do with the use of funds from the loans. Term loans are usually obtained for purchasing equipment. Loan amortisations are more desirable because loan repayments can be geared to the cash flows being generated by the equipment.

In this section two different loan amortisation procedures will be considered: full amortisation and one that results in a balloon payment.

Full Amortisation. Under full amortisation, the borrower makes periodic payments until the loan and interest component are fully paid. To explain the example cited previously, assume that Central Manufacturing Corporation borrows Rs 800,000 for 10 years at an interest rate of 9 per cent. The interest rate is the effective interest rate on the remaining balance. In addition, the bank making this term loan requires that the loan be repaid in 10 equal installments which would include interest as well as payment on the principal.

The annual payment required to repay this loan can be determined by using Equation 2.4.

$$P_O = P \times IFAP_{n/i} \qquad \text{.................................}(2.4)$$

Where, P_O is the present value of an annuity of P rupees received every year for n years and discounted at one per cent. In the term loan situation, the annual payment is P rupees and is found by

$$P = P_O \times IFA_{n/i} \qquad \text{.................................}(2.5)$$

In the example cited, P_O is Rs 800,000. The annuity factor, rounded off to four decimal places, for Re 1 received every year for 10 years and discounted at 9 per cent is 6.4177 ($PVIFA_{10,\ 9\%}$). Then

P = Rs 800,000 / 6.4177 = Rs 124,655.25.

After Central has made 10 annual payments of Rs 124,655.25, it will have fully repaid the term loan and the bank will have been provided with its 9 per cent interest rate.

Table 2.4 shows how this annual payment is divided between interest and payment on principal. At the time of loan, or at time O, the beginning balance is Rs 800,000. At the end of the first year, an annual payment of Rs 124,655.25 is made. This amount includes interest of Rs 800,000 × 0.09% = Rs 72,000. The remaining payment, Rs 124,655.25 - Rs 72,000 = Rs 52,655.25 is applied to the beginning balance to pay off a portion of the loan. The first-year ending balance is Rs 800,000 - Rs 52,655.25 = Rs 747,344.75. The first-year ending balance becomes the second-year beginning balance. Interest on this is computed at 9 per cent. The difference between the second-year payment and interest is used to reduce the second-year beginning balance. This process continues until the final payment is made at the end of the tenth year and the loan is completely repaid.

Table 2.4: Term Loan Amortisation[a]

1	2	3	4=2×0.09	5=3–4	6=2–5
End of Year	Beginning Balance	Annual Payment	Interest at 9 %	Loan Repayment	Ending Balance
0	Rs 800,000.00	Rs –	Rs –	Rs –	Rs 800,000.00
1	800,000.00	124,655.25	72,000.00	52,655.25	747,344.75
2	747,344.75	124,655.25	67,261.03	57,394.22	689,950.53
3	689,950.53	124,655.25	62,095.55	62,559.70	627,390.83
4	627,390.83	124,655.25	56,465.17	38,190.08	559,200.75
5	559,200.75	124,655.25	50,328.07	74,327.18	484,873.57
6	484,873.57	124,655.25	43,638.62	81,016.63	403,856.94
7	403,856.94	124,655.25	36,347.12	88,308.13	315,548.81
8	315,548.81	124,655.25	28,399.39	96,255.86	219,292.95
9	219,292.95	124,655.25	19,736.37	104,918.88	114,374.07
10	114,374.07	124,655.25	10,281.18[a]	114,374.07	--

[a] For the tenth year only, interest is the difference between annual payment balance. This rounding-off error exists because only four decimals were utilised in the annuity factor used in computing the annual payment.

One word of caution related to Table 2.4 has to do with the rounding-off error. We used a rounded-off annuity factor of 6.4177; the actual annuity factor is 6.4176550. Rounding off the annuity factor changes the annual payment slightly. The net cumulative result is that when one calculates the interest for the last year, it becomes Rs 114,374.07 × 0.09% = Rs 10,293.67. It should be recognised that minor errors are caused by rounding-off annuity and discount factors. This error is remedied by either using more significant decimals or by treating interest expense in the last year as a residual item—the difference between the annual payment and the tenth-year beginning balance.

Balloon Payment Amortisation. On occasion, firms prefer to amortise less than the full amount of the loan. Amortising only a portion of the term loan results in the firm's making a relatively large or "balloon" payment when the loan matures. One reason for doing this may be that the unamortised portion of the loan on maturity may equal the anticipated salvage value of the equipment to be purchased with the term loan. Another reason is that with a balloon payment, the firm's annual payments are smaller, except of course for the last payment, which includes - and comprises - the entire remaining portion of the unamortised loan. A firm may choose a balloon payment with the idea of refinancing the unamortised loan at maturity.

Assume that Central Manufacturing and the lending bank agree to amortise Rs 600,000 of the Rs 800,000, with the unamortised portion or Rs 200,000 due at the end of the tenth year. One way to evaluate this term loan is to view it as two separate loans—one for Rs 600,000 and one for Rs 200,000. The annual payment for Rs 600,000 portion is determined by using equation 2.5;

P = Rs 600,000 / 6.4177 = Rs 93,491.44

The Rs 200,000 portion is not repaid until the last year. Interest due every year for 10 years on this amount is Rs 200,000 × 0.09% = 18,000. Total annual payment for the first 9 years on this loan is Rs 93,491.44 + Rs 18,000 = Rs 111,491.44. The tenth and final payment would include the unamortised portion of the loan also and would equal Rs 111,491.44 + Rs 200,000 = Rs 311,491.44.

In this section, we have considered two alternative term loan repayment procedures. Variations would include situations in which the applicable interest rate is not fixed or the annual payment amount is not fixed. The technique for amortising term loans of these types is similar to the procedure outlined in Table 2.4.

Advantages and Disadvantages of Term Loans

As with any financing procedure, term loans are not without their advantages and disadvantages.

Advantages. The relationship between borrower and lender is one-to-one, and it is easy for them to negotiate loan terms that meet the special need of the borrower. Repayment schedules, annual payments, and maturity date can be negotiated to meet the borrower's needs. The borrower also finds it easy to negotiate with one lender and does not have to go through a SEBI registration as is the case with typical bond financing. The lending institution also may not seek certain financial information that the firm may be hesitant to divulge. Term loans can be arranged more quickly than long-term loans. The firm or borrower is assured of funds for a number of years, which is not the case with borrowing on a credit line. Finally, smaller firms with limited access to capital markets find term loans very convenient.

Disadvantages. The borrower may feel that, at times, term loan provisions are too restrictive. The limitations on issuing new debt may hinder the firm's ability to finance future growth. Another disadvantage of term loans is that at times the cost may be high. If the loans involve issuance of options on warrants that are exercised, then the effective cost of the loan to the borrower increases. Despite these disadvantages, term loans are a major source of financing.

Spot Quiz on Intermediate Term Loans

1. Term loans, because they are a relatively new concept, are a rapidly growing source of financing. T ❑ F ❑

2. Term loans and leases are similar because both create a liability. T ❑ F ❑

3. Term loans require that the loan be fully paid by the maturity date. T ❑ F ❑

4. Some term loans have costs that are not known until the loan matures. T ❑ F ❑

5. Variable interest rates on term loans are always advantageous for the lender. T ❑ F ❑

6. The provisions of term loans are designed to protect the financial interests of the lending institution. T ❑ F ❑

7. A term-loan lender views a fully amortised loan as an annuity. T ❑ F ❑

8. Balloon payment term loans may be desirable for a firm that anticipates large cash flows around the time the loan matures. T ❑ F ❑

Lease Financing

Firms are generally interested in acquiring the use of equipment. One way to acquire use is to buy the equipment. The same result can also be achieved by leasing the equipment. A lease is a contractually established obligation by the lessee to pay the lessor a series of payments for the use of certain assets. In this section, we shall consider types of leases, lease capitalisation, and the advantages and disadvantages of leasing.

Type of Leases

There are two major types of leases – operating and financial.

Operating Lease. An operating or service lease is one that allows the lessee to cancel the lease deal at his convenience. Telephone service is an example of an operating lease. The telephone user can, at his or her convenience, discontinue telephone service. Another example of a service lease is leasing copying equipment from companies such as Xerox Corporation and A. B.

Dick Corporation. These companies typically lease their equipment on a 30-day cancellation notice basis. If a lessee cancels a service lease, the equipment is leased to another lessee. The lessor expected to recover the costs plus profits over the economic life of the equipment. Operating lease payments usually include charges for servicing and maintaining the leased equipment.

Financial Lease. A financial lease is a non-cancelable, contractual obligation of the lessee to pay the lessor a fixed amount for a specified time period for the use of certain assets. A financial lease includes the following features:

1. The lease is non-cancelable. The lessee cannot "walk away" from the lease without becoming liable for the remaining lease payment.

2. The lease is fully amortised. A fully amortised lease is one that returns to the lessor all his costs plus a reasonable return.

3. A financial lease does not include repair and maintenance services. A variation of the financial lease in which the lessor pays the maintenance and insurance costs is called a maintenance lease.

A special type of financial lease is a sale and leaseback arrangement. In a sale and leaseback, a firm sells an asset to another firm, which leases the asset back to the first firm. Special features of a sale and leaseback arrangement are as follows:

1. Assets involved can be either old or new. A firm could sell an old fully depreciated plant and then lease it back. Another firm could buy a new IBM computer, sell it to a finance company, and then lease it right back.

2. Assets are sold at or close to appraised market value.

3. The leaseback arrangement calls for lease payments that return all costs plus a fair return to the lessor. That is, the lease is fully amortised.

Sale and leaseback arrangements and financial leases are identical. The practical distinction is that financial leases involve assets new to the firm whereas sale and leasebacks typically involve assets that the firm is already using.

Lease Capitalisation

Financial leases call for the lessee to make periodic payments to meet contractual obligations. As such, it is not conceptually different from a loan. Lease capitalisation involves capitalising the lease payments at an appropriate capitalisation rate and showing the capitalised amount as a liability. An entry equal to the capitalised lease obligations is shown on the assets side of the balance sheet.

The capitalisation rate is generally equal to the lessee's marginal cost of borrowing. For example, a corporation leases a computer system for 6 years. Lease payments are to be made in six annual payments of Rs 340,000 each. The first payment is made on the day that the computer is installed. The second payment is due 2 years from today, and so on. Payments three through six are capitalised at the firm's marginal borrowing rate of 9 per cent. The capitalised value of payments 3 through 6 is Rs 340,000 (0.84168 + 0.77218 +0.70843 + 0.64993) = Rs 1,010,555. The balance sheet entry for this leasing transaction would be

Assets		Liabilities	
Net leased assets	Rs 1,350,555	Current liabilities	
		Lease obligation	Rs 340,000
		Long-term liabilities	
		Lease capitalisation	Rs 1,010,555

These entries would be adjusted each year as the firm makes its lease payment.[7] Keep in mind that the net capitalised value of the lease of Rs 1,350,555 + Rs 340,000 = Rs 1,690,555.

Cost of Leasing

The typical situation in leasing involves a decision either to borrow and buy or to lease the equipment. The best alternative of buying or leasing is

7. The discussion on lease capitalisation is necessarily sketchy here; the reader is referred to any standard managerial accounting text for a more detailed accounting treatment.

the one with the highest net present value. This situation is discussed in the last section of the chapter. Another situation could be when the item available is for lease only and cannot be purchased. Here the leasing analysis becomes intermingled with the capital budgeting decision itself. All leases, however, involve a rate of return to the lessor. One way to conceptualise a before-tax cost of leasing is to view the lessor's cost of leasing. Consider the computer system lease example given previously. Assume that the computer system costs the lessor Rs 1.68 crore and that the investment tax credit is passed along to the lessee. Maintenance and service costs are also borne by the lessee. From the lessor's viewpoint, the lease involves an outflow of Rs 1.68 crore at t = 0 for the purchase, an inflow of Rs 340,000 at t = 0 from the first lease payment, another Rs 340,000 at t -1 for the second payment, and so on. The rate of return for the lessor is that discount rate which equates the sum of the present values of lease payments with Rs 1.68 crore. Or

$$\text{Rs } 1{,}680{,}000s = E^5\, t = 0 \text{ Rs } 340{,}000\ (1+ r)^{-t}$$

$$= \text{Rs } 340{,}000\ (E^5\ t = 0\ (1+ r)^{-t}$$

$$= \text{Rs } 340{,}000\ (1+ E^5\ t =1\ (1+ r)^{-t} \qquad ....(2.6)$$

$$= \text{Rs } 340{,}000\ (1 + IFA5/r)$$

Equation 2.6 can be restated in terms of the annuity factor IFA as

$$IFA5/r = (\text{Rs } 1{,}680{,}000/\text{Rs } 340{,}000 - 1 = 3.94118 \quad ...(2.7)$$

The IFA $_{5,\ 8\%}$ is 3.99271 and IFA $_{5,\ 9\ \%}$ is 3.88965. By interpolation r is found to be 8.5 per cent. A way of identifying the leasing cost is to consider this 8.5 per cent return to the lessor as the lessee's cost of leasing. It should be recognised that in calculating the cost of leasing this way, we are ignoring tax effects and consequently depreciation as a tax shield. This method, however, does provide us with a reasonable perspective on leasing cost.

Equation 2.7 can be generalised to estimate the lessor's rate of return on any lease. If it is assumed that the first lease payment is made at the time the equipment is installed, then

$$IFAn\text{-}1/r = C/L - 1 \qquad ....(2\text{-}8)$$

where

n = length of lease

C = cost of equipment

L = annual lease payment

r = lessor's rate of return on the lease

The annuity factor can be used to solve for r as shown in the example given previously.

One interesting factor to note is that the gross lease capitalised value does not necessarily have to equal the cost of the equipment being leased. The answer lies in the fact that the lessors' rate of return is generally different from the lessee's lease capitalisation rate.

Advantages and Disadvantages of Leasing

Leasing equipment possesses a variety of advantages and disadvantages for the lessee.

Advantages of Leasing. Lease financing is viewed to possess a number of advantages for the lessee. Perhaps one of the major advantages of leasing is that it provides for the use of equipment with 100 per cent debt financing. That is, a firm that is leasing equipment does not have to make a down payment. Such is not the case when a firm borrows to buy the same equipment. Very rarely will a lending institution provide a loan equal to the purchase price of the equipment. More typically, it will require the firm to take an equity position equal to 10 or 20 per cent of the equipment's purchase price (called 'margin' by banks in India). Some, however, argue that this advantage may be illusory, because 100 per cent financing provided by leasing uses up more of the firm's debt capacity than buying the equipment with an 80 per cent loan.

The current trend in financial reporting is towards full disclosure of financial obligations created by leasing arrangements. Once firms are required to capitalise lease obligations and to integrate lease capitalisation fully into their financial statements, the advantage of 100 per cent financing in leasing will diminish significantly.

Another advantage of leasing is that it provides the lessee with flexibility in acquiring the use of specialised equipment that may become obsolete for the lessee but may be still a productive asset for another firm. Items such as computers and copying machines fall in this category. A third generation

IBM equipment may become obsolete as far as a large manufacturer is concerned but may be readily utilised by a small manufacturer. A firm may prefer to lease a computer and then let the lessor handle the subsequent lease of the computer to another firm. The lessor has specialised skills in doing this and can do a better job of leasing the equipment again.

Another advantage of leasing is that the provisions typically associated with term loans are not present in lease financing. A firm that does not wish to conform to minimum current ratio requirements, and so forth, may find the lack of these restrictions in lease financing sufficient motive to prefer leasing to borrowing.

A final advantage in leasing is that the lessor and lessee can negotiate over who utilises the investment tax credit. A firm that is not able to fully utilise the tax credit may let the lessor retain the credit and settle for lower annual lease payments. This planning flexibility is not available with borrowing and buying when the tax credit goes to the buyer.

Disadvantages of Leasing. The major disadvantage of leasing is that the residual value of the leased asset at the termination of the lease belongs to the lessor. The typical leasing arrangement calls for a full amortisation of the cost of the equipment. One frequently encounters examples where the cost of leasing an automobile covers complete amortisation over 4 years of the automobile cost. If, after 4 years, the lessor can sell the leased automobile for more than zero rupees, he or she gained at the expense of the lessee. Another example is full amortisation of costs in a sale and leaseback of a building and the land on which it is constructed. While the building will generally depreciate in value, very rarely will the land value decline to its eventual fully amortised cost of zero rupees. On the contrary it will probably appreciate handsomely over the given period.

Another disadvantage of leasing is that typically the lessor's rate of return is higher than the lessee's cost of borrowing.

This makes borrowing a more desirable alternative than leasing.

Spot Quiz on Lease Financing

1. The principal difference between an operating lease and a financial lease is that the former is cancelable whereas the latter is not. T ❑ F ❑

2. A sale and leaseback arrangement is a disguised form of an operating lease. T ❑ F ❑

3. Properly capitalised leases constitute a proper measure of the firm's debt obligations in leasing transactions. T ❑ F ❑

4. The rate of return to the lessor can be considered as the cost of leasing to the lessee. T ❑ F ❑

5. Leasing is advantageous because leasing costs are generally lower than borrowing costs. T ❑ F ❑

Comprehensive Example

In this chapter, it has been indicated that leasing and borrowing are equivalent alternatives for financing the use of equipment. The firm would prefer to use that alternative which has the lowest cost. In this section, an example is presented that provides the foundation for evaluating a lease versus borrowing situation.

Wilson Industries is a relatively small manufacturing firm located in the southeastern part of the country. In early 1999, it was considering acquiring the use of a reproduction machine. After evaluating equipment by seven different manufacturers, it had come to the conclusion that the Aztec 4 was the most suitable machine for its needs. Consequently, it had asked the Aztec sales personnel to provide information on alternative financing plans available through Aztec's financing subsidiary. The Aztec financing subsidiary presented the two alternatives.

Alternative 1 was to lease the Aztec 4 equipment for 7 years, which was the machine's expected useful life. The annual lease payment would be Rs 14,700 and would include service and maintenance. Lease payments would be due at the beginning of the year. On checking with its lawyer, Wilson found that the lease would be fully tax deductible. Furthermore, the investment tax credit would be passed along to Wilson.

Alternative 2 would allow Wilson to purchase the Aztec 4 equipment through a 100 per cent loan from Aztec's financing subsidiary. The cost of the machine is Rs 50,000. Wilson would make seven annual payments of Rs 9,935 each to repay the loan of Rs 50,000. Payments would be due at the end of the year.

Wilson Industries marginal tax rate is 44 per cent. It has estimated that the equipment has an expected salvage value of Rs 1,000. However, this salvage value could range from zero rupees to Rs 2,000. Wilson plans to depreciate the equipment by using the straight-line method. On inquiry Wilson has been told that a service and maintenance Lease on the Aztec 4 is available for 7 years for Rs 3,700 annually. Should Wilson borrow and buy the equipment or should it Lease?

To answer this question, we need to determine the alternative with the lowest cost on a net present value basis. The after-tax cost of the Lease is readily determined. The after-tax cost of borrowing and buying is more complex. First, we can ignore the investment tax credit, since its effect on the two alternatives will be the same. Second, to make the alternatives fully comparable we need to recognise service and maintenance costs for the borrowing alternative. Third, since the equipment is purchased, it can be depreciated. Annual depreciation on a straight line basis would be

Depreciation = Rs 50,000 - Rs 1,000/7 = Rs 7,000

The equipment would be depreciated at an annual rate of Rs 7,000 toward a salvage value of Rs 1,000 at the end of the seventh year. Finally, the Rs 9,935 payment on the loan has to be separated into an interest expense portion and a loan repayment portion. Following the procedure discussed earlier, we first calculate the annuity factor

$IFA_{7\ years,\ 1\%}$ = Rs 50,000/Rs 9,935 = 5.03271

From PVIFA table, we find that this annuity factor is for a discount rate of almost 9 per cent. Knowing this discount rate, we can separate the Rs 9,935 payment into interest and principal portion, as shown in Table 2.5.

One issue still existing is the discount rate to be used in the analysis. The discount rates should reflect the risking of the Cash flows. The Cash flows in the Lease or borrow decision are deterministic with the exception of the salvage value. It is appropriate to use the after-tax cost of debt financing for discounting all Cash flows except the salvage value. The after-tax cost of debt is 9 per cent × (1 - 0.44) = 5 per cent. Since the expected salvage value has some uncertainty around it, a discount rate higher that 5 per cent – say 12 per cent – is justified.

Table 2.5: Lease Versus Borrow Loan Payment Components

Year	Balance	Payment	Interest [a]	Repayment
1	Rs 50,000	Rs 9,935	Rs 4,500	Rs 5,435
2	44,565	9,935	4,011	5,924
3	38,641	9,935	3,478	6,457
4	32,184	9,935	2,897	7,038
5	25,146	9,935	2,263	7,672
6	17,474	9,935	1,573	8,362
7	9,112	9,935	823	9,112

[a] At 9% the last-year interest expanse is the difference between payment and balance.

The lease or borrow analysis is summarised in Table 2.6. At t = 0, the only outflow is the first lease payment. At t = 1, total payments associated with borrowing and buying are the sum of the maintenance; interest, and depreciation are tax deductible. Column 6 shows the tax shield provided by these deductions. Net outflows associated with borrowing are shown in column 7. Column 9 shows the benefit of ownership or cost savings associated with ownership. The last column shows the present value of the ownership benefit. The last row shows the recovery of the salvage value, which is discounted at 12 per cent. The sum of the present values is Rs 6,224 and indicates that alternative 2 – borrowing and buying – is more desirable than the leasing alternative.

Table 2.6: Lease Versus Borrow Summary of Analysis

Year	Loan	Maintenance	Interest [a]	Depreciation	Tax Shield 6 = (3+4+5) × 0.44	Outflows 7=2+3– 6	After-tax Lease Cost [b]	Ownership Benefit 9=8– 7	Interest Factor [c]	Present Value
1	2	3	4	5	6	7	8	9	10	11
0	--	--	--	--	--	--	Rs 8,232	Rs 8,232	1.00000	Rs 8,232
1	Rs 9,935	Rs 3,700	Rs 4,500	Rs 7,000	Rs 6,688	Rs 6,947	8,232	1,285	.95238	1,224
2	9,935	3,700	4,011	7,000	6,473	7,162	8,232	1,070	.90703	971
3	9,935	3,700	3,478	7,000	6,238	7,397	8,232	835	.86384	721
4	9,935	3,700	2,897	7,000	5,983	7,652	8,232	580	.82270	477
5	9,935	3,700	2,263	7,000	5,704	7,931	8,232	301	.78353	263
6	9,935	3,700	1,573	7,000	5,400	8,235	8,232	(3)	.74622	(2)
7	9,935	3,700	823	7,000	5,070	8,565		(8,565)	.71068	(6,087)
8	Salvage					(1,000)		1,000	.45235	452
										Rs 6,224

[a] From Table 2.5.

[b] Rs 14,700(1 - 0.44) = Rs 8,232.

[c] At 5% except for salvage, which is 12%.

Summary

Two major issues involved in managing the firm's use of short-term financing are:

(1) How much short-term financing should the firm use? And (2) what specific sources of short-term financing should be selected? The earlier chapter answered the first of these two questions. The objective of this chapter is to answer the second of the above questions.

In general, three basic factors should be considered in selecting a source of short-term credit: (1) the effective cost of credit, (2) the availability of credit in the amount needed and for the period of time when financing is required, and (3) the influence of the use of a particular credit source on the cost and availability of other sources. These three issues have been taken up in the chapter. To begin with, problem of estimating the cost of short-term credit has been discussed. It has been illustrated that the effect of compounding is to raise the effective cost of short-term credit.

Short-term credit sources can be classified into two basic groups: unsecured and secured. Unsecured loans include all those sources that have as their security only the lender's faith in the ability of the borrower to repay the funds when due. Three major sources of unsecured short-term credit: trade credit, unsecured bank loans, and commercial paper have been described at length in the chapter. Secured loans involve the pledge of specific assets as collateral in the event the borrower defaults in payment of principal or interest. Prominent sources of secured credit covered herein are accounts receivable loan, inventory loan and trade credit. The qualitative and the quantitative attributes of the various secured and unsecured credit options have been elaborately dealt with in the chapter along with their comparative assessment.

The last section discusses in detail the various types of term financing options available to firms. A comparative analysis of the term loans and the lease financing option has been made therein. The cost aspect, the interest payment and the principal repayment schedule under these two alternatives have been illustrated. Also, the leasing vs borrowing and owning decision situation has been comprehensively illustrated in the last section of the chapter.

Questions

1. Explain the similarities between term loans and leases.

2. What is meant by a term loan? How is it different from borrowing on a credit line and bond financing?

3. If you were seeking a term loan, would you prefer a fixed interest rate or a variable rate? Why?

4. Which term loan provision seems to be most restrictive from the borrower's viewpoint? Why?

5. If you were a bank commercial lending officer, what sorts of restrictions would you want to impose on a small firm seeking a term loan? Would your answer be different if this loan were being sought by a major company? If not, why?

6. What is the difference between a fully amortised term loan and a term loan with a balloon payment? Under what conditions would you want to seek the latter type of term loan?

7. What are the similarities and dissimilarities, if any, between the following concepts:

   a. Operating lease

   b. Financial lease

   c. Sale and leaseback

   d. Maintenance leases

8. How can one estimate the cost of leasing?

9. Explain the advantages and disadvantages of leasing.

PROBLEMS

1. A firm takes out an 8-year term loan for Rs 1.7 crore. It has to repay the loan by making eight year-end annual payments of Rs 313,800

each. Calculate the interest rate that the bank is charging on this loan.

2. A firm has borrowed Rs 5.0 crores on a 10-year term loan. The bank is charging 8.5 per cent interest on this loan. The loan is to be repaid in 10 year-end equal installments. Calculate the installment payment that would fully amortise this loan.

3. A firm has taken out a Rs 2.0 crore loan; 80 per cent or Rs 1.6 crore of the loan is to be repaid in five equal year-end installments of principal and interest; 20 per cent or Rs 40,00,000 is to be repaid at the end of the fifth year. The bank is charging 10 per cent interest on this loan. Calculate the amount of the first-year installment.

4. A firm with a 6-year Rs 2.0 crore term loan is repaying Rs 1.4 crore of the loan in six year-end annual payments. The interest rate being charged by the bank is 7 per cent. Calculate the amount of the final balloon payment.

5. A firm has leased a computer system that requires it to make annual payments of Rs 390,000 every year for the next 4 years. The firm has already made the first payment and has three more lease payments remaining. Show the balance sheet entries for capitalising this lease. The firm's borrowing rate is 8 per cent.

6. A leasing firm is willing to lease a fleet of trucks to a transportation company. For leasing trucks with a value of Rs 600,000 for 7 years, it requires seven annual payments of Rs 108,000 each. The first payment would be due at the time the trucks are made available to the firm. Other payments would follow at 1-year intervals. Calculate the leasing firm's rate of return.

7. A computer manufacturer is willing to lease a Rs 3.7 crore computer for 5 years with five year-end annual lease payments of Rs 950,000 each. Calculate the lessor's rate of return (Hint: Equation 2.5 has to be slightly modified to accommodate year-end rather than beginning-of-year payments).

8. Marion Machine Company (MMC) can either lease a computer-controlled metal fabricator or obtain a term loan from a bank and purchase the fabricator. The fabricator can be leased on a fully amortised 10-year lease for Rs 110,000 per year. The lease payments would be

due at the beginning of the year and would include maintenance and repairs. The investment tax credit would be passed along to MMC.

The Marion Machine Company can also obtain a bank term loan and purchase the fabricator. The fabricator can be bought for Rs 800,000 and would be depreciated on a straight-line basis over 10 years toward a zero salvage value. The bank would provide a term loan of Rs 800,000 for 10 years at 9 per cent interest. The loan would be repayable in 10 equal installments of Rs 124,655 each year at year end. The purchase would not include maintenance services. The company has estimated that maintenance and service costs would be Rs 5,000 a year for the first 5 years and Rs 6,500 a year for the last 5 years. The MMC marginal tax rate is 44 per cent.

a. From the data provided, and on a net present value basis, identify the better of the lease or borrow-and-buy alternatives.

b. What additional qualitative factors need to be taken into consideration before MCC decides to lease or to borrow-and-buy?

9. Columbia Mills, Inc. (CMI) is planning to either lease a computer system or buy it from the manufacturer. The computer can be purchased for Rs 2.2 crore. The purchase would be financed by a bank term loan for Rs 2.2 crore. The loan would be repayable in five equal installments of Rs 565,604 each, payable at year end. The computer would be depreciated at an annual rate of 20% on written down value at the beginning of the year for 5 years. Columbia Mills' marginal tax rate is 44 per cent.

Columbia Mills can also lease this computer system for 5 years for an annual lease payment of Rs 551,000 payable at year end. Under either the purchase plan or the lease plan, the computer manufacturer would be willing to provide maintenance services for 5 years for Rs 22,000 annually. If the equipment is leased, the investment tax credit would be passed along to CMI.

a. Calculate the annual interest payments for the bank loan.

b. Which alternative, lease or buy, appears to be more desirable on a net present value basis? Assume that the salvage value is as risky as the firm's average cash flow. Columbia Mills' marginal cost of capital is 10 per cent.

c. What qualitative factors should be considered before CMI decides to lease or to borrow and buy?

Answers to Spot Quizzes

Intermediate-Term Loans

1. Term loans have been in use for a long time. T ❑ F ☑
2. They are similar in this respect. T ☑ F ❑
3. Some term loans involve balloon payments. T ❑ F ☑
4. Some term loans have a variable interest rate. T ☑ F ❑
5. Sometimes they are not. T ❑ F ☑
6. After all, it is their money. T ☑ F ❑
7. The amount lent is the "initial investment" for the annuity. T ☑ F ❑
8. It makes the loan repayment easier. T ☑ F ❑

Lease Financing

1. Definitional. T ☑ F ❑
2. A sale and leaseback is a financial lease. T ❑ F ☑
3. Lease capitalisation represents debt obligations. T ☑ F ❑
4. The lessee provides this return to the lessor by leasing. T ☑ F ❑
5. Leasing costs are not generally lower than borrowing costs. T ❑ F ☑

ANNEXURE
Working Capital Control and Banking Policy

The purpose of commercial bank lending in India has traditionally been seen as the provision of short-term finance for business. Banks have been providing the working capital finance to meet the short-term financing needs of the Indian corporate sector. To ensure the smooth flow of credit from the banks to the industry, RBI has constituted various committees to review the prevailing norms pertaining to the flow of credit from the banking sector to the industry from time to time. Some of the prominent committees along with their TOR and their recommendations are mentioned below.

Tandon Study Group

Tandon Study Group (or 'Tandon Committee', as it subsequently came to popularly called) was constituted by RBI in July 1974 to frame guidelines for rational allocation and optimal use of bank credit.

The committee was set up in the background of growing demand for bank credit by different sectors of the economy. It was felt that cheap credit available from banks was being misutilised for building up disproportionate stocks of materials so as to realise trading profits by the manufacturing firms. Moreover, the prevalent cash credit system was being misused by firms, indulging as they were in surreptitious double financing.

The practice under the cash credit system was to lend to the extent of 75% of the value of inventory and receivables, the remaining 25% being the margin. This value of inventory included purchases of material on credit. Thus, this amounted to double financing—from creditors as well as banks. Also, bank lending under the system was focused on the security available in the form of inventory and receivables and bore no relationship with the operations of the borrower. As the result, those borrowers who had large inventory build-ups – hardly a laudable trend – were entitled to higher financing, whereas those borrowers who had low inventory and receivables blockages due to better inventory handling and efficient collecting systems were given short shrift.

The Terms of Reference of the Group were:

(i) To suggest guidelines for commercial bank to follow-up and supervise credit from the point of view of ensuring proper end-use of funds and keeping a watch on the safety of the advances, and also to suggest the type of operational data and other information that may be obtained by banks periodically from such borrowers and, in turn, by the Reserve Bank of India from the leading banks.

(ii) To make suggestions for prescribing inventory norms for different industries both in the private and public sectors and indicate the broad criteria for deviating from these norms.

(iii) To make recommendations for obtaining periodical forecasts from borrowers of (a) business/production plans, (b) credit needs.

(iv) To suggest criteria regarding satisfactory capital structure and sound financial basis in relation to borrowings.

(v) To make recommendations as to whether the existing pattern of financing working capital requirements by cash credit/overdraft system, etc., requires to be modified. If so, to suggest suitable modifications.

(vi) To make recommendations on any other related matter as the Group may consider germane to the subject of enquiry of any other allied matter which may be specifically referred to it by the Reserve Bank of India.

Observations and Recommendations

The Study Group submitted its report to the RBI in 1975. The main recommendations can be broadly classified under two heads — recommendations on banks' lending norms and those related to inventory and receivables norms.

Lending norms

The Group identified working capital gap viz., the borrower's requirements of finance to carry current assets (based on norms) other than those financed out of his other current liabilities, could be bridged partly from his owned funds and long term borrowings and partly by bank borrowings. It suggested that the maximum permissible level of bank borrowings could be worked out in three ways:

First Method

Under the first method, the difference between the acceptable level of current assets and the anticipated quantum of other current liabilities (i.e., other than bank finance, viz., largely comprising sundry creditors) would be calculated, and this will be termed as the "Working Capital Gap" (WCG). And, the Net Working Capital (NWC), [or the margin, or the Owner's Equity (OE)], should be a minimum 25% of the working capital gap. Thus, under the first method, the banker would finance maximum upto 75% of the working capital gap.

Second Method

Under the second method, the Net Working Capital (NWC) should be a minimum 25% of the total value of the acceptable level of current assets. The remaining 75% would first have to be financed by the other current liabilities (mainly Sundry Creditors) and the banker may finance the balance amount of the working capital requirements.

Third Method

The third method is similar to the second method, differing only to the extent of the composition of the acceptable current assets. Under this method, the acceptable current assets would mean the total current assets (as commonly understood by us) less the value of the core assets. Core Assets, according to the Tandon Committee, constitute "the absolute minimum level of the raw material, goods in process, finished goods and stores, which are in the pipe line, so to speak, to ensure a continuity of production". The entire core assets, however, were to be financed only out of the Owner's Equity (OE).

The three alternatives may be illustrated by taking the following example of a borrowers' financial position, projected at the end of the next year:

Table 1: Balance Sheet

Current Liabilities		Current Assets[1]	
Creditors for purchase	100	Raw materials	200
Other current liabilities	50	Stocks-in-process	20
	150	Finished goods	90
Bank borrowings, including bills discounted with bankers	200	Receivables including bills discounted with bankers	50
		Other current assets	10
	350		370

The 1st method would mean the banker financing upto a maximum of 75% of the working capital gap of 220[2], i.e., 165 and the borrower providing at least 55 out of his long-term funds, i.e., owned funds plus long-term borrowings. This method will give a minimum current ratio of 1:1.

1 As per suggested norm or past practice, whichever is lower in relation to projected production for the next year.

2 Working capital gap = CA -CL. Current assets =370 and Current liabilities, except bank loan = 220. Thus WC gap = 220

It is presumed that the amount of permanent Current assets (the minimal amount that remains invested in the Current assets all through the year) is 95.

The 2nd Method would mean the borrower financing a minimum of 25% of total Current assets (.25* 370=92.5) through long-term funds and the gap, i.e., maximum of 127.5 (277.5-150), would be provided by the bank. This would give a current ratio of at least 1.3:1.

Table 2: Permissible Levels of Bank Finance

1st Method		2nd Method		3rd Method	
Total current assets	370	Total Current assets	370	Total current assets	370
Less: Current Liabilities other than bank borrowings	150	Less: 25% or above from long-term sources	92.5	Less: Core current assets from long-term sources	95[1]
			277.5		275
Working capital gap	220	Less: current liabilities other than bank borrowings	150	Real current assets	275
				Less: 25% or above from long-term sources	69
			127.5		206
Less: 25% or above from long-term sources	55	Working capital gap	220	Less: current liabilities other than the bank borrowings	150
					56
Maximum bank borrowings permissible	165	Maximum bank borrowings permissible	127.5	Working capital gap	220
				Maximum bank borrowings permissible	56
Excess borrowings	35	Excess borrowings	72.5	Excess borrowings	144
Current ratio 1.17:1		Current ratio 1.33:1.		Current ratio 1.79.1	

The 3rd Method would mean a further reduction in bank borrowing and strengthening of the current ratio. This method will provide the largest multiplier of bank finance.

Inventory and Receivable norms

The committee suggested that the borrowers be allowed to retain only the reasonable level of Current assets, particularly Inventory and Receivables. The banker should finance only the normal level of Inventory based on the production plan, lead time, economic ordering levels and reasonable factor of safety. These levels of Inventory and Receivables to be financed should be in tune with the practices of borrower's firm and industry. The committee gave the following norms for Inventory and Receivables in different industries:

It is presumed that the amount of permanent Current assets (the minimal amount that remains invested in the Current assets all through the year) is 95.

SUGGESTED NORMS FOR INVENTORIES AND RECEIVABLES AS PER THE TANDON COMMITTEE

Notes

Sl. No.	Industry	Raw Materials (Including stores and other items used in the process of manufacture)	Stocks in process	Finished goods	Bills Receivable, Bills purchased and discounted
	1	2	3	4	5
1.	(a) Cotton and (b) Synthetic Textiles	(a) Cotton 2, (Bombay and Ahmedabad Areas) 3, Eastern Areas (Bihar, Orissa, West Bengal and Assam) 2.5, (other than the above areas) (b) Other Raw Materials 2, (all over India).	0.75, Composite textile mills 0.50, other mills	2.25	2.25
2.	Man-made Fibre	1.5	0.5	1.75	1.75
3.	Jute Textiles	2.5	0.25	(a) 1 (for domestic sales) (b) 1.5 (for exports)	1.50
4.	Rubber Products	2	0.25	1.75	1.75
5.	Fertilizers (a) for nitrogenous plants (b) for phosphatic plants	2 0.75 (units near refinery) 1.50 (units away from refinery) 2 (units in port areas) 3 (units away from port areas)	0.25 negligible "	1. (where stocks are in plant size); 1.5 (where stocks are also in uncountry centres) "	1.75 1.25 1.25
6.	Pharmaceuticals	2.75	0.5	2	1.25
7.	Dyes and Dyestuffs	2.25	1	0.75	2.25
8.	Basic Industrial Chemicals	2.75	0.25	1	1.75
9.	Vegetable and Hydrogenated Oils	1	Negligible	0.75	0.75
10.	Paper	2-6, Bamboo & Wood (to be built up in stages, from November to May, and thereafter, to be brought down) 2.25, Chemicals	"	1 (for controlled sales and 0.25 for free sales)	0.75
11.	Cement	2.25 Gypsum, 1.25 Limestone 0.75 Coal, 1.5 Packing Materials	0.5	1	1
12.	Engineering (Automobiles & Ancillaries)	2.25	0.75	2.5	2.5
13.	Engineering (Consumer Durables)	2	0.75	2.5	2.5
14.	Engineering: (ancillaries, other than automobile ancillaries) and component suppliers	2	0.75	2.5	2.5
15.	Engineering: Machinery Manufacturers and other Capital Equipment suppliers (other than heavy engineering)88	2.75	1.25	3.5	3.5
16.	Silk & Art Silk Mills (a) Weaving mills (b) Processing mills (including composite mills & others); (not applicable for job work units)	1. (Synthetic Yarn) 0.5 (Cloth processing mills) 2. (Other Raw Materials, vide note 1)	(a) 0.5 (b) 0.75	(a) 1.5 (b) 2.5	
17.	Woolen Mills	3 (Raw wool, rags & waste) 1 (Synthetic fibre/yarn) 2(Other materials, vide note 1)	1.25 (off season) (busy season)	4 (Apl. Sept) (Oct. mar.)	

Contd...

18.	Bulbs, Fluorescent Tubes & Dry Cell Batteries	4* 2.5**	0.5	3	
19.	Storage Batteries	4* 2.5**	1	3	
20.	Fans	3* 1**	0.5	4 @	
21.	Transformers	2* 0.5**	2 1.5	2 @@	
22.	Switchgears	2* 0.5**	0.5 1.5	2 @@	
* Imported ** Indigenous @ In Off-Seasons @@ During seasons					

Notes

1. Raw materials are expressed in Terms of "so many months of consumption". These include stores and other items used in the process of manufacture.
2. (a) Stock-in-process are expressed in Terms of "so many months of cost of production".

   (b) In individual cases, however, the bank may deviate from the norm, for the stocks-in process, if it is satisfied that the actual process time involved, in any particular unit, say, in view of the nature of production past experience and technology employed, is more than the norm suggested.
3. (a) Finished Goods,* and Receivables, are expressed in Terms of so many months of "cost of sales", and "sales", respectively. These figures represent only the average levels. Individual items of Finished Goods and Receivables, for different periods, could, however, exceed the indicated norms, so long as the overall average level of Finished Goods and Receivables does not exceed the amounts, as determined in Terms of the norm.

   (b)* The norm prescribed for Receivables relates only to inland sales, on short -term basis, (i.e., excluding Receivables arising out of deferred payment sales and exports).
4. Stocks of spares are not included for norms, since in financial Terms, they are not significant in many industries. Banks will, therefore, ascertain the requirements of spares for individual units. They should, however, keep a watchful eye if the level of spares exceeds 5% of the total inventories.
5. ** Heavy Engineering will include supply of whole or substantial plants, involving long manufacturing period, i.e., sugar, cement, steel and textile plants.

Chore Committee

The committee was set up by RBI in 1979 to review the operation of the Cash credit system with reference to the gap between sanctioned credit limits and the extent of their utilization. The TOR for the group was to review the Cash credit system and to suggest modifications in the system to make the system more amenable to rational management of funds by commercial banks, and/or alternative types of credit facilities, which would ensure greater credit discipline and also enable banks to relate credit limits to increase in output or other productive activities.

The group made the following recommendations:

(a) ***Reduced dependence on credit:*** The group was of the view that the borrowers' dependence on bank credit should be reduced, for which it recommended the firms to be placed in the second method of lending as given by Tandon committee.

(b) *Separation of credit limit into 'peak level' and 'normal peak level' limits::* Banks should appraise and fix separate limits for the 'peak level' and 'normal peak level' credit requirements for all the borrowers in excess of Rs. 10 lacs, indicating the relevant periods. The borrower should indicate in advance his need for the funds during a quarter, within the sanctioned limits for these two periods. Any deviation in utilisation beyond 10% tolerance limit should be treated as an irregularity and attract necessary action.

(c) *Continuance of the existing lending system:* The existing system of extending credit – a combination of the three types of lending, viz., cash credit, term loan and bill discounting – should be retained. However, it acknowledged the need for some directional changes to ensure that wherever possible, the use of cash credit is supplanted by loans and bills. It further suggested the introduction of necessary corrective measures to remove the impediments in the use of bill system of finance and also to remove the drawbacks observed in the cash credit system.

(d) *Information system:* All the borrowers enjoying working capital limits of Rs. 50 lacs and over from the banking system should be asked to submit quarterly statements.

Marathe Committee

With the incorporation of the guidelines of the Tandon Committee and the Chore Committee, bank lending to industry came increasingly under the direct supervision of the Reserve Bank of India. In 1982, it was felt that an independent review of the Credit Authorization Scheme (CAS) which had been in operation for several years would be useful and accordingly, the Reserve Bank of India appointed a Committee in November 1982 to review the working of the Credit Authorization Scheme. The Committee, which came to be referred as the Marathe Committee, submitted its report in July 1983.

The Marathe Committee was set up to examine the operational aspects of Credit Authorization Scheme. The major recommendations of the Marathe committee were in the area of providing incentive for borrowers to comply with all the requirements of the scheme (including compliance with the information system), and for the banks to improve the quality of credit appraisal. It recommended that banks be allowed discretion to deploy credit in CAS cases.

The committee highlighted the need for viewing CAS within the broader perspective of ensuring orderly credit management and improving the quality of bank lending so that all borrowings, whether large or small are in conformity with the policies and priorities laid down by RBI. The committee were of the view that the different criteria for lending to the borrowers above the cut off point, as compared to those who did not come within the purview of the Scheme, came about only because of administrative limitations or convenience. The committee suggested suitable organizational changes to reduce the time purview of the Scheme, came about only because of administrative limitations or convenience. The committee suggested suitable organizational changes to reduce the time taken by the commercial banks in processing applications. If the banks, the committee felt, were able to evolve an operational culture that was immune to unhealthy pressures and which would display in-built discipline in conforming to the broader parameters of policy laid down by RBI, the need for a regulatory role for the Reserve Bank in respect of individual credit limits would diminish, if not disappear altogether.

Kannan Committee Report

With a view to free the banks from rigidities of the Tandon Committee recommendations in the area of Working Capital Finance and considering the ongoing liberalizations in the financial sector, IBA constituted a committee on 'Working Capital Finance' including 'Assessment of Maximum Permissible Bank Finance (MPBF)', headed by K. Kannan, Chairman and Managing Director of the Bank of Baroda.

The Committee examined all aspects of working capital finance and came up with far reaching recommendations on the modalities of assessment of working capital finance, in its report submitted to IBA on February 25, 1997. It observed that in view of deregulations and liberalizations being witnessed by the commercial banks India, it was imperative that micro-level credit administration be handled by each bank individually with their own risk perceptions, risk analyses and risk forecasting. In its report, the committee pointed out that the following areas required to be given greater attention, along with the credit granting and monitoring. These areas were:

(1) Regular interface with the borrower to have a better understanding of his business/ activity; and problems/constraints faced by him and the future action plan envisaged;

(2) Periodical obtaining of affidavits from the borrowers, declaring highlights of their assets, liabilities and operating performance (in lieu of subjecting even the high rated/high valued borrowers to several routine inspections/verifications) in order to bestow faith-oriented, rather than *ab initio* doubt-oriented approach in monitoring the credit dispensation.

(3) Periodical exchange of information between/among financing banks/financial institutions to pick-up the alarm signals at the earliest.

(4) Establishing within a time bound programme a "Credit Information Bureau" to provide updated information of existing/new borrowers before taking a credit decision. (Modality of Information Bureau in advanced countries could be taken as a guide for floating an appropriate Credit Information Bureau).

Accordingly, the Committee recommended that the arithmetical rigidities imposed by Tandon Committee in the form of MPBF- computation, so far in vogue, should be done away with and banks be given freedom to evolve their own system of working capital

As a result of the recommendations of the committee, RBI advised the banks to follow cash budget system for assessing the working capital finance in respect of large borrowers. The turnover method could continue to be used as a tool of assessment relative to small borrowers. It also directed that working capital credit limit may henceforth be determined by banks according to their perception of the borrower and the credit needs. Banks should lay down, through their boards, transparent policy guidelines for credit dispensation in respect of each broad category of economic activity.

New System of Assessment of Working Capital Finance

With the advent of the era of economic liberalisation and integration of the Indian economy with the global economy, two major shifts were discernible in the banking sector. The first was the emergence of the concept of universal banking, while the second involved erosion of the dichotomy between the capital and money market segments of the financial markets.

In the light of the said developments, the Kannan Committee expressed doubts over the wisdom of continuing with separate assessment/fixations of various sub-limits, within the overall working capital limits. The Committee felt that Line of Credit System (LCS), instead, as is prevalent in many advanced countries, should replace the existing system of assessment/fixation of sub-limits within total working capital credit requirement. A Line of Credit is not a credit facility per se; it is an outer limit for total (funded and non-funded) working capital finance, and within this outer limit, various types of working capital fund-based as well as non-fundbased credit facilities (illustrative list furnished in Table 3) with appropriate limits should be made available to the borrower.

Table 3

(1)	Cash Credit including bills-acceptance/Latter of credit for purchases.	with sub-divisions into respectively (i) hypothecation of stock and (ii) hypothecation of book debts
(2)	Inland Bills Purchased	with further sub-division into sub-limit for (i) documentary bills (ii) clean bills (iii) usance bills and (iv) sight bills
(3)	Export credit – FCNR (B)	With further sub-divisions into (i) Packing Credit (ii) PCFC (III) FBP etc.
(4)	Letter of credit for purchase other than Capital goods	with subdivisions into usance (L/C and sight L/C
(5)	Guarantee	with subdivisions into Performance Guarantee, Financial Guarantee, bid bond guarantee, advance money guarantee, etc.

The committee suggested that the entire Current Assets be considered as the prime security for the confirmed Line of Credit - LCS (i.e., fixed / outer limit of working capital finance - whether funded finance or non-funded finance) and any excess drawings/ requirement over and above the confirmed LCS may be subjected to additional rate of interest, say, upto 2.00%, to take care of the bank's cost of managing the uncommitted funds/obligation. However, specific long-term working capital requirements such as Sales to Electricity Boards, Bills Discounting under IDBI/SIDBI scheme, etc., guaranteed by State/Central Government be allowed to continue to be separate as per prevailing norms. The financing pattern in this regard would continue to be assessed taking into account quantum of Deferred Receivables as per prevalent practice.

In the above context, the committee suggested that the existing system of assessment of working capital finance may be replaced by a new system of assessment of working capital finance. The new system was proposed to be applicable to all borrowers engaged in legally permitted economic/financial activities, except those given in the following table (Table 4).

Table 4

NBFCs (Non Banking Finance Companies)	For whom, separate guidelines for assessment of W/C finance are devised by RBI
Construction Companies / Contractors	For whom separate guidelines for assessment of W/C finance are suggested by RBI
Tea Companies	For whom Cash budget system is used to assess E/C finance
Ship breaking companies	Existing system of W/C finance is to be continued.
Diamond Industry	Existing system of W/C finance is to be continued.
Small Scale Industrial Undertakings requiring W/C funded finance upto Rs. 2 crores	For whom RBI has directed to use "Turnover Method" propounded by Nayak Committee
Small borrowers (all sectors) requiring: Working Capital finance upto Rs. 2.00 Lacs (Rupees Two Lacs)	Most of such borrowers are usually covered under one or the other Schemes sponsored by various Governments/local bodies. Therefore, "financing-requirements of such borrowers shall be met as per the directives of the relevant sponsored scheme.
Specific long-term working capital requirements such as Bills discounting under IDBI/SIDBI – schemes, etc.	Existing separately set out guidelines to continue to be in force.

**Note: In Case of All Non-Priority Sector Borrowers, not covered under above points from '1' to '8', the Working Capital Credit requirement shall be assessed as per the Turnover Method applicable for SSI-Borrowers requiring W/C finance upto Rs. 200.000 lacs.

As a consequence of the proposed withdrawal of the existing system of working capital finance based on "MPBF-system", though a large leeway is available to the modifications, strengths, and to remove weaknesses of existing MPBF-system, simultaneously doing away with its rigidities as regards (i) computation of working capital bank finance and (ii) supervision and monitoring of the credit dispensed by the banks so that the proposed new system ensures faster credit delivery with inherent need and merit based flexibilities.

Therefore, the Committee proposed a shift in emphasis from "Liquidity Level Lending to Cash Deficit Lending". Cash deficit lending has been aimed at perceiving the borower's requirement, rather than to assess, after the deserving risk-analysis and risk-forecasting on case-to-case basis with perusal of the acceptability of the borrower's overall financial status, projected level of liquidity and activity, market reports, industry/activity profile and the economic strata to which a particular borrower belongs. As such, it was suggested by the committee that the new system of working capital finance be known as Desirable Bank Finance (DBF). The Committee recommended that the DBF - method be put in force immediately, with the aim of making it fully operational over a period of 3-4 months, i.e., with effect from April 1, 1998 in order to afford, wherever necessary, adequate breathing time to bank staff and borrowers for developing familiarity with DBF method and also to coincide with the start of the new financial year for most of the borrowers as well as of the bank to afford operational convenience.

CHAPTER III

Management of Cash

Learning Objectives

- Cash flow process
- Motives for holding cash
- Objectives of cash management and decisions made to achieve them
- How to maximise the availability of cash through expediting collections and deferring disbursements
- Determination of optimal working capital balance and deciding the mix between cash and marketable securities

Chapter Organization

- The chapter begins with the basic issues involved in the management of a firm's cash position. The cash flow process in a typical firm has been discussed along with the motives for holding cash. The objectives and the decisions involved in the management of cash have also been taken up in the first section of the chapter.
- The second section of the chapter deals with the management of collections and disbursements through quick collections and slow disbursements. The methods that firms adopt to cut down the amount and the duration of blockage of funds in the working balance have been suggested in the section.
- Determination of the optimal level of working balance and investment of surplus cash in marketable securities has been covered in the last section of the chapter.

CHAPTER 3

Management of Cash

One of the important components of working capital management is management of cash. The importance of cash management stems from the flow of cash in and out of the organization. The basic features of cash combined with the uncontrollable nature of its flow necessitate that finance managers frame policies and programmes for the management and proper utilisation of cash. Before looking into the various facets of cash management, it is necessary to know the cash flow process in an organization.

Cash Flow Process

A thorough understanding of why and how a firm holds cash requires an accurate conception of how cash flows into and through the enterprise. Figures 3.1 (a) and 3.1 (b) depict the process of resources generation and disposal in a typical manufacturing setting.

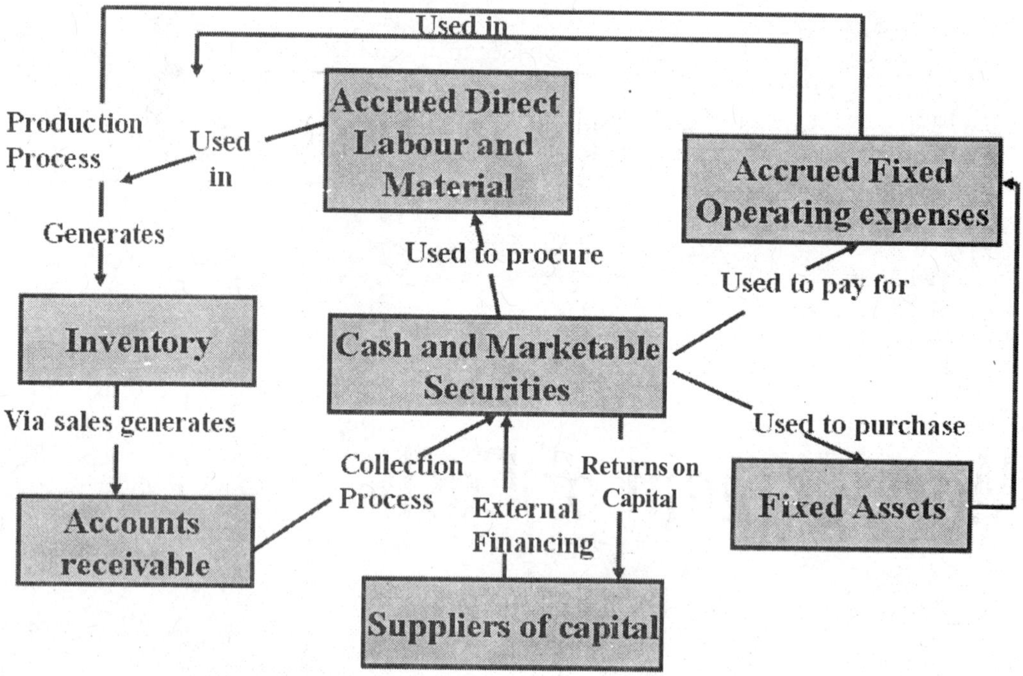

Figure 3.1 (a): Resource Flow in a Manufacturing Firm

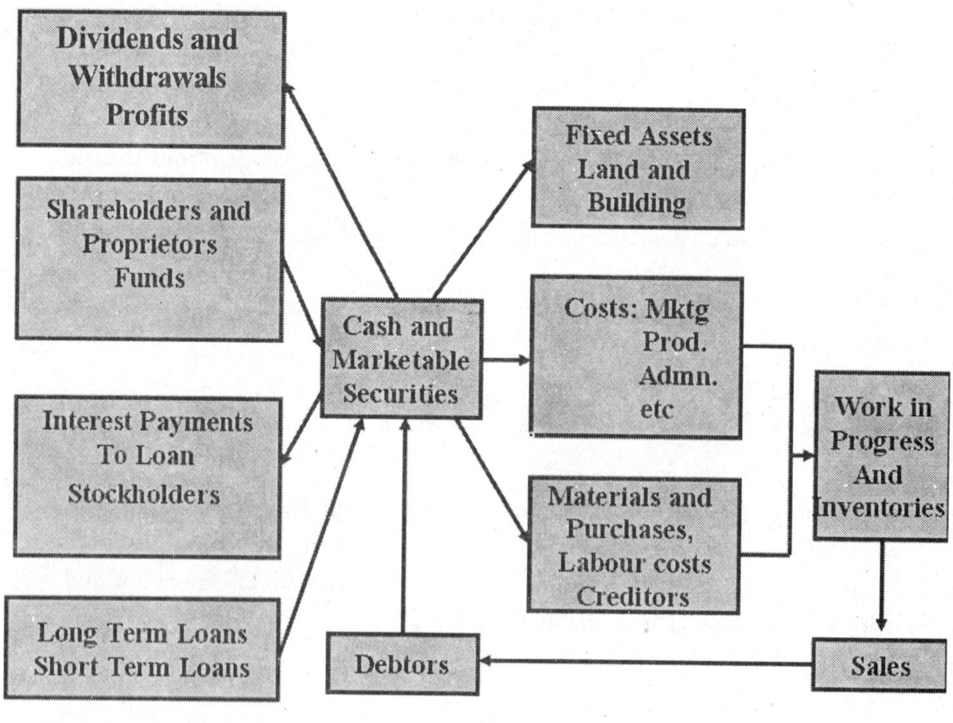

Figure 3.1 (b): Flow of Funds through a Firm

The firm experiences irregular increases in its cash holdings from several external sources. Funds can be obtained in the financial markets from the sale of securities such as bonds, preference shares and equity shares or through debt contracts with lenders such as commercial banks. These irregular cash inflows do not occur on a daily basis. They tend to be episodic, in that the financing arrangements that give rise to them are effected at wide intervals. The reason is that external financing contracts usually involve huge sums of money stemming from a major need identified by the company's management, and these needs do not occur every day. For example, a new product might be in the process of launched, or a plant expansion might be required to provide added productive capacity.

In most organizations, the financial officer responsible for cash management also controls the transactions that affect the firm's investment in marketable securities. As excess cash becomes temporarily available, marketable securities will be purchased. When cash is in short supply, a portion of the marketable securities portfolio will be liquidated.

Whereas the irregular cash inflows are from external sources, the other main sources of cash to the firm arise from internal operations and occur on a more regular basis. Over long periods, the largest receipts will come from accounts receivable collections and to a lesser extent from direct cash sales of finished goods. Many manufacturing concerns also generate cash on a regular basis through the liquidation of scrap or obsolete inventory. In the automobile industry, large and costly machines called chip cruisers grind waste metal into scrap that brings considerable revenue to the major producers. At various times, fixed assets may also be sold, thereby generating some cash inflow. This is not a large source of funds except in unusual situations where, for instance, a complete plant renovation may be taking place.

Apart from the investment of excess cash in near-cash assets, the cash balance will experience reductions for three key reasons. First, on an irregular basis withdrawals will be made to (1) pay cash dividends on preferred and common shares, (2) meet interest requirements on debt, (3) repay the principal borrowed from creditors, (4) buy the firm's own shares in the financial markets for use in executive compensation plans or as an alternative to paying a cash dividend, and (5) pay tax. Again, by an "irregular basis" we mean items not occurring on a daily or highly frequent schedule. Second, the company's capital expenditure program will designate that fixed assets be acquired at various intervals. Third, inventories will be purchased on a rather regular basis to ensure a steady flow of finished goods off the production line. Note that the investment in fixed assets involves depreciation. This indicates that a portion of the cost of fixed assets is charged against the product coming off the assembly line. This cost is subsequently recovered through the sale of finished goods inventory, as the product selling price will be set by management to cover all of the costs of production, including depreciation.

The variety of influences we have mentioned that constantly affect the cash balance held by the firm can be synthesized in terms of the classic motives for holding cash, as identified in the literature of economic theory.

Motives for Holding Cash

In a classic economic treatise, John Maynard Keynes segmented the firm's or any other economic unit's demand for cash into three categories: (1) the transactions motive, (2) the precautionary motive, and (3) the speculative motive.

Transactions Motive

Balances held for purposes of transactions allow the firm to dispense with cash needs that arise in the ordinary course of doing business. Transactions balances would be used to meet the irregular outflows as well as the planned acquisition of fixed assets and inventories.

The relative amount of transactions cash held will be significantly affected by the industry in which the firm operates. If revenues can be forecast to fall within a tight range of outcomes, then the ratio of cash and near cash to total assets will be less for the firm than if the prospective cash inflows might be expected to vary over a wide range. In this regard, it is well known that utility concerns can forecast cash receipts quite accurately, owing to demand for their services arising from their quasi-monopoly status. This enables them to stagger their billings throughout the month and time them to coincide with their planned expenditures. Inflows and outflows of cash are thereby synchronised. Thus, we would expect the cash holdings of utility firms relative to sales or assets to be less than those associated with a major retail chain that sells groceries. The concern experiences a large number of transactions each day, almost all of which involve an exchange of cash.

The Precautionary Motive

Precautionary balances are a buffer stock of liquid assets. This motive for holding cash is related to the maintenance of balance to be used to satisfy possible, but as yet indefinite, needs.

In our discussion of transactions balances, we saw that cash flow predictability could affect a firm's cash holdings through synchronisation of receipts and disbursements. Cash flow predictability also has a material influence on the firm's demand for cash through the precautionary motive. The airline industry provides a typical illustration. Air passenger carriers are plagued with a very high degree of cash flow uncertainty. The weather, rising fuel costs, and continual strikes by operating personnel make cash forecasting a most difficult activity for any airline company. The upshot of this problem is that because of all the things that might happen, the minimum cash balances desired by the management of the air carriers tend to be large.

In addition to cash flow predictability, the precautionary motive for holding cash is affected by the firm's access to external funds. Especially important are those cash sources that can be tapped on short notice. Book building relationships and established lines of credit can reduce the firm's need to keep cash on hand. This unused borrowing power will obviate somewhat the need to invest in precautionary balances.

In actual business practice, the balance for precautionary motive to a large extent is maintained by the holding of a portfolio of liquid assets, not just cash. In large corporate organization, funds may flow either into or out of the marketable securities portfolio on a daily basis. Because actual rate of return can be earned on the near-cash assets, compared with a zero rate of return available on cash holding, it is logical that the precautionary motive will be met in part by investment in marketable securities.

The Speculative Motive

Cash is held for speculative purposes in order to take advantage of expected profit making situations. Construction firms that erect private dwellings will at times accumulate cash in anticipation of a significant drop in lumber costs. If the price of building supplies does drop, the companies that build up their cash balances stand to profit by purchasing materials in large quantities. This will reduce their cost of goods sold and increase their net profit margin. Generally, the speculative motive is the least important component of a firm's preference for liquidity. The transactions and precautionary motive account for most of the reasons why a company holds cash balances.

Decisions that concern the amounts of liquid assets to be held, rest with the finance officer responsible for cash management. Factors that can be expected to influence the finance officer's investment in cash and near cash have just been reviewed. Not all of these factors affect every firm. Moreover, factors that do affect many companies will do so in differing degrees. Since the executives ultimately responsible for making cash management choices will have different risk-bearing preferences, we might expect that patterns of liquid asset holding among firms would exhibit considerable variation. Such is the case, as shown by Table 3.1.

Bharat Power is an electric utility and as such operates within an environment where cash flows are highly predictable relative to other industries. We see that Bharat Power holds a very small proportion (3 per cent) of its total assets in the form of liquid assets. Even firms that operate in a regulated setting, however, can experience sudden shifts in their liquidity postures. At the end of 1998, Bharat Power had a liquid asset to total asset ratio of 0.5 per cent, but at the end of 1991, it stood much higher at 3.1 per cent. By the end of 1992, this ratio decreased to 0.3 percent (Table 3.1)

Table 3.1: Liquid Asset Positions of Selected Firms (in Per cent) for 1992

Ratio	Bharat Power	Car Corporation	Bharat Corporation	Bombay Refineries
Cash to total assets	0.2	1.8	2.6	0.8
Marketable securities to total assets	0.1	12.5	3.4	7.2
Total liquid assets to total assets	0.3	14.3	6.0	8.0

The Car Corporation competes in a more risky arena than does a utility like Bharat Power. We would expect Car Corporations' cash management policies, then, to be quite different from those of Bharat Power. Competition from foreign manufacturers coupled with the recession spelled troubled economic times for the domestic automobile manufacturing industry.

At the end of 1992, 14.3 per cent of this firm's total assets were held in the form of cash and marketable securities. Notice that the great bulk of Car Corporation's liquid assets are held in the form of marketable securities rather than cash. There is an important advantage to the type of liquid asset mix displayed by Car Corporation. Marketable securities earn a positive rate of return, while mere holding of cash earns a zero return for the Car Corporation. It seems fair to state that Car Corporation's need for precautionary cash balances far exceeds that of Bharat Power.

It is useful to review the liquid asset positions of the Bharat Corporation and the Bombay Refineries together. There are some differences in their end-product markets to be sure, but they compete in essentially the same energy industry. Both firms are heavily involved in crude oil exploration, crude oil production, and the distribution of petroleum products. Still, their cash management policies as displayed at the end of 1992 in their liquid assets are rather unlike. The percentage of liquid assets to total assets totaled 6.0 per cent for Bharat Oil and 8.0 per cent for Bombay Refineries. Furthermore, their liquid asset mix also differs widely. The marketable securities to total asset ratio for Bharat Oil was 3.4 per cent; for Bombay Refinery it was much larger at 7.2 per cent. To understand the cash management policies of firms, it takes more than knowledge of the industry class in which a firm operates. The executives of both the companies perceive the liquidity needs of the respective firms quite differently. It also seems that their risk-bearing preferences with respect to the chances of running out of cash are also different.

The examples given above show that the liquid asset holding of some specific firms are only snapshots at a fixed point in time. This tends to obscure the fact that assets are acquired, wasted, and sold every day. This dictates that we view the management of cash and near cash as a dynamic process. The flow of cash never ceases. The cash inflows and outflows affecting the size of the firm's cash reservoir occur simultaneously. This ensures that the overall problem of cash and marketable securities management will be complex. In order to cut through this complexity, it is imperative that the firms' cash management system be designed to operate within clearly defined objectives.

Cash Management Objectives and Decisions

Risk Return Trade-off

A company-wide cash management program must be concerned with minimising the firm's risk of insolvency. In the context of cash management, the term 'insolvency' is used to describe the situation where the firm is unable to pay its maturing liabilities on time. A company is said to be technically insolvent if it lacks the necessary liquidity to make prompt payment on its current debt obligations. This problem could be met quite easily by carrying large cash balances to pay the bills that come due. Production, after all, would soon come to a halt should the payments for raw material purchases be continually late or omitted entirely. The firm's suppliers would cut off further shipments. In fact, the fear of irritating a key supplier by not being able to make payment of a trade payable on the due date undoubtedly causes some finance managers to invest in too much liquidity.

The management of the company's cash position, though, is one of those major problem areas where you are criticized if you don't and criticized if you do. True, the production process will eventually be halted should too little cash be available to pay bills. If excessive cash balances are carried, however, the value of the enterprise in the financial marketplace will be suppressed in terms of the large cost of income forgone. The explicit return earned on idle cash balances is zero.

The finance manager must strike an acceptable balance between holding too much cash and too little cash. This is the focal point of the risk-return trade-off. A large cash investment minimises the chances of insolvency but penalises the company's profitability. A small cash investment frees excess balances for investment in both marketable securities and longer-lived assets; this enhances company profitability and thereby the value of the firm's common shares but increases the chances of running out of cash. The ability to walk this financial tightrope calls for deep knowledge of industry trends, cash inflow/outflow position of the firm and an almost uncanny ability on the finance manager's part to foresee major deviances from usual patterns.

Objectives

The risk-return trade-off can be reduced to two prime objectives for the firm's cash management system:

1. Enough cash must be on hand to dispense effectively with the disbursal needs that arise in the course of doing business.

2. The firm's investment in idle cash balances must be reduced to a minimum.

Evaluation of these operational objectives and a conscious attempt on the part of management to meet them, gives rise to the needs for some typical cash management decisions.

Decisions

Two conditions would allow the firm to operate for extended periods with cash balances near a level of zero: (1) a completely accurate forecast of net cash flows over the planing horizon, and (2) perfect synchronisation of cash receipts and disbursements.

Cash flow forecasting is the initial step in any effective cash management programme. This is usually accomplished by the finance function's evaluation of data supplied by the marketing and production functions in the company. The device used to forecast the cash flows over the planning period is the cash budget. Cash-budgeting procedure is explained later. It is emphasized, though, that the net cash flows pinpointed in the formal cash budget are mere estimates, subject to considerable variation. Thus, a totally accurate cash flow projection is only an ideal, not a reality.

Cash inflows and outflows of firms are not synchronised. Some inflows and outflows are irregular while others are more continual. Some finished goods are sold directly for cash but more likely the sales will be on account. The receivables then will have to be collected; raw materials have to be purchased before a cash inflow is realised, but several suppliers are probably used, and each transaction may have its own payment date. Thus business collections do not coincide with raw material payment dates. So the second criterion that would permit operation of the firm with extremely low cash balances is not met in actual practice either.

Given that the firm will, as a matter of necessity, invest in some cash balance, certain types of decisions related to the size of those balances dominate the cash management process. These include formulation of answers to the following questions:

1. What can be done to speed up cash collections and slow down or better control cash outflows?

2. What should be the composition of a firm's marketable securities portfolio?

3. How should investment in liquid assets be split between actual cash holdings and marketable securities?

The remainder of this chapter dwells on these three questions

Managing Collections and Disbursements

To size up our problem of cash management, let us examine the flow of cash through a firm's accounts. It is useful to think of the process as cycle in which cash is used to procure inputs, from which output is produced, which are then sold to customers, who later pay their bills. The firm receives cash from its customers and the cycle repeats.

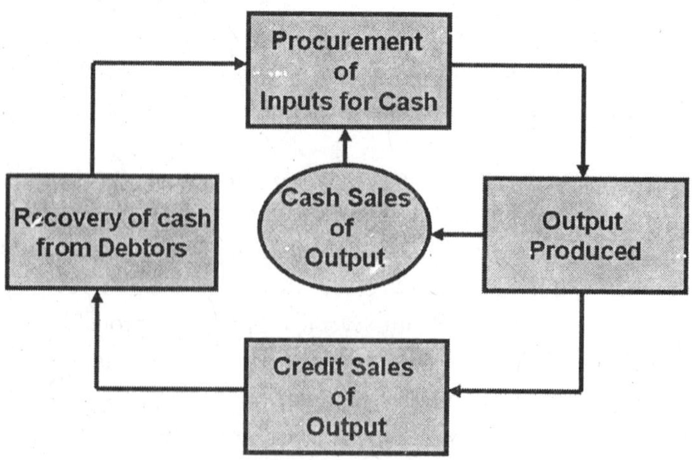

Figure 3.2: Cash Cycle

Opportunities to improve efficiency in collecting and disbursing funds centre on flows through the current section of the balance sheet. Let us assume that XYZ Corporation orders raw materials at point A and receives those 14 days later at B. Terms of 2/10, net 30 are offered, so the firm pays the invoice 10 days later at C. However, it takes 2 days for the cheque to clear, and XYZ's bank account is not debited until point D. XYZ turns over its inventory six times per year, so 60 days after the materials are received, the product is sold and the customer is billed, the collection period is 30 days, 28 for the customer to pay and 2 for the cheque to arrive by mail (G). XYZ processes the payment and deposits it 2 days later at H. Another 2 days elapse while XYZ's bank collects the funds from the customer's bank.

The firm's total financing requirements are affected by the total time lag from point B to point I. The firm itself can control some factors that determine the various lags, but some it cannot. Some of the lags affect the cash balance, while others affect other components of working capital such as accounts receivable and inventory. In addressing ourselves to Cash management, we are concerned with time periods BCD and FGHI. Time period AB is beyond the firm's control and does not directly affect its financial statements, although it may affect production schedules. Time period BE is determined by the firm's production process and inventory policy, and affects the total investment in inventory. Time period EF is determined by the firm's credit terms and the payment policies of its customers, and affects the total investment in accounts receivable. We will examine the management of inventory and accounts receivable in the next chapter.

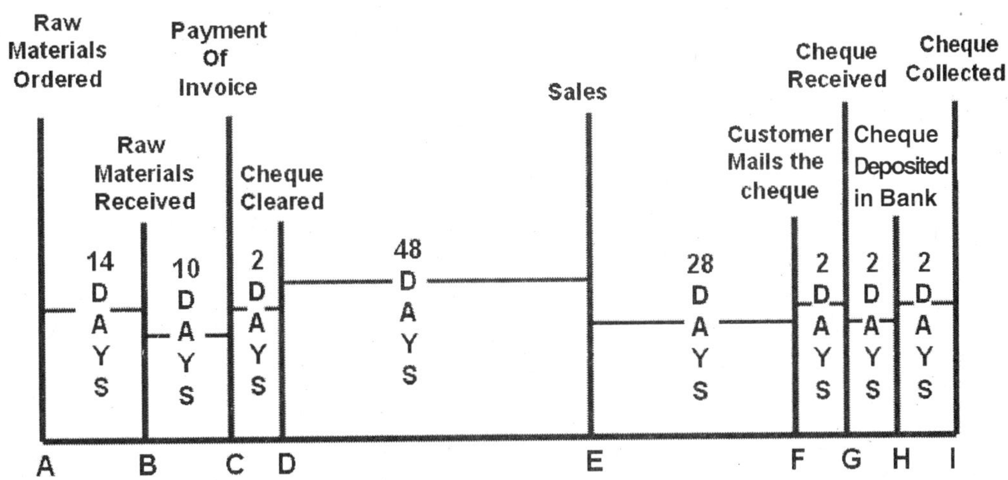

Figure 3.3: Working Capital Cycle of a typical Manufacturing Firm

Our present task is to examine what can be done to improve the efficiency of a firm's cash management. We will focus on three areas: concentrating working balances, speeding collections, and controlling disbursements.

Concentrating Banking

Many firms need only a single bank account. Larger firms that operate over wide geographical areas usually need more than one, sometimes dozens. Where many accounts are needed, concentration accounts can be used to minimise the total requirement for working balances. Suppose a company has a number of branch offices, each with a local bank account. Branches collect accounts receivable and make deposits in their local accounts. Each day, funds above a certain predetermined minimum level are transferred to a central concentration account, usually at the firm's headquarters. The daily transfer of funds can be made either by a depository transfer check or by Fax/TT; the latter is faster but more expensive.

The funds transferred to the concentration account are available for disbursements and for other purposes. As we will see later, the more variable a firm's cash flows, the higher the requirement for working cash balances.

By pooling its funds for disbursement in a single account, the aggregate requirement for working balances is lower than it would be if balances were maintained at each branch office. Concentration in short, permits the firm to "store" its cash more efficiently.

Speeding Collections

Another means of conserving cash is to reduce the lag between the time the customer mails the cheque and the time the funds become collected, that is, from points F to I in figure 3.3. Of the 6 days lag in figure 3.3, 2 days are due to mail time, 2 days are due to processing time within XYZ Corporation, and 2 days are due to collection time required by the bank. We will have more to say later about collection within the banking system. Let us now focus on the 4 days lag from F to H.

Small firms that operate over scattered geographical areas can often do little to reduce mail time. However, improvements can be made in processing time within the firm. Suppose XYZ Corporation has credit sales of Rs 5 crores per year. With approximately 250 working days per year, XYZ's collections average Rs 200,000 per working day. If XYZ could reduce such credit sales even by Rs 20,000, (XYZ's borrowing cost was 9 per cent) saving of about Rs 1,800 per year would be realised. This potential saving could be compared to the cost of faster processing to determine whether the change in processing should be made. We can conclude that internal processing should be speeded up to the point at which the costs of further improvement exceed the savings.

A second step that may be advantageous is to establish a lock-box system, which often can reduce mail and processing time still further. The firm first establishes a number of collection points, taking account of customer locations and mail schedules. At each location, the firm rents a post office box and instructs its customers to remit to the box. The firm's local bank is authorised to pick up mail directly from the box. The bank does so, perhaps several times a day and deposits the cheques in the firm's account. The bank's computerized system prepares a record of names and amounts and other data needed by the firm for internal accounting purpose, even as it enters the cheques for collections/clearing on the respective schedules.

The lock-box system results in two benefits to the firm. First, the bank performs the clerical tasks of handling the remittances prior to deposit, services which the bank may be able to perform at lower cost. Second, and often more important, the process of collection through the banking system begins immediately upon receipt of the remittance and does not have to wait until the firm completes its processing for internal accounting purpose. In terms of the activities in Figure 3.3, the activity represented by HI now takes place simultaneously with GH. The firm processes remittances for internal accounting purpose using data supplied by the bank and can schedule this processing at any time without delaying collection. Using a lock-box systems, as much as 4 days in mailing and processing time can be reduced.

Banks charge for their services in connection with a lock-box plan either via fees or compensating balance requirements. Whether the savings will outweigh the costs for a particular company depends mainly on the geographical dispersion of customers, the amount of the average remittance, the firm's cost of financing.

We see that a major advantage of speeding collections is freeing of blocked cash and thereby reduction in the firm's total financing requirements. There are other advantages as well. By transferring clerical functions to the bank, the firm may reduce its costs, improve internal control, and reduce the possibility of fraud. By getting cheques to banks on the day when they are written dropped or soon thereafter, the incidence of cheques getting dishonoured for insufficient funds in the drawers' accounts may be reduced.

Collection Time in the Banking System

We have made several references to the time required to collect a cheque through the banking system (HI in Figure 3.3) but we have made no proposals to shorten it. Let us look at the process of cutting down the collection time in the banking system. Suppose a customer in New Delhi, purchases electronics equipment from a firm in Mumbai, and remits a cheque drawn on a New Delhi Bank. The seller deposits the cheque in a bank in Mumbai, but the funds are not available for use until the cheque has been presented physically to the New Delhi bank, a process that depends on mail service between the two cities and may take several days. A very extensive clearing network has been established in India that involves the commercial banks and the RBI. In the majority of cases, collection times have been reduced to 2 days or less using the facilities of the direct inter-bank clearing. In the matter of cheque clearing, the banks are the experts, and firms usually can rely on their banks to minimise the time requirements. Time norms for outstation collections (clearing is basically a local phenomenon) have been laid down by RBI, ranging from ten days from metro-to-metro collections, to about 3 weeks in case of remote branches in the interior. Banks not staying within these parameters are likely to face RBI censure, or adverse comments from auditors.

Controlling Disbursements

Just as speeding up collections turns accounts receivable into cash as soon as possible, thereby reducing the firm's financing requirements, slowing disbursements also has the same effect. In an earlier chapter, we discussed trade credit as a source of funds. There, we concluded that the proper policy was to pay within the terms agreed upon, and taking cash discounts when offered. We also concluded that there is no point in paying sooner than agreed. By waiting as long as possible, the firm maximises the extent to which accounts payable are used as a source of funds, a source which requires no interest payment.

Firms with expense-generating activities over a wide area often find it advantageous to make disbursements from a single central account. In that way, schedules can be tightly controlled and disbursements can be made on exactly the right day. An alternate arrangement is to disburse from decentralised locations, but to wire transfer the exact amount needed in each local account for all disbursements scheduled that day needs to be ascertained accurately by the Finance Department at the Head Office.

Some firms find it advantageous to exploit the "cheque book float", which is the time between the writing of a cheque and its presentation for collection, represented by CD in Figure 3.3. If this lag can be exploited, it offsets at least partially the lag in the other direction in collecting cheques from customers (HI). Because of lag CD, a firm's balance on the bank's books is higher than in its own cheque book. Knowing this, a firm may be able to reduce its working cash requirements. Banks understand cheque book float also, and can be expected to set compensating balances and fees based on balances on their (the banks) books. If a firm exploits cheque book float too far, it increases the likelihood of cheques being dishonoured for insufficient funds and the accompanying displeasure of both bank and payee.

Determining the Appropriate Working Cash Balance

Let us assume the firm is now collecting, and disbursing its cash as efficiently as possible. Given its long-term financial structure and fixed assets, its total cash position at any time is determined by its operating plan. If a firm's total cash is more than what it needs for operating purposes, it would be faced with a surplus working capital position.

The Neptune Company projected a total cash balance as high as Rs 4,89,000 in November. Should all these funds be kept in Neptune's current account?

Since current accounts earn no interest, it is to Neptune's advantage to leave only the amount necessary to operate, and to invest the remainder temporarily in interest-bearing liquid assets until needed.

Our problem, then, is to determine how much cash a firm should maintain in its current account as a working balance. We will address this question here, and in the next section discuss the investment of amounts above the working balance.

The working balance is maintained for transaction purposes like paying bills. If the firm maintains too small a working balance, it may run out of cash. It then must liquidate marketable securities, if available, or borrow. Liquidating marketable securities and borrowing, both involve transaction costs.

If, on the other hand, the firm maintains too high a working balance, it foregoes the opportunity to earn interest on marketable securities, that is, it incurs what economists refer to as an 'opportunity cost'. Thus, the answer we seek is the optimal working balance, rather than the minimum. Finding the optimum involves a trade-off of transaction costs against opportunity costs. If a firm tries to keep its working balances low, it will find itself selling securities (and later repurchasing securities) more often than if it aims at a higher level of working balances, that is, transaction costs fall as the working balance level rises. Opportunity costs, on the other hand, rise as the level of working balances rises. There is one point where the sum of the two costs is at a minimum as shown in Figure 3.4. This is the optimal level of working balance that efficient management should try to find.

Optimal Level of Working Balance

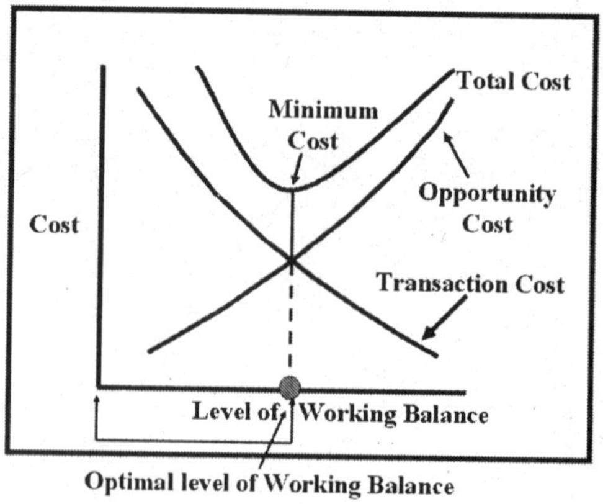

Figure 3.4: Optimal Level of Working Balance

Compensating Balance Requirements

If a firm uses bank credit as a source of financing, the question of the optimal current account balance may have a simple answer: it may be dictated by its compensating balance requirements to compensate for various services such as processing cheques and standby commitments to lend.

In some cases, a firm may determine with very little analysis that its optimal working balance is below the bank's compensating balance requirement. In such cases, the latter figure becomes the firm's minimum current account balance. In other cases, where the answer is not so clear or where compensating balances are not required, we must put pencil to paper to determine the appropriate working balance.

Finding the Optimal Working Balance

Having done all we can to improve our collection and disbursement procedures, let us now take the pattern of receipts and disbursements as given. Over any time period, a firm's beginning and ending cash balances are related as follows:

Ending balance = Beginning balance + Receipts - Disbursement

If receipts and disbursements were constant each day, we would know with certainty the amount of each component daily and our problem would be simple. Since receipt always would exceed disbursements by the same amount, we could withdraw the ending balance each day and use it for other purposes. In practice, we have two problems: variability and uncertainty. In most firms, receipts and disbursements vary both over the month and over the year. Over a month, receipts and disbursements for current operating expenses are likely to show some variation, perhaps in a regular pattern. In seasonal firm, the amounts also will vary over the year. Less frequent outlays such as those for capital expenditure, taxes, and dividends, introduce still more variability. Some of this variability may be predictable, but some probably is not. Let us examine these two problems of variability and uncertainty separately.

Variability

Suppose both receipts and disbursements vary and are not synchronised, but the variations are completely predictable. Determining the appropriate working balance in the face of non-synchronous but predictable cash flows is a problem of minimising total costs. If we set the balance too low, we incur high transaction costs; one might say we make too many trips to the bank. If we set the balance too high, we lose too much interest on marketable securities.

The determination of the optimal working balance under conditions of certainty can be viewed as an inventory problem in which we balance the costs of too little cash (transaction costs) against the costs of too much cash (opportunity costs). If the cash shortage becomes severe enough, we may begin to forego cash discounts on purchases, adding another element of opportunity cost.

Formal models of the cash balance problem have been developed using inventory theory. Inputs to such a model are the total net cash outflow over the period of time in question, the transaction costs of replenishing the cash balance by selling securities or borrowing, and the interest rate that can be earned on securities. The answer given by the model tells us how often and in what amounts funds should be transferred to the checking account from other sources.

Uncertainty

Receipts and disbursements are very seldom completely predictable. If we go to the opposite extreme and assume receipts and disbursements, or the difference between them, to be completely random, a different kind of model can be developed using the technique of control theory. In addition to information on transaction costs and interest rates on securities, we need a measure of the variability of net cash flows. Using these data, we can determine the optimal maximum and minimum balances in the firm's checking account, denoted by levels X and Y in Figure 3.5

In Figure 3.5, the firm's working cash balance fluctuates randomly in response to random inflows and outflows. At time t, the balance reaches the lower control limit Y. At that point, (Y-ß) value of marketable securities are sold and the proceeds transferred to the working balance. Such a transaction brings the firm's working cash balance to the return point (R). The balance continues to fluctuate, gradually rising to the maximum level X at t+3. At this point, (X-a) amount of cash is invested in marketable securities and the firm's working cash balance comes down to the level of return point (R) again. The control limit model thus gives an answer in terms of maximum and minimum balances and provides a decision rule, rather than a fixed schedule of transfers as done in the simple inventory model. One of the important insights of the control limit model is that, where cash flows are uncertain, the greater the variability the higher the minimum balance (X in Figure 3.5).

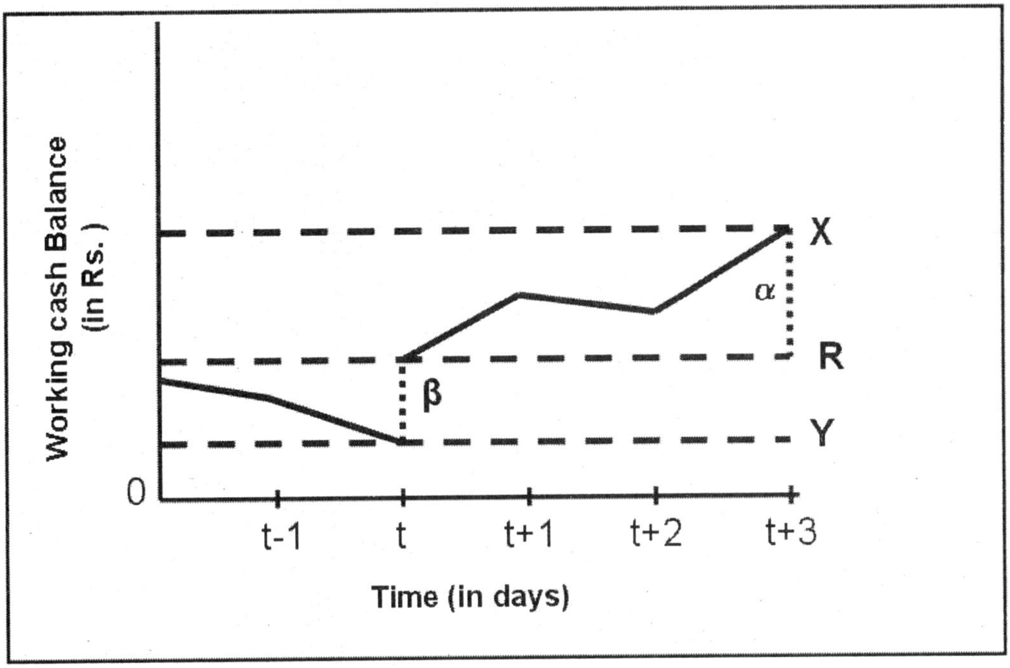

Figure 3.5: Control Limits approach to determine the working cash balance.

Using Mathematical Models

Formal mathematical models such as those mentioned above are useful for increasing our understanding of the cash management problem and providing insights and qualitative guidance. The models tell us which factors are important and make the trade-offs explicit. We see, for example, that transaction costs play a central role. If transaction costs were zero, the firm would require no working cash balance at all; it simply would sell securities or borrow to pay every bill.

Are formal mathematical models also useful for quantitative applications? In practice, the cash flow patterns of most firms are partly predictable and partly random. Neither the inventory model nor the control limit model is strictly applicable. By combining the insights from formal models with the techniques of cash budgeting and pro forma analysis, many firms can arrive at reasonable answers by experience and experiment. In deciding how far to go in analysing the problem, we must consider the cost of the analysis. Except in the case of very large firms, quantitative solutions to the cash balance problem using formal mathematical models are likely to be uneconomical. Often, the cost of obtaining the necessary input data and operating the model exceeds the savings over solutions that can be attained by experience and experiment. As always, we must keep an eye on the cost of our analytical techniques as well as on the benefits.

Planning Cash Requirement

In most cases, to search for the optimal working cash balance probably overstates our capabilities; we must be content to get reasonably close. Perhaps we should substitute the word "appropriate" for "optimal."

The current account balance that the firm should maintain is the compensating balance requirement or the optimal working balance, whichever is greater. Some firms, especially those with seasonal sales patterns, may find that the appropriate working balance varies somewhat over the year. As a firm grows, the appropriate working cash balance will also grow, although probably not proportionally.

Once we have settled on the appropriate balance to be maintained in the current account, we can integrate cash management into the financial planning process. The projected current account balance goes into the pro forma balance sheet. Any excess cash over that figure may then be invested in interest-bearing assets.

Investing Idle Cash

Cash in excess of requirements for working balances normally is invested in interest-bearing assets that can be converted readily into cash. A firm might hold excess cash for two principal reasons; first, the firm's working capital requirement may vary over the year, perhaps in a fairly predictable manner if the variation is due to recurring seasonal factors. From the pro forma balance sheet, it was apparent that excess cash would build up during seasonal lows in accounts receivable and inventory, and would be needed later to finance a re-expansion of receivables and inventory during the next seasonal high. We can view the excess cash as a part of the firm's transaction balances. Even though the cash is temporarily idle, there is a predictable requirement for it later. Second, excess cash may be held to cover unpredictable financing requirements. In a world of uncertainty, cash flows can never be predicted with complete accuracy. Competitors act, technology changes, products fail, strikes occur, and economic conditions vary. On the positive side, attractive investment opportunities may suddenly appear. A firm may choose to hold excess cash to finance such needs if and when they occur. We noted earlier that cash held for such purposes is referred to as a precautionary balance and is usually invested in interest-bearing assets until needed.

An alternative exists to the holding of excess cash for either of the two purposes described above. The firm can simply borrow short-term to finance variable requirements as they arise. Under such a policy, the firm would never hold excess cash. A firm's choice between short-term borrowings versus liquid assets as a means of financing variable requirements will depend on policy decisions with respect to the firm's long-term financial structure, particularly the mix of short-term and long-term funds. We will discuss overall financial structure and the relationship between maturity structure and liquidity later. Here, we take as given the long-term structure and the amount available for investment in interest-bearing assets.

Investment Criteria

A firm might invest excess cash in many types of interest-bearing assets. To choose among the alternatives, we must establish criteria based on our reasons for investing excess cash in the first place. We are investing either temporary transaction balances or precautionary balance or both. When we need the cash, we want to be able to obtain it – all of it – quickly. Given these objectives, we can rule out equity shares and other investments with returns that are not contractual and with prices that often vary widely. Debt securities, with a contractual obligation to pay, are our best candidates. In selecting among debt securities, there are three principal characteristics we should examine: default risk, maturity and marketability.

Default risk refers to the possibility that interest or principal might not be paid on time and in the amount promised. If the financial markets suddenly perceive a significant risk of default on a particular security, the price of such a security is likely to fall substantially, even though default may not have actually occurred. Investors in general are averse to risk, and the possibility of default is sufficient to depress the price. Given our purposes in investing excess cash, we want to steer clear of securities that stand any significant chance of defaulting. In an uncertain world, although there is no guarantee against the default risk, still there are securities available with sufficiently low, almost negligible, default risk. In selecting securities, we must keep in mind that risk and return are related, and that low-risk securities provide the lowest returns. We must give up some return in order to purchase safety.

Maturity refers to the time period over which interest and principal payments are to be made. A 20-year bond might promise interest semi-annually and principal at the end of the twentieth year. A 6-month bank certificate of deposit would promise interest and principal at the end of the sixth month.

The prices of fixed-income securities vary with the interest rates. A rise in market rates produces a fall in price, and vice versa. Because of this relationship, in addition to default risk, debt securities are subject to a second type of risk – interest rate risk. A government bond, though free of default risk, is not immune to interest rate risk. The longer the maturity of a security, the more sensitive its price is to interest rate changes and the greater its exposure is to interest rate risk. For this reason, short maturities are generally best for investing excess cash.

Marketability refers to the ease with which an asset can be converted into cash. With reference to financial assets, the terms 'marketability' and 'liquidity' are often used interchangeably. Marketability has two principal dimensions – price and time – that are interrelated. If an asset can be sold quickly in large amounts at a price that can be determined in advance within narrow limits, the asset is said to be highly marketable or highly liquid. Perhaps the most liquid of all financial assets are Treasury Bills. On the other hand, if the price that can be realised depends significantly on the time available to sell the asset, the asset is said to have low liquidity. The more independent the price is of time, the more liquid the asset. Besides price and time, a third attribute of marketability is low transaction costs.

Yields

All the characteristics we discussed above – default risk, maturity, and marketability – affect yield. In general, lower the default risk and better the marketability, lower the yield. Securities with these desirable characteristics have higher prices, and since price and yield are inversely related lower yields.

The relationship between maturity and yields is more complex and changes over time. On an average, short maturity securities yield less, other factors being equal, because they are subject to less interest rate risk. Rates on short maturities, however, are more volatile than those on longer maturities, and at times exceed the latter.

At any point in time, rates on the major types of money-market securities discussed above are fairly close to one another. For equal maturities, the differentials usually are small and are due to small differences in default risk and marketability.

Over time, the entire structure of short-term rates varies significantly. Such variations are related to the business and monetary cycles, the demand for funds by individuals and firms, and the credit policies of the RBI.

Summary

The term 'cash' in this chapter refers to total liquid assets, made up of working cash balance plus interest-bearing securities and deposits. Firms hold cash (liquid assets) for two reasons: to execute financial transactions and for precautionary purposes. The overall problem of cash management comprises three steps: (1) collecting and disbursing funds efficiently, (2) determining the appropriate working cash balance, and (3) investing the remaining excess cash.

Steps to improve the efficiency of collection and disbursement must focus on the cash cycle of the firm. Concentration accounts can be used to reduce the requirement for working balances. Collection time can be reduced by the use of a lock-box system. Disbursements should be made within credit term but no sooner than required.

A working cash balance is required for various business purposes so its adequacy is very important for the business. Determination of the optimal level of working cash balance is a *sine qua non* for efficient business operations. In some cases, bank compensating balance requirements may determine the minimum working balance. Where this is not the case, finding the optimal balance involves a trade-off between transaction costs (high for low working balances) and opportunity costs (high for high working balances). By combining the qualitative insights from theoretical models with techniques such as cash budgeting and proforma analysis most firms can arrive at reasonable answers with some experimentation.

Firms hold liquid assets over and above working-balance requirements for two main reasons: as temporarily idle transaction balances to meet the transaction requirements and as precautionary balances. Vehicles for investing such cash reserves should be evaluated on the basis of default risk. Maturity, marketability and yields on such short-term money-market instruments vary over the business cycle and tend to average slightly less than those of longer-maturity issues.

Questions

1. What are the principal motives for holding cash and liquid assets?

2. From the standpoint of cash management, on what parts of the cash cycle should attention be focused?

3. What are the advantages of concentration banking?

4. How can a firm speed the collection of cash?

5. Suppose a firm's cash inflows and outflows are variable but completely predictable. How are the concepts of inventory theory applicable to such a problem?

6. Suppose a firm's cash inflows and outflows are completely random. What approach might a firm use to set its minimum working balance?

7. Why might a firm have idle cash?

8. Discuss the criteria that a firm should use in choosing assets in which to invest idle cash.

Problems

1. Harshad and Co. has credit sales of Rs 2 crore per year. Collections average Rs 8,000 per day (250 working days per year). Suppose Harshad could reduce its internal processing time by one day. What would be its annual savings, assuming a cost of funds of 9 per cent?

2. Shoppers Stop is a national retailing concern that sells primarily on a credit basis. Collections from the southern region average Rs 100,000 a day and the total float (amount of time it takes from payment mailing to the time when shoppers obtains the use of the funds) is averaging 5 days for customers in this area. The opportunity cost on short-term funds is considered to be 8 per cent.

    a. ICICI bank has offered to set up a lock-box system which will reduce float by 3 days for a compensating balance of Rs 200,000. Would you recommend that Shoppers Stop accept the offer?

    b. The bank also proposes an alternative of a flat annual fee of Rs 10,000. Which option should shoppers prefer?

3. M/s. Gokuldas & Co. purchases Rs 3 crores of raw materials each year on terms of net 30. The purchasing agent currently is paying each invoice 20 working days after its date to make sure that payment is received by suppliers in 30 days. A study shows that payments delayed until the 25th working day and still leave enough time for receipt by the 30th day. How much would the company save annually by making this change, assuming a 9 per cent cost of funds?

4. The MHF Company currently maintains an account with HDFC Bank for collections in the southern marketing area. The bank handles collections of Rs 500,000 per day in return for a compensating balance of Rs 300,000.

    a. The company is considering an alternative of opening two separate accounts in the southern area. It has been projected that total processing time could be reduced by 1½ days if accounts are maintained in Lord Krishna Bank and Bank of Madurai, each requiring a compensating balance of Rs 300,000. Would you recommend the two-bank system to MHF Company?

    b. If HDFC Bank offers to drop the required compensating balance in favour of a flat fee, what is the maximum fee MHF Company should be willing to pay to leave its business with that bank?

5. Max Company currently maintains a centralised billing system at its home office to handle average daily collections of Rs 300,000. The total time for mailing, processing, and clearing has been estimated at 5 days.

    a. If the firm's opportunity cost on short-term funds is 8 per cent, how much is this time lag of 5 days costing the company?

    b. If management has designed a system of lock-boxes with regional banks that would reduce float by 2½ days and home office credit department expense by Rs 30,000 annually, what is the largest total amount of required compensating balance that the firm should be willing to accept with the lock-box arrangement?

CHAPTER IV

Receivables Management

Learning Objectives

- The significance of accounts receivable management in the overall financial management of firms
- Credit policy and its constituents – credit terms, credit standards and collection efforts
- Impact of change in the components of credit policy on the other financial variables and consequently on the firm's overall financial performance
- The practical techniques that firms can take recourse to strike at optimal credit terms and to ensure that sales are made to credit worthy customers
- The procedures that firms follow to expedite their collections from receivables

Chapter Organization

- The chapter examines the significance of accounts receivable management and focuses on the decision variables involved in it.
- Thereafter, credit policy has been dealt with in detail including the different components of credit policy and their impact on the financial position of the firm. Also, models and decision tools like credit scoring, discriminant analysis, heuristic approach, etc., that aid in evaluating the credit-worthiness of the credit applicant have been illustrated in the chapter.
- The last section of the chapter discusses in detail the collection policies and procedures.

CHAPTER 4

Receivables Management

In the previous chapters, we developed a general overview of working-capital management and took an in-depth look at the management of cash and marketable securities. In chapter 4 & 5, we will focus on the management of two very important components of working capital: accounts receivables and inventory.

Much of our concern with accounts receivable and inventory is derived from the fact that they make up a large portion of the firm's assets; they actually compose 25.12 and 7.45 per cent, respectively, of a typical firm's assets. Thus, because of their sheer magnitude any change in their levels affects profitability. For example, an increase in accounts receivable - that is, additional extension of trade credit - not only results in higher sales but also requires additional financing to support the increased investment in accounts receivable. The costs of credit investigation and collection efforts and the chance of bad debts are also increased. With respect to inventory management, a larger investment in inventory leads to more efficient production and speedier delivery and hence increased sales. However, additional financing is required to support the increase in inventory and in handling and carrying costs.

In studying the management of these current assets, we will first examine accounts receivable management in this chapter, focusing on its importance, what determines the investment in it, what are the decision variables involved and how do we determine them. After examining accounts receivable management, we will turn to inventory management in the next chapter, examining its importance and the order quantity and order point problems, which in combination determine the level of investment in inventory.

All firms by their very nature are involved in selling either goods or services. While some of these sales will be for cash, a large portion will involve the use of credit. Whenever a sale is made on credit, it increases a firm's accounts receivable. Thus, the importance of accounts receivable management depends upon the degree to which the firm sells on credit. Table 4.1 lists, for selected industries, the percentage of total assets made up by accounts receivable.

From Table 4.1 we can see that accounts receivable typically comprise slightly over 25 per cent of a firm's assets. In effect, when we discuss management of accounts receivable, we are discussing the management of one-quarter of the firm's assets. Moreover, since cash flows from a sale cannot be invested until the account is collected, control of receivables takes on added importance; efficient collection determines both profitability and liquidity of the firm.

Size of Investment in Accounts Receivable

The size of the investment in accounts receivable is determined by a number of factors. First, the percentage of credit sales to total sales affects the level of accounts receivable held. Although this factor certainly plays a major role in determining the investment in accounts receivable, it is generally not within the control of the finance manager. In essence, the nature of the business tends to determine the blend between credit sales and cash sales. For a large grocery store, sales tend to be made exclusively on a cash basis, while for most construction/lumber supply firms, sales are primarily on credit. Thus, the nature of the industry business, and not the decision of the finance manager, tends to determine what proportion of sales is made on credit.

The level of sales is also a factor in determining the size of the investment in accounts receivable. Very simply, the more the sales, the greater will be accounts receivable. As the firm experiences seasonal and permanent growth in sales, the level of investment in accounts receivable will naturally increase.

Thus, while the level of sales affects the size of the investment in accounts receivable, it is not a decision variable for the finance manager.

Table 4.1: Accounts Receivable as a Percentage of Total Assets for Major Industries

Industry	Accounts Receivable Relative to Total Assets
All industries	25.12%
Motor vehicles and equipment manufacturing	46.59
General merchandising stores-retail	31.14
Total construction	27.35
Building materials, garden supplies, and mobile home dealers-retail	24.96
Apparel and accessory stores-retail	16.12
Automotive dealers and service stations-retail	13.78
Agricultural, forestry, and fishing	8.92
Transportation	7.11
Food stores	6.59
Hotels and other lodging places	6.29

Source: Internal Revenue Service, U.S. Treasury Department, Statistics of Income, 1977, Corporate Income Tax Returns (Washington, D. C. Government Printing Office, 1982), pp. 27-34.

The final determinants of the level of investment in accounts receivable are the credit and collection policies—more specifically, the terms of sale, the quality of customers, and collection efforts. The terms of sale specify both the time period during which the customer must pay and the terms; that is, is there a discount for paying early, and if so, how much? The type of customer or credit policy also affects the level of investment in accounts receivable. For example, the acceptance of poorer risks and their subsequent delinquent payments may lead to an increase in accounts receivable. The strength and timing of the collection efforts can affect the period for which past-due accounts remain delinquent, which in turn affects the level of accounts receivable. Collection and credit policy decisions may further affect the level of investment in accounts receivable by causing changes in the sales level and the ratio of credit sales to total sales. However, the three credit and collection policy variables are the only true decision variables under the control of the finance manager.

Every business day, credit managers across the country face the same issue: a new client is requesting prompt clearance of his application to allow him to buy materials. The sales department is feverishly lobbying for a quick approval on the credit application so that the company can nail down a sale. If credit for the client is approved, he may buy and default, causing the company a loss. If the credit is not approved, the sale and the profit potential go to a competing firm. This implies that a well-functioning credit granting and receivables management policy is vital for a firm.

The management of accounts receivable deals with establishing viable credit and collection policies. A very liberal credit policy will increase sales and also bad-debt losses. On the other hand, a conservative credit policy will reduce bad-debt losses but also reduce sales. A good credit policy should seek to strike a reasonable balance between sales and bad-debt losses. A collection policy should be designed to keep the level of investments in receivables at an appropriate level. In this section, we consider general guidelines for credit and collection policies. The last section discusses credit and collection procedures as they apply to individual accounts.

Credit and Collection Policies

A firm needs to invest in and manage accounts receivable because it sells some or all of its output on credit. A firm that chooses not to extend credit will not have any receivables to manage. Very few firms actually operate on a "cash and carry" basis. The more typical situation is that firms do grant credit, make sales on credit, and have to manage accounts receivables.

The firm's credit policy will influence (a) the sales level; (b) the investment level in cash, inventories, accounts receivable, and possibly physical investments; (c) bad-debt losses; and (d) collection costs. By credit policy is meant decisions with regard to credit standards – who gets credit and up to what amount – and the specific terms of credit. In this section we examine the influence of credit policy on sales, investments, and so forth, and discuss credit standards and credit terms.

Influence of Credit Policy

Credit policy will directly influence sales, investment levels, bad-debt losses, and collection costs.

Sales: Sales vary directly with the extent to which credit terms are liberalised. The demand for a firm's products is greatly influenced by the ease with which the products can be purchased on credit. Sales will be at their lowest level if they are strictly for cash. Those who want to buy on credit will patronise other manufacturers who extend credit. Sales will start increasing as credit terms are liberalised. Sales will be at their maximum level when the firm does not screen buyers for credit worthiness. Rather, credit is extended to all who want to buy the firm's products.

Investment Levels: Sales on credit result in accounts receivable. As discussed above, sales are directly related to the liberality of credit terms. As credit terms are liberalised, sales increase and to service this increased level of sales properly, the firm needs to increase its investments in cash and inventories. Finally, if sales increase sufficiently, the firm may have to increase its productive capacity. As credit terms are made more liberal, the firm's investment in cash, accounts receivable, inventories, and perhaps physical investments increase in a complimentary fashion.

Bad-Debt Losses: Without credit sales the firm will not incur any bad-debt losses. With a very conservative credit policy, debt-debt losses will be nonexistent or minimal. As credit terms are liberalised, the firm begins to give credit to marginally less-credit-worthy clients. The liberalisation of credit terms results in increase in bad-debt losses.

Collection Costs: Collection costs are the clerical and administrative costs associated with granting credit and managing accounts receivable. When credit is not granted, collection costs are minimal. As credit terms are liberalised, the firm's volume of accounts receivable increases. The clerical and administrative costs of invoicing, collecting, and book keeping also increase as credit terms are liberalised. A second type of collection cost is the one related to efforts to collect on delinquent accounts. As credit terms are liberalised, delinquent accounts increase and the costs of efforts to collect on these accounts also increase.

Credit Terms

The credit terms or the terms of sale identify the possible discount for early payment, the discount period, and the total credit period. They are generally stated in the form a/b net c, indicating that the customer can deduct a per cent if the account is paid within b days; otherwise, the account must be paid within c days. Thus, for example, trade credit terms of 2/10, net 30 indicate that a 2 per cent discount can be taken if the account is paid within 10 days; otherwise it must be paid within 30 days; but what if the customer decides to forgo the discount and not pay until the final payment date? If such a decision is made, the customer has the use of the money for the time period between the discount date and the final payment date. However, failure to take the discount represents a cost to the customer. For instance, if the terms are 2/10, net 30, the analysed opportunity cost of passing up this 2 per cent discount in order to withhold payment for an additional 20 days is 36.73 per cent. This is determined as follows:

(Analysed opportunity cost of forgoing the discount)

$$= \frac{a}{1-a} \times \frac{360}{c-b} \qquad \text{.................(4.1)}$$

Substituting the values from the example, we get

$$36.73\% = \frac{.02}{1-.02} \times \frac{360}{30-10} \qquad \text{.................(4.2)}$$

In industry, the typical discount ranges anywhere from one-half per cent to 10 per cent, while the discount period is generally 10 days and the total credit period varies from 30 to 90 days. Although the terms of credit vary radically from industry to industry, the terms tend to remain relatively constant over time and they do not appear to be a frequently used decision variable.

As discussed previously, credit policy has a direct influence on sales, investment levels, bad-debt losses, and collection costs. From a managerial view-point and looking strictly at the relationship between credit policy and sales, one could conclude that a very liberal credit policy is highly desirable. However, the relationship between credit policy and investment levels, bad-debt losses, and collection costs implies that a very conservative credit policy is desirable. An appropriate credit policy balances profits from increased sales due to more liberal credit terms with increased costs due to increased investments, bad-debt losses, and collection costs. The ideal credit policy allows for the liberalisation of credit terms to the point where the marginal revenues from a new category of credit accounts is exactly equal to the marginal costs of selling and servicing such accounts.

In practice, it is not feasible to establish the ideal credit policy. However, firms do consider alternative credit terms to see what influence they have on profits. Our focus here will be to look at certain specific credit terms and see how they might affect profits and what guidelines a firm could use to enhance its profitability. The three specific components of credit terms are credit period, credit discount, and discount period.

Credit Period: The credit terms are specified on the invoices sent out by firms. A typical credit term may state: 2/10, net 30. As discussed earlier in the chapter, the first number "2" is the credit discount and indicates that a 2 per cent discount may be taken if the invoice is paid within the number of days specified by the second term, i.e., 10 days. The second term "10" is the discount period and indicates the number of days during which the credit discount can be taken. The last number "30" indicates the credit period. The credit period specifies the number of days that a firm can take to pay the invoice without being considered to be delinquent. With terms of 2/10, net 30 the credit period is 30 days and the full amount of the invoice is due within 30 days.

One way to liberalise credit terms is to increase the credit period. Conversely, credit terms can be tightened by shortening the credit period. Mitsui Corporation is currently selling on credit terms of 2/10, net 30. Its annual gross sales are at the level of Rs 36 million currently. All sales are on credit. Fifty per cent of its clients take the 2 per cent discount and pay on the tenth day. The other 50 per cent, who do not take the discount, on an average pay after 30 days. The sales volume between discount takers and non-discount takers is evenly divided. The company's management is considering two alternative credit plans: plan A would change the credit terms 2/10, net 45; plan B would extend the credit period even further, making the terms 2/10, net 60. Plan A is expected to increase sales by 5 per cent from current levels, whereas plan B would increase sales by 7 per cent. Mitsui's margins on sales before credit-related costs and taxes are 20 per cent. Investments in accounts receivable carry a 12 per cent pre-tax cost.

In trying to decide whether to keep the present credit plan or switch to either of plans A or B, management recognises that an occasional result of extending the credit period will be that more customers will take the discount. However, they feel that with the present plans there will be no change in the rupee volume of sales on which the discount is taken. That is, all incremental sales will be paid for after the 10-day discount period. In addition, management feels that 1 per cent of all incremental sales under plan A and 2 per cent under plan B will prove to be uncollectible. No additional credit costs will be involved in clerical or administrative functions. Which credit period policy appears to be the most desirable?

The variables to be considered in deciding between the present credit terms and plans A and B are profits on increased sales, increases in accounts receivables, increases in the cost of financing the additional receivables, and increased in bad-debt losses. The effects of the three credit terms on these variables are summarized in Table 4.2. The analytical approach is incremental. That is, given the existing credit terms we focus on the incremental profits and costs of plans A and B. Under plan A, sales increase by 5 per cent or 0.05 per cent × Rs 36 million = Rs 1.8 million. Sales would increase by Rs 2.52 million under plan B. Marginal profits before taxes and credit-related expenses are 0.2%. × Rs 1.8 million = Rs 3,60,000 for plan A and Rs 504,000 for plan B.

Increases in accounts receivable cannot be calculated by just looking at incremental sales. The reason is that when the credit period is extended, the existing buyers who are not taking the discount and are paying after 30 days will also take advantage of the extended credit period and not pay for 45 days. Incremental investment in receivables is estimated by calculating total receivables first. For present credit terms, 50 per cent of sales are paid for in 10 days, the other 50 per cent in 30 days. The average sale is outstanding for 0.5(10) + 0.5(30) = 20 days. Daily sales are Rs 36 million / 360 days = Rs 100,000. Total accounts receivable equal 20 days × Rs 100,000 = Rs 2 million.[1]

Table 4.2: Analysis of credit terms: changing credit periods for Mitsui Corporation

	Present	Plan A	Plan B
1. Increase in sales (%)	0 %	5 %	7 %
2. Increase in sales (Rs=1×Rs 36 crore)	Rs. 0	Rs 1,800,000	Rs 2,520,000
3. Margin on sales (%)	20%	20%	20%
4. Marginal profits (Rs = 2 × 3)[a]	Rs. 0	Rs 360,000	Rs 504,000
5. Average sales outstanding	20 days	28.34 days	36.65 days
6. Daily sales	Rs 100,000	Rs 105,000	Rs 107,000
7. Total receivables (5 × 6)	Rs 2,000,000	Rs 2,975,000	Rs 3,921,600
8. Increase in receivables	0	975,700	1,921,600
9. Increase in investment costs (8×12 %)	0	117,084	230,592
10. Increase in bad debt losses (2 × x%)	0	18,000	50,400
11. Increase in costs (9+10)	0	135,084	280,992
12. Increase in profits (4 – 11)	0	224,916	223,008

[a] Before credit related costs and taxes.

1. Sales are assumed to be reasonably equitably distributed among buyers. Also, it is assumed that the daily sales volume is constant.

Under plan A total sales are Rs 36 million + 1.8 million = Rs 37.8 million. The rupee amount subject to payment by the tenth day remains at Rs 18 million or Rs 18 million/ Rs 37.8 million = 47.6 per cent. The other 52.4 per cent now takes 45 days to pay. The average sale will be outstanding for 0.476 (10 days) + 0.524 (45 days) = 28.34 days. Daily sales are Rs 37.8 million/360 days = Rs 105,000. Total receivables are Rs 105,000 × 28.34 days = Rs 2,975,700.

Under plan B, total sales are Rs 38.52 million. The percentage of discount takers is Rs 18 million/ Rs 38.52 million = 46.7 per cent. The average sales is outstanding for 0.467 (10 days) + 0.533 (60 days) = 36.65 days. Daily sales are Rs 38.52 million / 360 days = Rs 107,000 and receivables are Rs 107,000 × 36.65 days = Rs 3,921,600.

Incremental receivables for plan A are Rs 2,975,700 - Rs 2,000,000 = Rs 975,700 and are Rs 1,921,600 for plan B. The before-tax cost of financing these receivables is 12 per cent. Therefore, the increase in investment costs for plan A is Rs 975,700 × 0.12 = Rs 117,084 for plan A and is Rs 1,921,600 × 0.12 = Rs 230,592 for plan B. The incremental bad debts losses would be 0.01x 1.8 million = 18,000 for plan A and 0.02 × Rs 2.52 million = Rs 50,400 for plan B.

The total incremental credit associated costs for plan A are Rs 117,084 + Rs 18,000 = Rs 135,084 and are Rs 280,992 for plan B. The incremental profits after adjusting for credit costs are Rs 224,916 for plan A and Rs 223,008 for plan B. Both plans are superior to the present plan. However, plan A is slightly preferable to plan B.

Credit Discount: The credit discount is offered as an inducement for the credit buyer to pay promptly. The credit buyer's opportunity cost of not taking the discount is given by:

$$\frac{360 \text{ days} \times \text{credit discount}}{\text{credit period} - \text{discount period}}$$

For terms of 2/10, net 30 the opportunity cost of not taking the discount is 360 days × 2 per cent / (30-10) = 36 per cent. Obviously, this opportunity cost has to be high enough to motivate a financially strong credit buyer to take the discount. For example, terms of 1/10, net 70 imply an opportunity cost of 6 per cent. At this cost, firms will prefer to use trade credit rather than borrow from banks and the credit discount is no longer a viable credit policy instrument.

Although changing the credit discount has some influence on demand, its most visible impact is on reducing the average collection period and the level of accounts receivable. Assume that Mitsui is considering changing its credit terms from 2/10, net 30 to 2.5/10, net 30 in plan C or 3/10, net 30 in plan D. Either of the new plans would not affect the sales volume. However, under plan C, 70 per cent of the credit buyers would take the credit discount and, under plan D, 90 per cent would take the discount.

Should Mitsui switch to either plan C or D if the previously given information on investment cost is applicable here?

The analysis here would be similar to the one done for the credit period. Gross sales volume under either the present credit terms or plan C or D remain at Rs 36 million. Sales for which discounts are taken are 50 per cent or Rs 18 million for the present plan, and Rs 25.2 million and Rs 32.4 million for plan C and D, respectively (see Table 4.3). The credit discount for the present plan is 2 per cent or 0.02 × Rs 18 million = Rs 360,000. For plan C it is 0.025 × Rs 25.2 million = Rs 630,000 and is Rs 972,000 for plan D. The incremental cost of going to a more liberal credit discount under plan C is Rs 630,000 - Rs 360,000 = Rs 270,000 and is Rs 612,000 for plan D.

The increase in credit costs due to giving a larger credit discount reduces the level of investments in accounts receivable. Total receivables under the present plan were calculated to be Rs 2 million in Table 4.2. Under plan C, the average collection period is 0.7 (10 days) + 0.3 (30 days) = 16 days. Since daily sales are Rs 100,000, total receivables are Rs 16,00,000. Under plan D, total receivables are [0.9 (10 days)] × Rs 100,000 = Rs 12,00,000. Under plan C, receivables decrease by Rs 20,00,000- Rs 16,00,000 = Rs 400,000. The decrease in investments under plan D is Rs 20,00,000 - Rs 12,00,000 = Rs 800,000.

Table 4.3: Analysis of Credit Terms: Changing Credit Discounts for the Mitsui Corporation.

	Present	Plan C	Plan D
1. Gross sales volume	Rs 36,000,000	Rs 36,000,000	Rs 36,000,000
2. Sales with discounts (%)	50%	70%	90%
3. Sales with discounts (Rs = 1 × 2)	Rs 18,000,000	Rs 25,200,000	Rs 32,400,000
4. Credit discounts (%)	2%	2.5%	3.0%
5. Credit discounts (Rs = 3 × 4)	Rs 360,000	Rs 630,000	Rs 972,000

Contd..

6. Increase in discounts	0	Rs 270,000	Rs 612,000
7. Total receivables	Rs 20,00,000	Rs 16,00,000	Rs 12,00,000
8. Decrease in receivables	0	Rs 400,000	Rs 800,000
9. Decrease in investment costs (8 × 12 %)	0	Rs 48,000	Rs 96,000
10. Increase in profits (9–6)	0	(Rs 222,000)	(Rs 516,000)

The cost of investments in receivables is 12 per cent. Cost savings are Rs 400,000 × 0.12 = Rs 48,000 for plan C and Rs 96,000 for plan D. Cost savings less increase in discount costs give increase in profits before taxes. As shown in Table 4.3, neither plan C nor plan D results in increasing profits over the present levels. Consequently, Mitsui should not implement either plan C or plan D.

Discount Period: The analysis of changing discount periods is very similar to the analysis for changing credit discounts. As the discount period is increased, the opportunity cost of not taking a discount increases. Therefore, it becomes more attractive for a credit buyer to take the discount. However, as the discount period is extended, the existing discount takers take advantage of the liberalised credit terms and delay making their payments until the end of the new discount period. Whether extending the discount period is desirable is dependent on whether total receivables increase or decrease.

Continuing the Mitsui example, the firm can change credit terms to 2/12, net 30 or 2/15, net 30 under plans E and F, respectively. The per cent of sales subject to the discount would be 60 per cent in plan E and 80 per cent in plan F. Should Mitsui switch to either plan E or plan F? Gross sales would not be affected by these alternative plans.

Table 4.4: Analysis of Credit Terms: Changing Discount Periods for Mitsui Corporation

	Present	Plan E	Plan F
1. Gross sales volume	Rs 36,000,000	Rs 36,000,000	Rs 36,000,000
2. Sales with discounts (%)	50%	60%	80%
3. Sales with discounts (1×2)	Rs 18,000,000	Rs 21,600,000	Rs 28,800,000
4. Credit discounts (Rs = 3×2%)	Rs 360,000	Rs 432,000	Rs 576,000
5. Increase in discounts	0	Rs 72,000	Rs 216,000

Contd..

6. Total receivables	Rs 20,00,000	Rs 1,800,000	Rs 14,00,000
7. Decrease in receivables	0	Rs 2,00,000	Rs 6,00,000
8. Decrease in investment costs (7×12%)	0	Rs 24,000	Rs 72,000
9. Increase in profits (8–5)	0	(Rs 48,000)	(Rs 144,000)

Sales subject to discounts would be Rs 18 million, Rs 21.6 million, and Rs 28.8 million, for the present terms, plan E, and plan F, respectively. Credit discount at 2 per cent would be Rs 360,000 for the present plan and Rs 432,000 and Rs 576,000 for plans E and F, respectively. The increase in discounts for plan E would be Rs 72,000 and would be Rs 216,000 for plan F (Table 4.4).

The total receivables under plan E would be [0.6 (10 days) + 0.4 (30 days)] × Rs 100,000 = 1.8 million. The same entry would be [0.8 (10 days) + 0.2 (30 days)] × Rs 100,000 = Rs 1.4 million for plan F. A decrease in investment costs due to a decrease in receivables is Rs 24,000 for plan E and Rs 72,000 for plan F. Taking into consideration the increased discounts being given, we find that neither of the two new plans is acceptable.

Simultaneous Changes in Credit Terms

Most firms, from a practical standpoint, will consider changes in all credit terms simultaneously. For example, the Mitsui Corporation may seek to evaluate new credit terms in which the credit period, credit discount, and discount period all change simultaneously. As we have seen previously, extending the credit period influences sales most strongly, whereas changing the other two credit terms has a strong impact on the level of receivables outstanding. A firm considering changing all credit terms needs to carefully examine the potential impact of the changes, on incremental profits. Assume that Mitsui is considering changing from terms of 2/10, net 30 either to 2/15, net 45 in plan G or 2.5/15, net 60 in plan H. Under plan G, sales are expected to increase by 5 per cent, whereas with plan H sales would have a potential of increasing by 10 per cent. Marginal returns before credit-adjusted costs and taxes would be 20 per cent of sales.

Under the present credit terms, the average collection period is 20 days (as shown in Table 4.2). Under plan G, 45 per cent of sales would involve the discount. Those who take the discount would pay at the end of the discount period and others would, on an average, pay by the end of the credit period. Bad-debt losses would increase by 1 per cent of incremental sales for plan G and 2 per cent of incremental sales for plan H. Collection costs would increase by Rs 10,000 and Rs 30,000 under plans G and H, respectively. Which one of the two credit term plans appears to be better for Mitsui?

Under plan G, sales and marginal profits would increase by Rs 1.8 million and Rs 360,000, respectively. For plan H, sales would increase by Rs 3.6 crore and profits by Rs 720,000. These marginal profits are before credit adjusted costs and need to be adjusted for changes in the investment levels in receivables and in discount taken.

Given credit terms of 2/15, net 45, average collection period for plan G is 0.45 (15 days) + 0.55 (45 days) = 31.5 days. Since daily sales are Rs 37.8 million/360 days = Rs 105,000, total receivables for plan G would be 31.5 days × Rs 105,000 = Rs 3,307,500. Similarly, total receivables for plan H would be [0.40 (15 days) + 0.6 (60 days)] = 42 days × 39.6 million/360 = Rs 4,620,000 (see Table 4.4).

From total receivables, we can calculate incremental receivables and the cost of increased investments in receivables, as shown in Table 4.5.

Table 4.5: Analysis of Credit Terms: Changing Credit Terms for Mitsui Corporation

	Present	Plan G	Plan H
1. Increase in sales (%)	0%	5%	10%
2. Increase in sales (Rs = 1 × Rs 36 crore)	0	Rs 18,00,000	Rs 36,00,000
3. Margin on sales (%)	20%	20%	20%
4. Marginal profits (Rs = 2×3)[a]	0	Rs 3,60,000	Rs 7,20,000
5. Average collection period	20 days	31.5 days	42 days
6. Daily sales	Rs 100,000	Rs 105,000	Rs 110,000
7. Total receivable	Rs 20,00,000	Rs 33,07,500	Rs 46,20,000
8. Increase in receivable	0	Rs 13,07,500	Rs 26,20,000
9. Increase in investment costs (8×12%)	0	Rs 1,56,900	Rs 3,14,400
10. Increase in bad debt losses (2 × x%)	0	Rs 18,000	Rs 72,000

Contd..

11. Sales with discount (Rs)	18,000,000	17,010,000	15,840,000
12. Credit discounts (%)	2%	2.5%	2.5%
13. Credit discounts (Rs = 11 × 12)	360,000	340,000	396,000
14. Increase in discounts	0	19,800	36,000
15. Increase in collection costs	0	10,000	30,000
16. Increase in credit costs (9 + 10 + 14 + 15)	0	165,100	452,400
17. Increase in profit (4 – 16)	0	194,900	267,600

[a] Before credit-related costs and taxes.

For plan G, bad debt losses would be Rs 1.8 million × 0.01 = Rs 15,000 and Rs 72,000 for plan H. Cost of giving discounts and increased collection costs are shown in Table 4.5. Given the total credit related cost increases of Rs 165,100 for plan G, its profitability before taxes is Rs 360,000 - Rs 165,000 = Rs 194,900. Similarly, plan H would increase pretax profits by Rs 267,600. Of these two plans, plan H is the better one. Plan H is also the best plan among all eight plans discussed in this section.

Credit Analysis and Credit Limit

A second decision variable involves determining the type of customer who is to qualify for trade credit. Quite obviously, several costs are associated with extending credit to lower-quality customers. First, as the probability of customer default increases with the extension of credit to lower-quality customers, it becomes more important to identify which of the possible new customers would be a poor risk. Thus, more time is spent investigating the lower quality customer, and the costs of credit investigation increase.

Default costs also vary directly with the quality of the customer. As the customer's credit rating declines, the chance that the account will not be paid on time increases. In the extreme case, payment does not occur at all and the account must be written off. Thus, taking on lower quality customers results in increases in default costs.

Collection costs also increase as the quality of the customer declines. The increase in delinquent accounts will force the firm to spend more time and money in collecting them. In summary, the decline in customer quality results in increased costs of credit investigation, collection, and default.

In determining whether or not credit should be granted to an individual customer, we are primarily interested in the customer's short-run welfare. Thus, liquidity ratios, other obligations, and the overall profitability of the firm become the focal points in this analysis. Credit-rating services provide information on the financial status, operations, and payment history for most firms. Other possible sources of information would include credit bureaus, trade associations, chambers of commerce, competitors, bank references, public financial statements, and, of course, the firm's past relationships with the customer.

One way in which both individuals and firms are often evaluated as credit risks is through the use of credit scoring. Credit scoring involves the numerical evaluation of each applicant, in which an applicant receives a score based upon his or her answers to a simple set of questions. This score is then evaluated relative to a predetermined standard, its level relative to the standard determining whether or not credit should be extended. The major advantage of credit scoring is that it is inexpensive and easy to perform. For example, once the standards are set, a computer operator or clerical worker without any specialised training could easily evaluate any applicant.

The techniques used for constructing credit-scoring indexes range from the naïve, simple approach of adding up default rates associated with the answers given to each question, to sophisticated evaluations using Multiple Discriminant Analysis (MDA). MDA is a statistical technique for calculating the appropriate importance to be given to each question used in evaluating the applicant. Table 4.6 shows a credit "scorecard" used by a large automobile dealer. The weights or scores attached to each answer are based upon the auto dealer's past experience with credit sales. For example, the scorecard indicates that individuals with no telephone in their home have a much higher probability of default than those with a telephone. One caveat should be mentioned: Whenever this type of questionnaire is used to evaluate credit applicants, it should be carefully examined to be absolutely sure that it does not involve any (illegal) discriminatory questions.

Telephone						Score	Credit scorecard		
Home	Relative	None							
5	1	0					(Customer's Name)		
Living quarters							(Street Address)		
Own home no mortgage	Own home mortgage	Rent a house	Live with someone	Rent an apartment	Rent a room				
6	3	2	1	0	0		(City, State, Zip)		
Bank accounts							(Home/Office/telephone)		
None	1	More than							
0	4	6					(Credit scorer)		
							Credit scorecard evaluation		
Years at present address							Rupee amount Rs 0 - Rs 500		
Under ½	½-2	3-7	8 or more				0-18	19-21	22 or more
0	1	3	4				Reject	Refer to main credit	Accept
Size of family including customer							Rupee amount Rs 2001 - Rs 5000		
1	2	3-6	7 or more				0-21	22-24	25
2	4	3	0				Reject	Refer to main credit	Accept
Monthly income							Rupee amount : more than Rs 500		
Under	Rs 401 - Rs 6000	Rs 601 - Rs 900	Rs 901 - Rs 1200	More than Rs 1200			0-23	26-27	27 or more
0	1	2	6	8			Reject	Refer to main credit	Accept
Length of present employment									
Under ½ year	½-2	3-7 years	8 years or more						
0	1	2	4						
Per cent of selling price on credit									
Under 50	50-69	70-84	85-99						
5	3	1	0						

Contd..

Interview discretionary points (+ 5 to-5)									
If a previous loan customer, were payment received promptly?				Yes *					
Total				No					
Are you willing to take responsibility for authorizing				Yes *					
This loan?				No					

* refer to main credit if answer to either question is no.

Another model that could be used for credit scoring has been provided by Edward Altman, who used multiple discriminant analysis to identify businesses that might go bankrupt. In this landmark study Altman used financial ratios to predict which firms would go bankrupt over the period 1946 to 1965. Using multiple discriminant analysis, Altman came up with the following index:

$$z = 3.3\frac{\text{Credit}}{\text{Total Assets}} + 1.0\frac{\text{Sales}}{\text{Total Assets}} + 0.6\frac{\text{Market value of equity}}{\text{Book value of debt}}$$

$$+ 1.4\frac{\text{Retained earning}}{\text{Total assets}} + 1.2\frac{\text{Working capital}}{\text{Total assets}} \qquad \ldots\ldots\ldots\ldots\ldots(4.3)$$

Altman found that of the firms that went bankrupt over this time period, 94 per cent had Z scores of less than 2.7 one year prior to bankruptcy and only 6 per cent had scores above 2.7 per cent. On the other hand, of those firms that did not go bankrupt, only 3 per cent had Z scores below 2.7 and 97 per cent had scores above 2.7.

Again, the advantages of credit-scoring techniques are their low cost and ease of implementation. The credit scorer needs little or no training and with simple calculations can easily spot those credit risks that need more in the way of screening before credit should be extended to them.

A firm reviewing a request for credit needs to judge the credit applicant's willingness and ability to pay. If either of these two factors is missing, the firm would increase its chances of suffering losses on credit extended to the applicant. Willingness to pay is judged by the firm's past repayment behaviour. Its ability to pay is judged by the strength of its financial statements in relation to the amount of credit desired using credit scoring models or discriminant analysis.

Once the firm decides to grant credit to the customer, the next important issue facing the firm is that of establishing the credit limit. Heuristic or statistical procedures could be utilised for the purpose.

Heuristic Approach. The heuristic approach described here is based on a manufacturing company's actual experience. The formula or procedure described here has the weight of managerial experience and intuition behind it and therefore is heuristic in nature. There are eight factors that need to be considered in the decision to establish a credit limit and grant credit. The credit limit is the maximum amount of credit purchases allowed to the credit applicant at any one time and is stated as a per cent of tangible net worth. The lower limit is minus 15 per cent and is tantamount to denying new credit to the applicant. The upper limit is 80 per cent and is equivalent to the sum of the maximum percentage points on the eight credit-granting factors.

Credit Requirements. The first factor is the applicant's credit requirements, (C). This factor is a measure of the applicant's dependency on the creditor. If the applicant plans to buy less than 25 per cent of his requirements from the creditor, he gets 0 per cent toward his credit line. If he plans to buy between 25 and 50 per cent, he gets a 5 per cent allowance. If he plans to buy over 50 per cent he gets a 10 per cent allowance (see Table 4.6).

Pay Habits. The second factor is pay habits (P) and is a measure of the willingness and ability to pay. Payments during the discount period rate 10 per cent. Payments during the credit period are worth 5 per cent. Habitually late payments rate minus 5 per cent.

Years in Business. The third factor is years in business (Y) and is a measure of the ability of the firm to pay. Being in business less than 3 years has no effect on increasing the limits. If Y is between 3 and 10 years, the limit is increased by 5 per cent. If the firm has been in existence for more than 10 years, it rates 10 per cent.

Table 4.6: Heuristic Approach to Establishing the Credit Limit

Contributing factor	Rating	Contribution to Credit Limit : Per cent of Net Worth
Applicant credit requirements (C)	C < 25%	0
	25 < C < 50%	5

Contd..

	C > 50%	10
Pay habits (P)	Takes discount	10
	Pays on time	5
	Pays late	-5
Years in Business (Y)	Y < 3 years	0
	3 < Y < 10	5
	Y > 10	10
Profit Margin (M)	M < 5%	0
	M% < M < 14%	5
	M > 14%	10
Current Ratio (R)	R > 2.2:1	10
	1.5 < R < 2.2	5
	R < 1.5	0
Total debt total assets (T)	T < 1.3	10
	0.5 < T < 0.3	5
	T < 0.5	-5
Inventory Turnover (I)	I < 10	10
	5 < I < 10	5
	I > 5	0
Qualitative (Q)	Q = high	10
	Q = average	5
	Q = low	-5

Profit Margin. The fourth measure is the profit margin (M). If margins are less than 5 per cent, 0 per cent is contributed to the credit limit. Margins in excess of 14 per cent contribute 10 per cent to the credit limit.

Current Ratio. The fifth measure is the current ratio (R). A current ratio of over 2.2 to 1 is considered to be a good indication of ability to pay and helps contribute 10 per cent toward the credit limit. A current ratio of less than 1.5:1 is considered to be relatively weak and does not help increase the credit limit.

Total Debt to Asset Ratio. The sixth measure is the ratio of total debt to total assets (T) and represents the ability to pay. If T is less than 30 per cent, the applicant is viewed to be conservatively leveraged and adds 10 per cent to the credit limit.

On the other hand, a T of over 50 per cent implies increased financial riskiness and rates a minus 5 per cent toward the credit limit.

Inventory Turnover. The seventh factor is the inventory turnover (I). A higher inventory turnover implies high efficiency; I can help contribute anywhere from 0 per cent to 10 per cent toward the credit limit, as shown in Table 4.6.

Qualitative Factor. The last factor is a qualitative factor (Q) and lets the credit manager use discretion in subjective evaluation of the credit applicant's willingness and ability to pay.

It should be kept in mind that the factors mentioned here and their contribution to the credit limit is based on a particular firm's actual experience. The factors and their contributions to the credit limit may vary according to accounts payable, and the economic environment would also be considered in developing a heuristic credit evaluation decision model.

As an example, we can apply the heuristic model presented here to evaluate Kartik Metal. Assume that Kartik is requesting a credit line to buy less than 25 per cent of its raw materials requirements. What is the maximum credit line to establish for Kartik? The contributions of the various factors to the credit limit are shown in Table 4.7. The last factor, Q, is rated average because of Kartik's dependence on only 12 customers. Total contribution of the eight factors to the credit limit is 55 per cent of tangible net worth, or Rs 42,961 × 0.55 = Rs 23,629. Since the existing credit lines total Rs 5,000 + Rs 2,500 = Rs 7,500. Kartik can be extended additional credit up to Rs 23,629 - Rs 7,500 = Rs 16,129.

Table 4.7: Application of the Credit Limit Model for Kartik Metal Products

Factor	Kartik's Rating	Contribution to Credit Limit (per cent)
1. Kartik's requirement (C)	C < 25 %	0
2. Pay habits (P)	Takes discount	10
3. Years in business (Y)	Y > 10	10
4. Profit margins (M)	M = 4.6 % < 5 %	0

Contd..

5. Current ratio (R)	R = 2.89 > 2.5	10
6. Total debt to total assets (T)	T = 0.28 < 0.3	10
7. Inventory turnover (I) [a]	I = 12 > 10	10
8. Quantitative (Q)	Average	5
Total Contribution		55

[a] Based on sales; Rs 177, 250/Rs14, 619 = 12

Kartik's credit limit = Rs 42,961 / 0.55 = Rs 23,629.

Additional credit for Kartik = Rs 23,629 - Rs 7500 = Rs 16,129.

Statistical Approach. In quantitative approaches to credit analysis, the firm relies on financial information as well as on the payment records of firms that were granted credit in the past. Past customers can be readily classified into good risk and bad risk categories. The financial information on customers is used in conjunction with a statistical procedure called multiple discriminant analysis to develop a statistical credit scoring model. Discriminant analysis first of all provides an indication of those measures which are most important in distinguishing between good risk and bad risk customers. That is, the firm may start out by using 30 ratios and variables in its analysis. Discriminant analysis might indicate that only five of these ratios and variables are important in characterising good risk and bad risk customers. Second, discriminant analysis will develop weights for each ratio or variable to form a discriminant function that may look like:

Discriminant score = 3.5 (current ratio) + 1.7 (profit margins) + 7.1 (debt to assets) + 0.3 (inventory turnover) + 1.9 (quick ratio)

The 3.5, 1.7, and so forth, are weights developed by discriminant analysis. Current ratio, profit margins, and so forth, are discriminant variables identified as important by the model. The sum of the products of the weights and the variables is the discriminant score. The analysis selects weights such that discrimination between good risk and bad risk accounts is maximised. A perfect set of weights would create a discriminant score such that all bad risk firms would have scores on one side of the discriminant score. Once the discriminant credit scoring model has been developed, it can be applied to credit applicants. The weights can be used to calculate a score for the credit applicant. The credit applicant's score can be compared with the discriminant score to see whether the applicant falls in the good risk or bad risk category. If the applicant falls in the good risk category, a similar type of procedure to that described here can be used to establish a credit limit for the applicant.

Spot Quiz on Credit and Collection Procedures

1. Important credit analysis data can be gleaned from the applicant's financial statements. T ❑ F ❑

2. All applicants with the financial ability to pay should be given credit. T ❑ F ❑

3. The heuristic approach to credit analysis is based on utilisation of quantitative procedures. T ❑ F ❑

4. Discriminant analysis can be used successfully by a firm without any past credit-granting experience. T ❑ F ❑

5. Strict collection procedures should be utilised the moment an account becomes delinquent. T ❑ F ❑

Collection Policy

The key to maintaining control over the collection of accounts receivable is that the probability of default increases with the age of the account. Thus, control of accounts receivable focuses on the control and elimination of over-due receivables. One common way of evaluating the current situation is ratio analysis. By examining the average collection period, the ratio of receivables to assets, the ratio of credit sales to receivables (called the accounts receivable turnover ratio), and the amount of bad debts relative to sales over time, the finance manager can determine whether or not receivables are drifting out of control. In addition, an aging of accounts receivable provides a break-up both in rupee and in percentage terms of the proportion of receivables that are past due. Comparing the current aging of receivables with past data offers further insight into the degree of control that is being maintained over receivables portfolio. An example of an aging account or schedule appears in Table 4.8.

Table 4.8: Aging Account

Age Accounts receivable (days)	Rupee Value (in thousands)	Per cent of total
0-30	Rs 2340	39%
31-60	1500	25%
61-90	1020	17%
91-120	720	12%
Over 120	420	7%
Total	Rs 6000	100%

A ranking of measures used in monitoring accounts receivable compiled in a survey of 668 firms is provided in Table 4.9. This survey indicates that the aging account or schedule along with the accounts receivable turnover ratio and average collection period, which are actually variations of each other, serve as primary tools used in monitoring the payment behaviour of customers.

If changes are found in either the ratios or the aging of accounts, the manager should then look for any possible changes in the overall credit policy or laxness in the collection procedures that might have brought on this situation, and if changes are found, they should then be re-evaluated.

Table 4.9: Ranking of Measures used in Monitoring Payment Behavior of Customers

Measure	Number of Responses	Percentage Assigning Rank			
		1	2	3	4
Accounts receivable turnover	123	17.1%	22.8%	56.9%	3.3%
Collection period	156	28.2	53.8	17.9	0.0
Aging schedule	181	68.2	25.4	6.1	0.0
Other	10	80.0	0.0	20.0	0.0

Source: K. B. Smith and S. B. Sell, "Working Capital Management in Practice," In Readings on the Management of Working Capital, 2nd ed., ed. K. B. Smith (St. Paul, Minn.: West Publishing. 1980), pp.

Thus far, we have discussed the importance and role of accounts receivable in the firm and then examined the determinants of the size of the investment in accounts receivable. Since the credit and collection policies are the only discretionary variables for management, the primary focus has been placed on these determinants. In examining these decision variables, we have merely described their traits. In the appendix to this chapter these variables are analysed in a decision-making context, which is termed as marginal or incremental analysis.

When an account becomes delinquent, a firm can resort to a series of actions to try to collect on the account. These actions, discussed later in the chapter, include writing a letter, calling on the phone, calling in person, using a collection agency, and legal action. The particular collection procedures followed have a direct impact on bad-debt losses and the average collection period. The firm has an obvious interest in reducing both bad-debt losses and the average collection period, which lower total receivables and investment in receivables. In general, the more the firm spends on collection, the lower its delinquency costs (bad-debt losses) and the cost of maintaining excess receivables. However, the marginal productivity of collection expenditures decline as the firm expends more and more.

The discussion on collection policy has assumed that sales are independent of collection policy. Most firms recognise that instituting a very aggressive collection policy may be very irritating for some customers who are frequently slow in paying. An aggressive collection policy may therefore adversely affect sales. A second result of an aggressive collection policy may be to force more customers to prefer taking the discounts. These two factors need to be recognised before a firm implements a collection policy that equates marginal collection expenditures with marginal reductions in delinquency costs.

Spot Quiz on Credit and Collection Policies

1. Sales volume will be affected by the firm's credit policy. T ❑ F ❑
2. Marginal analysis provides an appropriate analytical foundation for managing credit and receivables. T ❑ F ❑
3. Extending the credit period is desirable because it raises the opportunity cost of not taking the discount. T ❑ F ❑

4. Raising the credit discount creates the same effect as shortening the discount period. T ❑ F ❑

5. The foundation for collection policy is conceptually different from credit policy. T ❑ F ❑

Credit and Collection Procedures

In the previous section we considered the firm's overall credit and collection policies. In this section we shall discuss how these policies can be applied to individual accounts.

Sources of Information

An individual or firm is requesting credit. What sources of information are available to judge the credit worthiness of the applicant? Sources that can be utilised are financing statements, bank references, and credit bureaus.

Financial Statements. A vital source of information is the applicant's financial statements. An applicant who is in a financially sound position would have no hesitation in making available his or her financial statements. Interim reports, if available, are more desirable than annual reports. The financial statements are useful for calculating various liquidity, leverage, efficiency, and profitability ratios that may be used in evaluating credit risk. If the firm is using a credit scoring model (discussed earlier in the chapter) or if the applicant is requesting a large amount of credit, financial statements are essential.

Credit Bureaus. Credit bureaus specialise in consolidating the experiences of other firms with the applicant. Credit bureaus compile a history of the applicant's credit payment performance as reported by the credit-granted firms. Financial information on a credit applicant may be obtained by credit bureau member firms who agree to provide credit bureaus with information on their clients.

In addition to these information sources, a firm may try to compile its own information. It may have its sales personnel prepare a report on the credit applicant. Alternatively, if the credit request is large enough, it may send a credit department employee to visit the credit applicant personally and garner as much financial information as possible.

Once the delinquent accounts have been identified, an effort should be made to collect them. A variety of collection procedures can be utilised by the firm in its efforts to collect on delinquent accounts. The initial efforts should be very low key and should become stricter as per the response from debtors. For example, over-due payment letters, called dunning letters, should be sent if payment is not received on time, followed by an additional dunning letter in a more serious tone if the account becomes three weeks past due, followed after six weeks by a telephone call.

Telephone Call. If letters are unsuccessful, a credit department employee, preferably the manager, should call the delinquent debtor and ask for prompt payment. The credit manager may also wish to communicate that legal action may be taken if payment is not forthcoming.

Personal Call. Some firms have either collection personnel or sales representatives visit delinquent debtors. These firms feel that a face-to-face confrontation with a delinquent debtor provides them with an edge over other creditors.

Collection Agency. If the preceding measures are unsuccessful, the firm may consider the services of a collection agency. The collection agency fee is typically high—usually 50 per cent of the amount collected. For small delinquent accounts, this may be the only feasible alternative open to a lender.

Legal Action. Legal action is usually costly and there is no guarantee of a payment. If a firm is in a very weak financial position, legal action will force it into bankruptcy. The firm may choose to use legal action as a negotiating tool to deal with large delinquent accounts. With a very large delinquent account, the firm may use the threat of legal action to appoint more competent management.

Questions

1. Explain briefly why receivables management is important.
2. What is meant by credit policy? How does credit policy influence the following?

   a. Sales

b. Investment in receivables

c. Bad-debt losses

d. Collection costs

3. How is credit policy translated into managerial action? What type of trade-off needs to be evaluated in setting credit terms?

4. What are the components of credit terms? Explain each component briefly.

5. How does changing credit period affect sales and credit related cost? Explain.

6. Would changes in the discount rate have the same effect on sales and credit related costs as changes in the discount period? Explain your answer briefly.

7. What is meant by collection policy? How is the conceptual foundation of collection policy similar to or different from credit policy framework? Explain briefly.

8. Evaluate the following statement: "A credit department that never has a delinquent account is an asset to the firm."

9. What sources of information can be utilised in credit analysis? Explain each source briefly.

10. Briefly explain the mechanics of a heuristic credit limit model that you know.

11. How can discriminant analysis be utilised in evaluating an applicant's credit worthiness?

12. Explain the sequence of procedures you would utilise in seeking payments on a delinquent account.

13. With respect to accounts receivable, how might the perspective of the finance manager differ from that of the credit manager?

14. Is the credit policy that maximises expected operating profit the optimal credit policy? Explain.

15. What is the objective of credit policy?

16. Discuss the problem of monitoring payment patterns in seasonal firms.

16. Suppose that the Delta Electric Company and a local bank both are considering extending credit to the same customer. Why might Delta and the bank arrive at different decisions?

17. What is the expected return on an investment in accounts receivable?

Problems

1. Desoto Industrial Products Company is currently allowing its customers credit terms of 2/10, net 30. It is considering changing credit terms to either 2/10, net 40 or 2/10, net 50. The first plan would increase sales by 5 per cent and the second by 8 per cent. Profit margins before credit-related costs and taxes are 18 per cent. The before-tax cost of investment in receivables is 14 per cent. Currently, with an annual sales volume of Rs 72 crores, 40 crores of sales are to firms taking the discount. Changing the credit period should not affect the rupee volume of sales subject to the discount. However, those customers who are not taking the discount presently will delay paying until the end of the new credit period. Show your calculations in support of your answer. Assume that with either of the new credit periods, bad-debt losses on incremental sales would be 2 per cent.

2. Lake View Manufacturers is considering changing its credit terms from 2/15, net 40 to either 2/15, net 30 (plan 1) or 2/15, net 50 (plan 2). Current sales of Rs 30 crore would decrease to Rs 28 crore for plan 1 and increase to Rs 31 crore for plan 2. Its average collection period is currently 25 days. For plan 1 it would become 18 days and would increase to 31 days for plan 2. Marginal profits before credit costs and taxes are 16 per cent of sales. Investment costs before taxes are 15 per cent.

   Under plan 1, bad-debt losses would decline by Rs 60,000 and would increase by Rs 20,000 under plan 2. Of the three credit plans existing and the two new ones, which one appears to be best? Assume that the cost of discounts taken is the same for all three plans.

3. Essar Steel with sales of Rs 600 crore is planning to induce quicker payments by changing its credit terms from 1/10, net 30 to 2/10,

net 30. Although this change would not affect sales volume, the per cent of sales with discounts would increase from 20 to 70 per cent. Investment costs before taxes in receivables are 20 per cent. Assuming that all buyers not taking the discount pay at the end of the credit period, should Essar Switch to the 2/10, net 30 plan? Show your calculations in support of your answer. Would your answer be different if it were known that increasing the discount would increase sales by Rs 3 crore and that profit margin before credit costs and taxes would be 20 per cent? Show your calculations, which should include the change in marginal profits before taxes.

4. The Star Fabricating Company is evaluating credit terms of 2/10, net 30 and 2.5/10, net 30. Sales under the first term are expected to be Rs 30 crore and Rs 31 crore under the second one. The average collection period for plan 1 would be 18 days and would be 16 days for plan 2. The per cent of discount sales under plans 1 and 2 would be 60 and 70 per cent, respectively. If profits before credit costs and taxes are 20 per cent of gross sales and before tax investment costs are 18 per cent, which plan should Star Fabricating select?

5. Kramer Corporation wishes to know whether changing from 2/10, net 30 to 2/15, net 30 would affect the firm's profitability. Gross sales are expected to remain at Rs 18 crores under the new plan. However, the per cent of sales with discounts would increase from 40 to 60 per cent. Investment costs before taxes are 20 per cent. Assume that all buyers not taking the discount pay at the end of the credit period. Should Kramer adopt the new plan? Show your calculations.

   Suppose that with the new plan, sales are expected to increase to Rs 18 crores with margins before credit-related costs and taxes on the new sales of 20 per cent. Given the above information, is your answer different from the one given under the assumption of no change in sales? Show calculations in support of your answer.

6. Systemic Systems is considering switching from terms of 2/10, net 30 to 1/10, net 40. It is expected that with the new term, gross sales would increase from Rs 110 crores to Rs 115 crores annually. Marginal returns before credit costs and taxes are 20 per cent. Currently, 50 per cent of gross sales are with discounts. This percentage is expected to decline to 20 per cent under the new credit terms. The average paying time for those who do not take the discount is going to equal the credit period. Under the new plan, bad-debt losses and collection

costs are expected to increase by Rs 30 lakhs and 41.2 lakhs annually, respectively. If investment costs before taxes are 18 per cent, should Systemic switch to terms of 1/10, net 40? Your answer should be supported by appropriate calculations.

7. Raman Industries is evaluating credit terms of 2/10, net 25 and 3/15, net 40. Under plan 1 gross sales would be Rs 65 crore with 80 per cent taking the discount. Under plan 2 gross sales are expected to be Rs 68 crore with 60 per cent taking the discount. Under plan 1, receivables are expected to equal Rs 3 crore and Rs 5 crore under plan 2. Investment costs before taxes in receivables are 16 per cent. Bad-debt losses under plan 1 and 2 are anticipated to be Rs 47,00,000 and Rs 11,00,000 annually, respectively. Collection costs would remain the same under either plan. If margins before credit costs and taxes are 19 per cent, which plan should Raman adopt? Show your calculations.

8. Techno Industry is applying for credit. Its abbreviated balance sheet is given.

Cash + receivables	Rs 7.0 crore	Account payable	Rs 4.0 crore
Inventory	5.0 crore	Other pebbles	2.0 crore
Net plant	13.0 crore	Long-term debt	4.0 crore
		Net worth	15 crore
Total assets	Rs 25.0 crore	Total claims	Rs 25.0 crore

Techno's most recent income statement showed that it earned Rs 1.2 crore on total sales of Rs 36.0 crore. Techno pays on time but does not take the discount all the time. It was incorporated in 1976 and its management is rated excellent. The credit line would be utilised to buy about 30 per cent of Techno's total raw materials requirements. If you were evaluating Techno's credit application, would you grant it credit? If not, why? If yes, what is the maximum credit you would allow Techno? Use Table in establishing Techno's credit limit.

9. The Candee Corporation is considering liberalising its credit policies to allow higher-risk customers to buy on credit terms of net 30. The credit department has been informed that variable costs will remain at 80 per cent of sales over the new potential sales levels. All new sales will be on credit, and the projected information for each risk class is as shown in the table. The scale of before-tax required returns reflects

the increased risk perceived for each risk class of customers. Which, if any, of the risk classes should Candee allow to buy on credit? (Assume a 365-day year.)

Risk Class	Required Return	DSO	New Sales (in Rs.)
3	0.24	38	500,000
4	0.30	45	400,000
5	0.39	58	300,000
6	0.50	70	200,000

10. Assume the credit department for Candee Corporation realised it had failed to include all the relevant costs in Problem 1 and the following additional information is submitted. Which risk classes should Candee allow to buy on credit?

		Increased Credit
Risk Class	Default Rate (Per cent)	Department Expense (in Rs)
3	4	5,000
4	7	5,000
5	12	5,000
6	20	5,000

11. The CBM Company currently offers credit terms of 1/10, net 30 on annual credit sales of Rs 30,00,000. An average of 50 per cent of the current customers take the discount, and the average collection period has consistently remained at 35 days. The percentage default rate has been 1 per cent. The company is considering two alternative changes in credit terms as outlined in the table. If sales are projected to remain stable under either alternative and the required before-tax rate of return on investment in accounts receivable is 0.20, what strategy would you recommend for CBM?

Credit Terms	Percentage Taking Discount	DSO	Default Rate (Per cent)
2/10, net 30	75	18	0.005
3/10, net 20	98	12	0.001

12. Delta Electric Company is considering a request from Bill's Electronics for open account credit in the amount of Rs 1,000 (figured

at Delta's selling price). Delta's gross margin on the particular merchandise to be purchased by Bill's is 17 per cent. Delta's salesperson expects Bill's to purchase Rs 5,000 of merchandise annually. On all sales, Delta will incur variable expenses of 2 per cent for the salesperson's commissions and 1.5 per cent for warehousing.

a. Calculate the annual expected return on the prospective account with Bill's.

b. Suppose Delta establishes 30 per cent pre-tax as the required rate of return on accounts in the risk class in which Bill's falls. Suppose also that there are two possible outcomes: (1) Bill's makes all payments on time, or (2) Bill's defaults immediately and Delta loses its entire investment. What must be the minimum probability of outcome (1) in order to give an expected return of 30 per cent pre-tax?

Answer to Spot Quizzes

Credit and Collection Policies

1. Credit terms affect sales volume. T ☑ F ❑
2. Incremental profits and credit related costs can be analysed. T ☑ F ❑
3. Extending the credit period lowers the opportunity cost. T ❑ F ☑
4. Raising the credit discount increases the buyer's opportunity cost of not taking the discount while shortening the discount period lowers it. T ❑ F ☑
5. Both are similar in terms of influence on profits. T ❑ F ☑

Credit and Collection Procedures

1. Financial statements are important sources of credit information. T ☑ F ❑
2. The willingness to pay also has to be considered. T ❑ F ☑

3. The heuristic approach is more intuitive than quantitative. T ☐ F ☑

4. Without historical data a firm cannot develop or test its own discriminant analysis, credit evaluation model. T ☐ F ☑

5. A gentle reminder is more appropriate initially. T ☐ F ☑

APPENDIX A

Marginal or Incremental Analysis of Credit Policies

Marginal or incremental analysis will be discussed here in terms of a systematic comparison of the incremental returns and the incremental costs resulting from a change in the firm's credit policy. Specifically, three categories of changes in credit policy will be considered: a change in the discount period, the risk class of customers who receive credit, or the collection process. Whenever the incremental return from a proposed change in the management of accounts receivable is greater than the incremental costs of the additional investment, the change should be implemented. To illustrate, let us follow through with an example.

Example: Assume that a firm currently has annual sales, all credit, of Rs 8 crores and an average collection period on non-bad-debt sales of 60 days. The current level of bad debts is Rs 240,000 and the firm's opportunity cost or required rate of return is 20 per cent. Further assume that the firm produces only one product, with variable costs equaling 75 per cent of the selling price. The company is considering an increase in the credit period. As a result, new sales will be generated, with an average collection period on non-bad-debt sales of 90 days, while old customers will change their payment habits to take advantage of the more generous credit period and increase their average collection period on non-bad-debt sales from 60 to 90 days. While these new customers will generate additional profits, they will also generate more bad debts (it is assumed the level of bad debts on the old customers will remain constant). In addition, in order to service new sales, it will be necessary to increase the level of average inventory from Rs 10,00,000 to Rs 10,38,000.

As a result of this relaxation of the credit period, profits will increase but so will the level of bad debts. In addition, the investment in receivables will increase because of additional credit sales and the slowdown in the cash collections from old customers as they take advantage of the more generous new credit terms. Finally, inventories will be increased. Marginal analysis quantifies and then compares the results of these changes to provide a decision on the desirability of the proposed credit policy change.

General Procedure

Marginal or incremental analysis involves a comparison of the incremental profit contribution (or benefits) from new sales with the incremental costs resulting from the change in credit policy. The decision concerning the change in credit policy is then made using the following rules (where the symbol α denotes change in):

if α Profit contribution α Costs > 0, then accept the change in credit policy

if α Profit contribution α Costs < 0, then recent the change in credit policy

if α Profit contribution α Costs = 0, then be indifferent as to the change in credit policy

Specifically, a four-step procedure for performing marginal or incremental analysis on a change in credit policy will be followed:

Step 1: Estimate incremental profit contribution.

Step 2: Estimate incremental costs (that is, the opportunity cost) associated with the delay in collection of accounts receivable caused by original customers paying later.

Step 3: Estimate incremental costs (that is, the rupee-level required return) associated with the increase in investment in receivables and inventory due to new sales.

Step 4: Compare the incremental revenues with the incremental costs.

To help simplify the analysis, Table A-1 defines a set of terms and symbols used, while Table A-2 provides a step-by-step analysis of the problem.

The major area of confusion in this analysis lies in the calculation of the incremental "investment" in accounts receivable which takes place in steps 2 and 3 and results in an opportunity cost to the firm in the form of lost income on funds that are blocked.

Table A-1: Marginal Analysis Definitions

S_{orig}	the original level of annual sales (Rs 80,00,000)
.. S	the incremental sales revenues resulting from the proposed change in credit policy (Rs 90,00,000 - Rs 80,00,000 = Rs 10,00,000)
B_{orig}	The level of bad debt losses on original sales (Rs 240,000)
.. B	The incremental bad debts resulting from the proposed change in credit policy (Rs 60,000)
.. ACP	The change in the average collection period on original collectible (non-bad-debt) sales (30 days)
.. ACP_{new}	The average collection period on new collectible (non-bad-debt) sales (90 days)
.. 1	The change in average inventory carried due to the increased sales level resulting from the proposed change in credit policy (Rs 38,000) valued at cost
V	Variable costs as a per cent of sales (assumed the same on both new and old sales = 75%)
R	The required return on the incremental investment in receivables and inventory due to increased sales resulting from the proposed change in credit policy (20%)
.. P	The incremental profit contribution (marginal benefits) resulting from the proposed change in credit policy = (.. S) (1-V) - .. B
OC	The opportunity cost associated with original customers changing their payments pattern = (R) (.. ACP). (S_{orig} - B_{orig}) (360 days)
DRR	The rupee-level required return on the incremental investment in receivables and inventory resulting from the proposed change in credit policy = {(ACPnew) [(.. S-.. B) /360] (V) + .. 1)}. R

Table A-2: Incremental Analysis of a Change in Credit Policy

Example:	Present credit policy	Proposed credit policy
Annual sale (all credit)	Rs 80,00,000	Rs 90,00,000
Average collection period on collection sales/original sales	60 days	90 days
Net sales		90 days
Bad debt losses		
Original sales	Rs 240,000	Rs 240,000
New sales		Rs 60,000
Variable costs	75%	75%
Average inventory (at cost)	Rs 10,00,000	Rs 10,38,000
Required return on incremental investment in receivables and inventory (R)	20%	20%

Analysis

Step1: Estimate the incremental profit contribution (.. P) resulting from the proposed change in credit policy.

Discussion: This is equal to the portion of incremental (new) sales that goes toward profits [α S(1-V)] less the increased loss to bad debts (α B)

Formula: α P = (new) (per cent of sales going toward fixed costs and profits) -

= (α S) (1-V) - α B

= Rs 1,000,000 (.25) - Rs 60,000

= Rs 250,000 - Rs 60,000

= Rs 190,000

Step 2: Determine the opportunity cost associated with the delay in collection of accounts receivable caused by original customers changing their payment patterns.

Decision: This involves multiplying the required rate of return on investment in receivable (R) times the incremental increase in collectible receivables due to original customers taking longer to pay [(α ACP) (S_{orig} - B_{orig}) / 360].

Formula: OC = (required return) (change in the average collection period on original collectible sales) (daily level of collectible sales from original customers)

= (R) (.. ACP) [(S_{orig} - B_{orig}) / 360]

= (.20) [30(Rs 80,00,000 - Rs 240,000) / 360]

= Rs 129,333

Step 3: Determine rupee-level required return on the marginal increase in investment in receivables and due to new sales.

Discussion: The marginal increase in investment in collectible receivable due to new sales (ACP new) [(α S - α B) / 360] (V) is added to the increased investment in inventory and receivable (R).

Formula DRR = [(Average collection period on collectible new receivables (non-bad-debt)) (daily level of new collectible sales) (Variable costs) + (new investment in inventory)] (required return)

= {(α ACP new) [(α S - α B) / 360] (V) + α1}.R

= [(90) (Rs 940,000/360) (.75) + Rs 38,000] (.20)

= [(90) (Rs 2611) (.75) + Rs 38,000] (.20)

= (Rs 176,250 + Rs 38,000) (.20)

= Rs 42,850

Step 4: Compare the incremental revenues with the incremental costs.

Formula: (Profit contribution from step 1.) (opportunity cost associated with original sales - from step

2) (required return associated with the investment in receivables associated with new sales from step 3)

= (a P) - (OC) - (DRR)

= Rs 190,000 - Rs 129,333 - Rs 42,850

= Rs 17,817

Decision = Since the benefits outweigh the costs by Rs 17,817, the proposed change in credit policy should be made.

Now, investment in accounts receivable. As mentioned earlier, the "investment" in accounts receivable increases in two ways: (1) an opportunity cost occurs as original customers take advantage of the more generous credit period and pay later, causing a delay in the collection of accounts receivable, and (2) new customers are attracted to the firm as a result of the more lenient credit policy thus further increasing accounts receivable. The increased investment represents funds that the firm can no longer invest elsewhere to earn a positive return. Thus the increased level of accounts receivable is a source of an opportunity cost. The opportunity cost arising from original customers taking advantage of the new credit period is based upon the full collectible sales value (the sales value less bad debts on those sales) of the receivables. What has happened is that the receipt of the collectible sales value of these receivables has been delayed, creating an opportunity cost. Before the introduction of the new liberal credit terms, the receivables would have been received 30 days earlier; thus if we multiply 30 days times the full daily collectible sales level, we get the increased investment caused by the delay in collection of original sales, which in turn creates the opportunity cost:

Increased investment due to delays in collection because original customers take advantage of the new longer credit period	=	Increase in the length of time (in days) that original customers' collectible receivable are outstanding	×	Daily level of original collectible sales

$$= (\alpha\ ACP) \times (S_{orig} - B_{orig})\ /360 \text{ days}$$

$$= (30 \text{ days}) \times (\text{Rs } 8{,}000{,}000 - \text{Rs } 240{,}000)\ /360 \text{ days}$$

$$= \text{Rs } 646{,}667$$

This calculation is actually part of step 2 in Table A-2 and this is repeated in that table. Note that level of bad debts for the firm's original customers is assumed not to change in the analysis presented here.

Although the opportunity cost of carrying new receivables caused by original customers' taking advantage of the new credit period is based upon the full collectible sales value, the cost of carrying new receivables due to new customers being attracted to the firm is based upon its variable cost; that is, the incremental investment in accounts receivable from new customers should be assessed at its cost to the selling firm. Since, at the margin, production and selling costs are the variable cost portion of the incremental or marginal receivables, and these are the only investment the firm makes in accounts receivable due to new sales, the incremental investment in accounts receivable is equal to the variable cost portion of these receivables. In effect, the variable costs are the only cash outflows associated with the new investment in receivables, for new customers. Thus,

$$\text{Marginal increase in investment due to attraction of new customers to the firm} = \text{Marginal increase in receivables due to new sales} \times \text{Per cent variable costs of the new sales}$$

$$= (\text{ACP new}) \times (\alpha\ S - \alpha\ B)/(360) \times (V)$$

$$= (90 \text{ days}) \times (\text{Rs } 940{,}000/360 \text{ days}) \times (.75)$$

$$= \text{Rs } 176.250$$

This calculation is actually part of step 3 in Table A-2 and thus is repeated in that table.

To summarise, the full collectible value of the original accounts receivable is the appropriate measure with which to calculate the opportunity costs resulting from a delay in the collection of receivables caused by change in the payment patterns by original customers, while only the variable cost portion of the cost of added accounts receivable is appropriate for the change in investment in receivables resulting from the bringing of new credit sales to the firm by the change in credit policy.[4]

4. Stephen E. Celec and Joe D. Icerman, "A Comprehensive Approach to Accounts Receivable Management," *Financial Review.* 15 (Spring 1980), 23-34, provides an excellent discussion of the state of the art of accounts receivable management.

Table A-2 summarizes the calculations associated with this problem.

Examining Table A-2, we find that the total marginal benefits are Rs 17,817 greater than the marginal costs. Thus, a change to the proposed credit policy is warranted. In summary, the logic behind this approach to credit policy is to examine the incremental or marginal benefits, the opportunity cost, and the required return associated with change in credit policy. If the change promises more benefits than costs, the change should be made. If, however, the incremental costs are greater than the benefits, the proposed change should be avoided. Graphically, investment should continue until marginal costs are equal to marginal revenues. In practice, this analysis is by no means easy. The inputs, such as sales and cost changes resulting from a given change in receivables policy, are extremely difficult to estimate. Moreover, in general the accuracy of these estimates usually leaves something to be desired. As a result, it is generally a good idea to change credit policies in a slow, controlled manner, making a minor change in one decision variable at a time, evaluating the results of this change, and then perhaps adjusting this variable further or changing another decision variable. In this way, major errors are avoided while the firm's credit policies move smoothly toward an optimum level.

Study Questions

1. What are the risk-return trade-offs associated with adopting a more liberal trade credit policy?

2. Explain the purpose of marginal analysis.

Study Problems

1. (Marginal Analysis) The J. Flowers Corporation is considering relaxing its current credit policy. Currently, the firm has annual sales (all credit) of Rs 5 crore and an average collection period of 90 days (assume a 360-day year). The current per cent of bad debt losses is 4 per cent and the firm's required rate of return on investment in receivables and inventory is 25 per cent. Flowers produce sports equipment on which the variable costs are 70 per cent of the selling price. Given the following information, should they adopt the new policy?

	Present Policy	Proposed Policy
Annual sales (all credit)	Rs 11,000,000	Rs 12,500,000
Average collection period on collectible sales:		
Original sales	45 days	55 days
New sales	--	55 days
Average inventory	Rs 900,000	Rs 975,000
Bad debt losses in per cent	5%	5% on original sales 8% on new sales

2. (Marginal Analysis) The S. Carison Corporation is considering a major change in its credit policy. Carison is a major manufacturer of sportswear on which 80 per cent of the selling price is variable costs. For any new investment in receivables and inventory, the firm would require a return of 30 per cent. Given the following information, should Carison adopt the proposed policy?

	Present Policy	Proposed Policy
Annual sales (all credit)	Rs 50,00,000	Rs 60,00,000
Average collection period on collectible sales:		
Original sales	90 days	120 days
New sales	--	120 days
Average inventory	Rs 800,000	Rs 875,000
Bad debt losses in per cent	4%	4% on original sales 8% on new sales

3. (Marginal Analysis) The D. Southard Company has annual sales of Rs 5 crore. All sales are on credit and the credit terms are net 30 days, which is also the average collection period. The company is studying the possibility of relaxing the credit terms in hopes of securing new sales for one year. The variable costs are 75 per cent and the required rate of return on investment in receivables and inventory is 25 per cent. Given the following information, which policy or policies should Southard adopt?

	Present Policy	Policy X	Policy Y
Annual sales (all credit)	Rs 50,00,000	Rs 56,000,000	Rs 60,00,000
Average collection period on collectible sales			
Original sales	30 days	45 days	60 days
New collectible sales for policy X		45 days	60 days
New collectible sales for policy Y			60 days
Average inventory	Rs 800,000	Rs 840,000	Rs 860,000
Bad debt losses in per cent	5%	5% on original sales 7% on new sales	5% on original sales 7% on new sales brought in by policy X 9% on new sales brought in by policy Y.

Summary

Much of our concern with accounts receivable is derived from the fact that it makes up around 25% of a typical firm's assets. Thus, because of their sheer magnitude any change in their levels affects profitability. In effect, when we discuss management of accounts receivable, we are discussing the management of one-quarter of the firm's assets. Management of accounts receivable focuses on credit policy and collection procedures.

Credit policy directly influences sales, investment levels, bad-debt losses, and collection costs. The demand for a firm's product is greatly influenced by the ease with which the products can be purchased on credit. As credit terms are made more liberal, the firm's investment in cash, accounts receivable, inventories, and perhaps physical investments increase in a complementary fashion. The decision to change the existing credit policy is taken based on the incremental analysis of the change in credit terms. An appropriate credit policy balances profits from increased sales due to more liberal credit terms with increased costs due to increased investments, bad-debt losses, and collection costs. The ideal credit policy allows for the liberalisation of credit terms to the point where the marginal revenues from a new category of credit accounts is exactly equal to the marginal costs of selling and servicing such accounts. One way to liberalise credit terms is to increase the credit period. Conversely, credit terms can be tightened by shortening the credit period. Credit policy can also be altered by changing the credit standards, i.e., by selling to customers with higher or lower risk profiles. Models and techniques like heuristic approach, credit scoring, etc., are put into practice for evaluating the credit worthiness of customers.

Active collection efforts are needed by firms to collect the accounts as and when they fall due. By examining the average collection period, the ratio of receivables to assets, the ratio of credit sales to receivables (called the accounts receivable turnover ratio), and the amount of bad debts relative to sales over time, the finance manager can determine whether or not receivables are drifting out of control. In addition, an aging analysis of accounts receivable provides a break-up both in rupees and in percentage terms of the proportion of receivables that are over-due. Comparing the current aging of receivables with past data offers further insight into the degree of control that is being maintained over receivables.

Once the delinquent accounts have been identified, an effort should be made to collect them. A variety of collection procedures can be utilised by the firm in its efforts to collect on delinquent accounts. The initial efforts should be very low key and should become stricter as per the response from debtors. Legal action is taken as the last resort in realizing the amounts due.

CHAPTER V

Inventory Management

Learning Objectives

- Purpose of holding inventory and types of inventory
- Ordering costs, carrying costs and total inventory costs. The relationship between these costs and the level of inventory
- How to determine the optimal level of inventory (Economic Order Quantity) under varying conditions of certainty and uncertainty

Chapter Organization

- Effective inventory management is the key to value creation for any business, particularly for manufacturing firms. This chapter discusses in detail the principles underlying effective inventory management. The chapter begins with basic aspects of inventory like the purpose of holding inventory and the types of inventory
- The different costs involved in the inventory have been taken up next in the chapter. The core issue of minimising the inventory costs has been unfolded with the introduction of the concept of Economic Order Quantity (EOQ)
- Finally, the EOQ concept has been taken up in the light of real life situations of uncertain demands and supplies. Also, the inventory management of seasonal firms has been discussed in the last section of the chapter.

CHAPTER 5

Inventory Management

Inventory management involves the control of assets being produced to be sold in the normal course of the firm's operations. The general categories of inventory include raw materials inventory, work-in-process inventory, and finished goods inventory. The importance of inventory management to the firm depends upon the extent of the investment in inventory. For an average firm, approximately 7.45 per cent of all assets are in the form of inventory. However, the percentage varies widely from industry to industry, as can be seen in Table 5.1, and thus the importance of inventory management and control varies from industry to industry also. For example, it is much more important in the automotive dealer and service station trade, where inventories make up 53.81 per cent of total assets, than in the hotel business, where the average investment in inventory is only 1.52 per cent of total assets.

Purposes and Types of Inventory

The purpose of carrying inventories is to uncouple the operations of the firm – that is, to make each function of the business independent of other functions – so that delays or shutdowns in one area no longer affect the production and sale of the final product. Since production shutdowns result in increased costs, and since delays in delivery can cause loss of customers, the management and control of inventory is an important duty of the finance manager.

Table 5.1: Inventory as a Percentage of Total Assets for Major Industries

Industry	Inventory relative to total assets
All industries	7.45%
Automotive dealers and service stations-retail	53.81
Apparel and accessory stores	41.14
Building materials, garden supplies, and mobile home dealers-retail	40.09
Food stores	33.52
Electrical and electronic equipment	19.57
Total construction	17.20
Agriculture, forestry, and fishing	9.82
Petroleum and coal products	7.01
Eating and drinking places	6029
Hotels and other lodging places	1.52

Source: Internal Revenue Service, U.S. Treasury Department, Statistics of Income, 1977, Corporate Income Tax Returns (Washington, D. C. Government Printing Office, 1982), pp. 27-34.

Actually, the decision-making process with respect to investment in inventory involves a trade-off between risk and return. Although the reduced investment in inventory saves money, there is always a risk that if the level of inventory is too low, the various functions of business may not be effectively uncoupled and delays in production and customer delivery may result in loss of sales for the firm. As the size of the inventory increases, the storage and handling costs in addition to the required return on capital invested in inventory will rise. Therefore, as the firm increases the level of inventory it holds, the risk of running out of inventory is lessened, but the inventory expenses are increased. To better illustrate the uncoupling function that inventories perform, we will look at several general types of inventories.

Raw Materials Inventory

Raw materials inventory consists of basic materials purchased from other firms to be used in the firm's production operation. These goods may include steel, lumber, petroleum, or manufactured items such as wire, ball bearings, or tires that the firm does not produce itself. Regardless of the specific form the raw materials inventory takes on, all manufacturing firms by definition maintain a raw materials inventory. Its purpose is to uncouple the production function from the purchasing function – that is, to make these two functions independent of each other, so that delays in shipment of raw materials do not cause production delays. In the event of a delay in shipment, the firm can satisfy its need for raw materials by liquidating its inventory. Another reason for maintaining raw material inventories is that firms find it economical to buy raw materials in large quantities. Most firms, therefore, maintain something in the form of raw materials inventory. Sometimes, firms maintain large raw material inventories in anticipation of a price increase by suppliers, materials shortage, a labour strike affecting the suppliers, and so forth.

Work-in-Process Inventory

Work-in-process inventory consists of partially finished goods requiring additional work before they become finished goods. The more complex and lengthy the production process, the larger will be the investment in work-in-process inventory. The purpose of work-in-process inventory is to uncouple the various operations in the production process so that machine failures and work stoppages in one operation will not affect the other operations. Assume, for example, there are ten different production operations, each one involving the piece of work produced in the previous operation. If the machine performing the first production operation breaks down, a firm with no work-in-process inventory will have to shut down all ten production operations. Yet, if a firm has such inventory, the remaining nine operations can continue to operate by drawing the input for the second operation from inventory rather than directly from the output of the first operation.

Finished Goods Inventory

The finished goods inventory consists of goods on which the production has been completed but that are not yet sold. The purpose of a finished goods inventory is to uncouple the production and sales so that sales remain unhindered of the stoppages/slowdown in the production process. With firms holding such an inventory, temporary bottlenecks in the production process can be absorbed and the sales can take place uninterrupted. In the auto industry, for example, if auto dealers did not carry an Inventory of cars, sales would virtually cease during a strike period. Another reason for maintaining inventories is that, in general, it is cheaper to produce in large quantities and at a steady rate over time. A lawn mower manufacturer may find that by manufacturing lawn mowers throughout the year, profits are increased. The Inventory of lawn mowers would increase during the winter and early spring months. As the mowers are sold in the spring, summer, and fall, the Inventory would be depleted. The economies would come from better utilization of plant capacity and a stable labour force. Maintaining Inventory is important for the firm because it allows the firm to service customer needs adequately. Maintaining Inventory also requires investment of capital. Excess investment in inventories adversely affects the firm's measures of financial performance and efficiency. For example, excess Inventory lowers the return on total assets and Inventory turnover ratio. Proper management of Inventory is an important managerial task.

Stock of Cash

Although we have already discussed Cash management at some length in Chapter 3, it is worthwhile to mention Cash again in the light of Inventory management. This is because the stock of Cash carried by a firm is simply a special type of Inventory.

In Terms of uncoupling the various operations of the firm, the purpose of holding a stock of Cash is to make the payment of bills independent of the collection of accounts due. When Cash is kept on hand, bills can be paid without prior collection of accounts.

The reason we have included Cash as a type of Inventory is that as we examine and develop Inventory economic ordering quantity (EOQ) models, we will see a striking resemblance between the EOQ Inventory and EOQ Cash model; in fact, except for a minor redefinition of Terms, they will be exactly the same.

The executive vice-president of International Heating and Air Conditioning Corporation identified his company's Inventory management programme as having two major objectives:[2]

1. Immediate – reduce the working capital required to support current inventories.

---

2. C.J. Slaybaugh, "Inventory Management Program, "Management Accounting, Vol. 53 (July 1971), p. 13.

2. Long-range – provide a group of techniques to facilitate continued sound inventory management.

He identified his company's inventory carrying cost at 20 per cent. Each rupee removed from inventory results in operational cost saving of 20 paise. The relatively large portion of total assets in the form of inventories combined with the costs of carrying or maintaining these inventories emphasises the importance of a good inventory management programme.

Spot Quiz on Role of Inventories

1. Finished goods inventory would exist even if the demand for the item were fixed, known, and constant. T ❑ F ❑

2. Not all firms maintain a work in process inventory. T ❑ F ❑

3. Prudent inventory management implies that maintaining very small inventories minimises costs. T ❑ F ❑

4. A manufacturer of custom, made-to-order items does not need to maintain an inventory. T ❑ F ❑

Investing in Inventory

Inventories represent another important use of a firm's funds and are therefore an important concern of the finance manager. At any point in time, a firm has a given investment in inventory. As in the case of accounts receivable, we will view a decision to expand inventories as an investment decision. Again, we will use valuation as our basic conceptual framework and will define the financial manager's responsibility as seeing to it that inventories are set at the level that maximises the value of the firm. As with receivables, we will find that the marginal return on investment in inventory declines as inventory is increased, and that the optimum lies at the point at which marginal E(R) equals the rate required by suppliers of funds.

Deciding Optimal Level of Inventory

Proper inventory management requires arriving at a balance between inventory carrying costs and adequately meeting demand. Extreme levels of inventory - too high or too low - are not desirable. Maintaining high levels of inventory enhances the firm's capability to meet demand. It also results in high carrying costs. Too little inventory, although resulting in lower carrying costs, increases the opportunity cost of being out of stock and increases customer dissatisfaction. In this section, we define costs associated with carrying inventory and then look at a model for managing inventory.

Inventory Carrying Costs

Inventory carrying costs are of three types: holding costs, reorder costs, and shortage costs. Inventory holding costs would include the following:

1. Cost of storing inventory
2. Cost of handling inventory
3. Cost of taxes on inventory
4. Cost of insuring inventory
5. Cost of obsolescence
6. Cost of "shrinkage" or theft
7. Cost of physical damage
8. Cost of auditing inventory
9. Cost of capital for the investment in inventory

The second type of inventory costs – reorder costs – are costs that are periodically incurred when inventory is replenished. Reorder costs include

1. Cost of processing orders
2. Cost of telephoning orders
3. Cost of typing orders
4. Mailing and stationery costs

5. Cost of receiving new shipment

6. Handling the accounts payable invoice

Many of these costs are incurred each time an order is placed.

The third type of inventory cost is the cost of being out of stock or a shortage cost. Shortage costs would include costs of lost sales, customer ill will, and processing special orders. Shortage costs are a function of the level of customer service that the firm wishes to provide its clients. Firms typically control shortage costs by maintaining adequate safety stocks—a topic to be discussed later.[3]

Inventory Decision Models

The use of inventories as buffer stocks has been studied extensively and a large body of inventory theory has been developed. Inventory theory has been found useful for studying a broad class of problems in addition to the problems of stocking raw materials and finished goods in a firm. Cash and liquidity, for example, can be viewed as inventories and analysed using inventory theory.

Inventory theory addresses two questions:

1. How much should be ordered?

2. When should it be ordered?

The first question, how much, arises because of friction, the existence of ordering costs, setup costs, and the like. The second question, when to order, arises because the life is full of uncertainties.

---

3. See William J. Baumol, "The Transactions Demand for Cash-An Inventory-Theoretic Approach," Quarterly Journal of Economics 65, 545-556 (Nov, 1952); Merton H. Miller and Daniel Orr, "A Model of the Demand for Money by firms," Quarterly Journal of Economics 80, 413-135 (Aug. 1966); and Yair E. Orgler, Cash Management (Belmont Ca.: Wadsworth, 1970).

Economic Order Quantity

Inventory models deal with the question of how much to order by defining an Economic Order Quantity (EOQ). The EOQ involves a trade-off between ordering costs (or setup costs) and Carrying Costs. A larger order quantity reduces the frequency of ordering and therefore total ordering costs, but increases the average Inventory level and therefore Carrying Costs. The optimal order quantity, the EOQ, is given by EOQ = root 2 ROK.

Where R is the usage per period in units, O is the ordering cost per order, and C is the carrying cost per unit per period.

To illustrate the use of the EOQ formula, consider an item that is used at the rate of 1,000 units per year. Ordering costs are Rs 25 per order and Carrying Costs are Rs 20 per unit per year. The EOQ then is

EOQ = v [2(1,000) (25)] /20 = 50 Units

Assuming that the usage rate is uniform, we can illustrate the ordering and usage process as in Figure 5.1. At time, 50 units are received and consumed over the period t_0 - t_1. At t_1, another 50 units are ordered, we can see that the average Inventory level is 25, so that total Carrying Costs for the year are 25 x 20 = Rs 500. We must place a total of 1,000/50 = 20 orders per year, so total ordering costs also are Rs 500 per year. The sum of ordering and Carrying Costs is Rs 1,000 per year. With a little arithmetic, we can verify that total costs are higher at any order quantity other than 50.

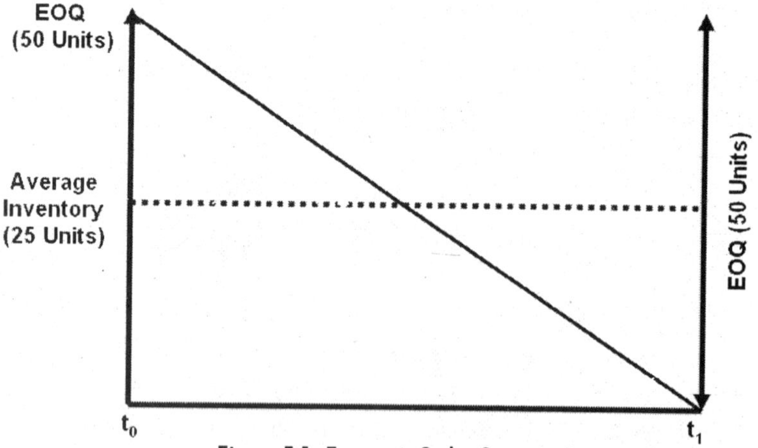

Figure 5.1: Economic Order Quantity 1

The EOQ formula is widely used in inventory control to determine optimal order quantities. To use the EOQ formula in quantitative applications, the cost of financing must be included as a component of carrying cost, which is often approximated using the interest cost of debt. However, investment in inventory is not riskless, so the interest rate may understate the real cost of financing, which is the return required by lenders and investors. The use of the interest rate may be a satisfactory approximation for the production manager in calculating order quantities for individual items. When the finance manager views inventory as an investment decision, he must take account of risk and require a return higher than the interest rate.

In addition to its usefulness in quantitative applications, the EOQ model yields several useful qualitative insights. We see the importance of friction costs; if ordering costs were zero, the EOQ would be zero. The firm would order continuously at the usage rate, holding no inventory at all. We see also that the EOQ and therefore the average inventory level varies with the square root of usage. Thus, a doubling of usage does not double the optimal inventory level, but increases it by root 2, or about 1.4 times.

The basic EOQ model discussed above assumes that delivery is instantaneous when an order is placed. If delivery lead time is known with certainty, the EOQ is unchanged. We simply place the order earlier by the number of days required for delivery. We will discuss the effects of uncertain delivery times in the next section. The availability of quantity discounts *does* alter the EOQ and can be handled by modifying the analysis. However, quantity discounts are of secondary importance to our discussion here, and we will not deal with them.

Consider two firms A and B. Both buy the same material and sell a similar finished product. Firm A buys very small quantities of raw materials and maintains a small finished goods inventory. Firm B buys very large quantities of raw materials and has a large inventory. Managers for both firms claim that their inventory management system is better. Are both right? Perhaps, but more likely both are mismanaging inventory. Firm A is successful in keeping holding costs down, but most probably its reorder costs are very high. The reverse would be true for firm B. Because B buys in large quantities, the total number of orders it places over a specified time period would be small and its total reorder costs would be low. However, its inventory holding costs would be high. A more reasonable approach would be to balance holding and reorder costs. Exactly such a result is accomplished by an inventory management model that identifies the right order quantity, the number of orders to be placed over a time period, and the average inventory to hold. The appropriate number of units that should be ordered is called the Economic Order Quantity or EOQ, and this Inventory management model is called the EOQ model.

Let H denote the Inventory holding costs per unit per time period: H is assumed to remain constant as Inventory increases. Some of the holding costs per unit such as insurance and storing would decline as Inventory increases. Other costs such as obsolescence, handling, and damage costs per unit would increase with increasing Inventory. Overall, H would remain constant and total holding costs would increase proportionally to the rate of increase in Inventory. Figure 5.2 shows total holding costs as a function of Inventory. As Inventory size increases, total holding costs increase proportionally.

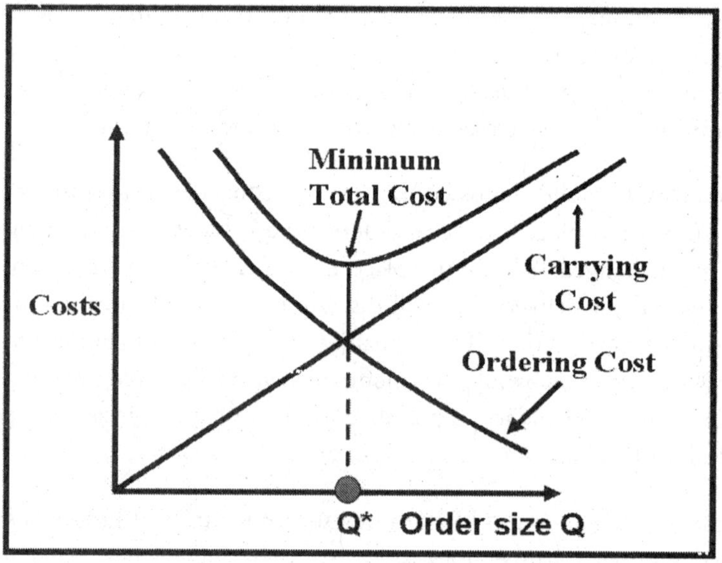

Figure 5.2: Inventory Costs and Economic Order Quantity

Examination of EOQ Assumptions

The major weaknesses of the EOQ model are associated with several of its assumptions, in spite of which the model tends to yield quite good results.

Where its assumptions have been dramatically violated, the EOQ model can generally be easily modified to accommodate the situation. The model's assumptions are as follows:

1. Constant or uniform demand although the EOQ model assumes constant demand; demand may vary from day to day. If demand is stochastic - that is, not known in advance - the model must be modified through the inclusion of a safety stock.

2. Constant unit price. The inclusion of variable prices resulting from quantity discounts can be handled quite easily through a modification of the original EOQ model, redefining total costs and solving for the optimum order quantity.

3. Constant carrying costs. Unit carrying costs may vary substantially as the size of the inventory rises, perhaps decreasing because of economies of scale of storage efficiency or increasing as storage space runs out and new warehouses have to be rented. This situation can be handled through a modification in the original model similar to the one used for variable unit price.

4. Constant ordering costs. While this assumption is generally valid, its violation can be accommodated by modifying the original EOQ model in a manner similar to the one used for variable unit price.

5. Instantaneous delivery. If delivery is not instantaneous, which is generally the case, the original EOQ model must be modified through the inclusion of a safety stock.

6. Independent orders. If multiple orders result in cost savings by reducing paper work and transportation cost, the original EOQ model must be further modified. While this modification is somewhat complicated, special EOQ models have been developed to deal with it.[3]

These assumptions have been pointed out to illustrate the limitations of the basic EOQ model and the ways in which it can easily be modified to compensate for them. Moreover, an understanding of the limitations and assumptions of the EOQ model will provide the finance manager with a strong base for making inventory decisions.

3. For example, R. J. Tersiree, Material Management and Inventory Control (New York: Elsevier North Holland, 1976).

Inflation and EOQ

Inflation affects the EOQ model in two major ways. First, while the EOQ model can be modified to assume constant price increases, many times major price increases occur only once or twice a year and are announced ahead of time. If this is the case, the EOQ model may lose its applicability and may be replaced with anticipatory buying—that is, buying in anticipation of a price increase in order to secure the goods at a lower cost. Of course, as with most decisions, there are trade-offs associated with anticipatory buying. The costs are the added carrying costs associated with the inventory that you would not normally be holding. The benefits, of course, come from buying the inventory at a lower price. The second way inflation affects the EOQ model is through increased carrying costs. As inflation pushes interest rates up, the cost of carrying inventory increases. In our EOQ model this means that C increases, which results in a decline in Q*, the optimal economic order quantity.

Safety Stocks

Now let us reintroduce uncertainty. In practice, uncertainty is likely to exist with respect to delivery times, production rates, and sales rates. Strikes occur, suppliers fail to deliver, and unexpected surges in demand appear. When delivery is delayed or usage increases unexpectedly, a stock-out is likely to occur. To reduce the likelihood of stock-outs, firms hold safety stocks, additional inventory over and above that prescribed by the EOQ formula.

Finding the optimal level of safety stock involves a trade-off between stock-out costs and carrying costs. When a stock out occurs, several kinds of costs may be incurred, some out-of-pocket and some opportunity costs. A stock-out in raw materials may cause production delays or stoppages and higher costs of scheduling and set-up. In continuous-process industries such as paper or synthetic fibers, a production stoppage would cause a loss of sales or, at a minimum, customer inconvenience. The relationship between on-time delivery and inventory level is not linear.

The cost of stock-out includes lost contribution as well as damage to the firm's reputation. Calculating stock-out costs is a difficult problem and one about which not much can be said of a general nature. In each situation, it is necessary to identify out-of-pocket and opportunity costs incurred because of the stock-out.

The optimal size of the safety stock depends on stock-out costs, carrying costs, and the probability that stock-outs will occur. The optimal level thus varies directly with

1. Stock-out costs either in lost contribution or production inefficiency
2. Uncertainty of usage of sales rates
3. Uncertainty of delivery times and
4. Inventory carrying costs

Analytically, the safety stock is determined by calculating the appropriate reorder point.

Quantitative models for calculating reorder points and safety stocks are widely used in inventory control systems. It is important to note that having a safety stock still does not eliminate the possibility of a stock-out. The safety stock is intended to give a known probability of a stock-out such that the expected cost of a stock-out (cost times probability) is balanced against the inventory carrying cost. The quantitative models show us the important effect of uncertainty—the greater the uncertainty, the higher the optimal level of inventory.

Total Inventory Costs

If we apply inventory theory as described above, in theory we will be led to minimise the total costs of inventory, including opportunity costs of stock-outs. Diagrammatically, we can view the relationships as in Figure 5.2. At inventory level Q*, the total out-of-pocket and opportunity costs of inventory are minimised. If another increment of inventory is added, carrying costs exceed the ordering and stock-out costs that are saved. Thus, at point Q*, operating profit is maximised.

The profit we have maximised in Figure 5.2 is expected profit. Although carrying and ordering costs can be estimated fairly accurately, stock-out costs may be subject to considerable uncertainty. Thus, we have not yet taken risk into account. Also, we have given no consideration to financing costs, that is, the return required by those who supply funds to the firm. As in case of accounts receivable, to take account of these factors we must evaluate expected return on investment.

Let Q* denote the number of items ordered each time an order is placed in the time period. Furthermore, we assume that demand is constant and that the amount of time it takes to deliver is known and is constant. Given these assumptions, the manager would place an order so that the delivery of the Q new units would coincide with depletion of the existing stock. This situation is represented in Figure 5.3. The lead time to delivery is b – a days. Therefore, an order for Q units is placed at the point marketed a. The inventory of Q units is in transit for time b – a. Delivery is Received just as the existing inventory is fully depleted. Since beginning inventory is Q* units and ending inventory is O units at the moment of replenishment, average inventory is depicted as per the equation below:

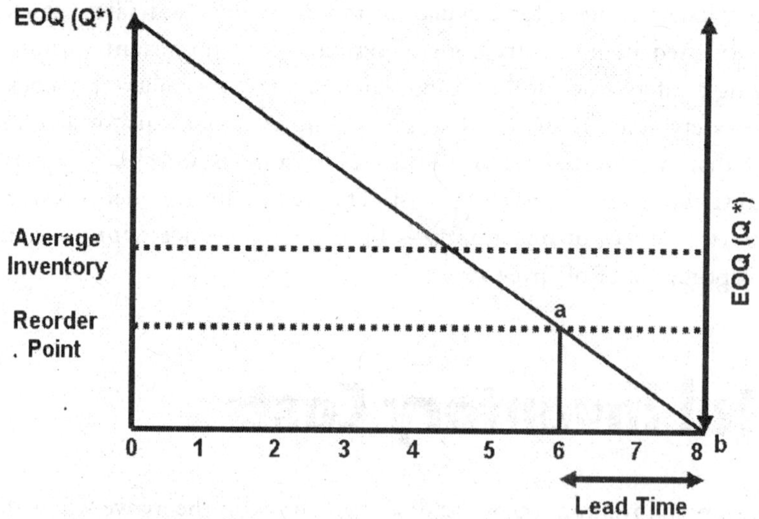

Figure 5.3: Inventory Pattern: Constant Demand.

Average inventory = Q / 2 ....(5.1)

Inventory holding costs per unit per time period were H. Since average inventory is Q/2.

Total holding costs = holding cost per unit × average inventory

$= H \times Q / 2 = HQ / 2$

We also know that since demand over the time period is D and since Q units are ordered each time an order is placed, the total number of orders placed over the time period is

Number of orders placed $= N = D / Q$ ....(5.2)

Turning our attention to reorder costs, we recognise that they remain constant from one order to the next, irrespective of the number of units ordered each time. Let R denote the costs of placing one order. Total order costs would equal R times N:

Total order costs = cost per order × number of orders placed

$= R \times N = RD / Q$

Total order costs decrease as number of units ordered each time increases. This happens because with more units being ordered each time, the number of orders placed decreases. Total order costs are shown in Figure 5.2 also. Figure 5.2 shows that total holding costs increase as inventory increases and total order costs decrease as inventory increases. Combining these two costs shows that total inventory costs decrease up to a point with increases in inventory. Beyond this point - labeled Q* in Figure 5.2 - total inventory costs increase with increasing inventory. Let T denote total inventory costs, then

$T = HQ / 2 + RD / Q$ ....(5.3)

Point Q* in Figure 5.1 where T is minimised is given by[4]:

Q = root 2 RD / H ....(5.4)

By using equation 5.4, we can identify the number of units that should be ordered each time to minimise inventory costs. Bradford Mills, Inc. anticipates that demand for an item it stocks will be 300 units for the

4. Q* is obtained by differentiating T in Equation 5.3 with respect to Q, setting the derivative equal to zero and solving for Q.

coming year. It costs Rs 40 per unit annually to carry it in inventory. Order processing costs are Rs 15 per order. To summarise:

H = Rs 40

D = 300 units

R = Rs 15

How many units should Bradford order each time?

Q* = root 2 × Rs 15 × 300 / Rs 40 = 15 units

Bradford should place an order for 15 units each time. Using equation 5.3, we can calculate Bradford's total inventory carrying cost for these items:

T = HQ / 2 + RD / Q

= Rs 40 × Rs 15 / 2 + Rs 15 × 300 / Rs 15

= Rs 600 annually

Using equation 5.1, we find that Bradford's average inventory for this item is 15/2 = 7.5 units. Similarly, by using Equation 5.2 we can determine that Bradford has to place 300 / 15 = 20 orders for this item every year. Incidentally, any order quantity other than 15 units will result in total inventory carrying cost being higher than Rs 600 annually.

The EOQ model presented here, despite the assumptions involved, is a useful managerial device for gaining a perspective on inventory management.

Varying Demand and Safety Stocks

In the discussion of the EOQ model, it was assumed that demand is constant and known. In real life, demand is unknown and tends to vary over time, not being able to meet demand results in lost sales, which carries an opportunity cost. In addition, the inability to satisfy demand may create customer ill will. Finally, a firm that is out of stock may try to fill an order by special order. All of these stock-out and shortage situations add to inventory carrying costs. An intuitive way to handle unanticipated demand is to carry safety stock or inventory over and above the quantity determined by using the EOQ model. This situation is shown in Figure 5.4. The firm maintains X units in safety stock. Its average inventory is X + Q*/2 units. When unexpected demand depletes a portion Y of its safety stock, it orders Q* + Y units on the next order.

How does one determine the optimal level of safety stock to maintain? A balance has to be struck between safety stock carrying costs and the inventory shortage costs. Safety stock levels are dependent on lead times to delivery, the probability distribution of the demand for the item, and customer service level policies. In general, a rule of thumb that gives approximately correct answers is

S = 1.85 root LD ....(5.5)

where

S = safety stock in units

L = average lead time to delivery as a fraction of the time period

D = demand per time period

Assume that for the Bradford example given previously, the average lead time was 2 weeks or 2 / 52 Safety stock would be

S = 1.85 root LD

= 1.85 root 2 / 52 * 300 = 6.28 = 7 units

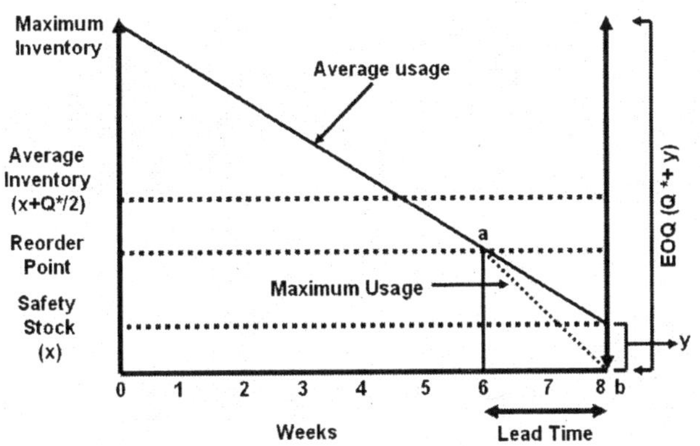

Figure 5.4: Inventory Pattern: Varying Demand

Spot Quiz on Inventory Management

1. In general, as inventory increases it is not feasible for total inventory holding costs to increase while inventory holding costs per unit remain constant. T ❑ F ❑

2. Reorder costs per order increase as number of units ordered each time increases. T ❑ F ❑

3. Inventory carrying costs can be minimised by carrying fewer units in inventory. T ❑ F ❑

4. For the Bradford example, placing 15 orders for 20 units each time will result in total inventory carrying costs of Rs 600 annually. T ❑ F ❑

5. One way to handle uncertain demand is to carry safety stock. T ❑ F ❑

Questions

1. Why is inventory management important?
2. Why would a firm want to maintain inventories?
3. What impact would the following factors have on a firm's inventories?
   a. Air freight rates are lowered and become competitive with trucking rates.
   b. A firm selling batteries as original equipment decides to sell them in the replacement market also.
   c. A raw material supplier increases discounts for quantity buying.
4. How would you characterize the difference between inventory holding costs and inventory carrying costs? Would decreasing one always result in decreasing the other one also?

Problems

1. Taxes Energy Resources Inc. is considering implementing the EOQ model for a new product. The anticipated demand is 800 units annually. Reorder costs are expected to be Rs 25 per order; the cost of holding the product in inventory is Rs 300 annually.

   a. Calculate the inventory carrying costs of ordering 10 units 80 times every year and ordering 20 units 40 times each year.

   b. Calculate the economic order quantity.

   c. Explain why the EOQ costs are lower than when either 10 or 20 units are ordered each time.

2. For the Bradford example given in this chapter, calculate the total inventory carrying cost when Bradford orders 6, 9, 12, 18, 21, and 24 units. Inventory carrying costs when 15 units are ordered each time are Rs 600 annually. Plot the inventory carrying costs with the associated various order lots. Explain why the costs are lowest with an order lot of 15 units.

3. Mankato General Corporation (MGC) wants to optimise its inventory management cost for a certain product it handles. It anticipates a demand of 10,000 units annually. Reorder costs are Rs 30 per order. The annual cost of holding the product is expected to be 25 per cent of the retail-selling price of Rs 40.

   a. Calculate the economic order quantity for the product. (Hint: Instead of equation 5.4, use the following equation):

      Q* = root 2 RD/FP

   where P = retail selling price of the item

   F = fraction of the retail selling price as holding cost

   b. Calculate the number of orders placed and average inventory.

   c. Calculate the number of units that Mankato should hold as safety stock if the average lead time to delivery is 5 weeks. What would happen to the size of the safety stock if average lead time to delivery were reduced to 3 weeks? Why?

4. Midwest Precision Control Corporation is trying to decide between two alternate order plans for its inventory of a certain item. Irrespective of the plan to be followed, demand for the item is expected to be 1,000 units annually. Under plan 1, Midwest would use a teletype for ordering; order costs would be Rs 40 per order. Inventory holding costs would be Rs 100 per unit per annum. Under plan 2, order costs would be Rs 30 per order and holding costs would remain the same. Which plan would result in the lowest total inventory carrying costs?

5. American Art Corporation is considering using airfreight rather than express to have one particular item shipped in. The annual demand is 600 units and the EOQ model indicates that 20 orders should be placed every year. Average lead time to delivery is 3 weeks with express delivery or 1 week with airfreight delivery. Inventory holding costs are Rs 100 per unit per year. What is the maximum amount of additional freight expense that American would be willing to incur to switch from express to airfreight?

6. Kemper & Johnson Ltd. has become the distributor for a new product. Anticipated demand in its marketing territory is 16,000 units annually. Kemper has estimated that order costs would be Rs 17 per order. Inventory holding costs would be Rs 47 per unit per year. Because the product is new and well received by its users, the manufacturer cannot fill an order from a distributor immediately. Consequently, the average lead-time to delivery is 6 weeks. Because of this large lead time to delivery, Kemper decided to maintain a safety stock in the item also. Calculate the total cost of carrying inventory and safety stock.

Answers to Spot Quizzes

Role of Inventories

1. Production economies of scale would take account of inventories. T ☑ F ☐

2. A retailer does not have a work-in-process inventory. T ☑ F ☐

3. Small inventories may not be desirable from an economic production lot viewpoint. T ☐ F ☑

4. A raw materials inventory is still necessary. T ☐ F ☑

Inventory Management

1. Total inventory holding costs are a function of number of units in inventory. T ☐ F ☑
2. Reorder costs per order remain fixed. T ☐ F ☑
3. Reorder costs may becomc very high. T ☐ F ☑
4. It is Rs 40 × 20/2 + Rs 15 × 300 / 20 = Rs 625. T ☐ F ☑
5. Safety stock serves to provide protection from the effects of uncertain demand. T ☑ F ☐

Calculating Expected Return

As in the case of accounts receivable, we will illustrate the calculation of expected return on inventory investment with an example. Southeastern Motors Inc., is a manufacturer of fractional horsepower electric motors used in hand tools, electric fans, appliances, and other similar applications, produced for stock according to a schedule jointly planned by the sales and production department.

Southeastern's sales totaled Rs 7.8 crore in 2003. In the past, inventories had been tightly controlled and were dictated to a considerable extent by production considerations. Inventory turnover in 2003 was 6.3 times, a figure considered quite good by industry standards. However, southeastern management had become increasingly concerned over sales lost due to stockouts of finished goods inventories. At year-end 2003, total inventories were Rs 800,000, of which Rs 200,000 was in finished goods.

Motivated by the problem of stock-outs, management initiated a study to determine whether finished goods inventories should be increased. From historical records of orders received and filled, management estimated that at the present inventory level, lost sales due to stock-outs were running at an annual rate of Rs 625,000. Since variable costs totaled about 60 per cent of sales, lost contribution amounted to about Rs 250,000.

The magnitude of the lost contribution figure convinced management that further study was necessary. Lost sales were estimated at four alternative levels of finished goods inventories, each of which represented an incremental increase over current levels. The results are listed in Table 5.2. The analysis showed that if finished goods inventories were increased from the current level of Rs 200,000 to Rs 278,000, lost sales would decline from Rs 625,000 to Rs 475,000 and an additional contribution of Rs 60,000 (last column in table 4) would be realised. Similarly, the additional contribution at inventory levels B, C, and D also was determined.

Table 5.2: Southeastern Motors Inc.: Lost Sales

(Thousands of Rupees)

Policy	Inventory level[a]	Lost sales	Lost contribution[b]	Incremental contribution
Current	200	625	250	-
A	278	475	190	60
B	414	303	121	69
C	620	153	61	60
D	868	63	25	36

[a] Finished goods inventory only.

[b] Variable costs equal 60 per cent of sales.

The next step in the analysis was to determine carrying costs at each inventory level. Carrying costs included warehousing, servicing, taxes, insurance, and record-keeping, and amounted to about 5 per cent of the value of the inventory. This figure excluded financing costs. Incremental operating profit was estimated as shown in Table 5.3 By moving to level A, carrying costs would increase by Rs 4,000. Subtracting this figure from incremental contribution Rs 60,000 gives a pretax increase in operating profit of Rs 56,000 after taxes.

Table 5.3: Southeastern Motors Inc.: Incremental Operating Profit

(Thousands of Rupees)

Policy	Inventory level	Carrying cost[a]	Incremental carrying cost	Incremental contribution[b]	Incremental operation profit	
					Before Tax	After Tax[c]
Current	200	10	-	-	-	-
A	278	14	4	60	56	28
B	414	21	7	69	62	31
C	620	31	10	60	50	25
D	868	43	12	36	24	12

[a] 5 per cent of inventory level.

[b] From Table 1.

[c] Taxes at 50 per cent.

From the data in tables 5.2 and 5.3, expected return on investment was calculated as in Table 5.4.

Table 5.4 Southeastern Motors Inc.: Expected Return on Investment in Additional Inventory

Policy	Inventory level (Thousand)	Incremental investment[a] (Thousands)	Incremental operating profit, after tax[b] (Thousands)	Incremental E(R) on investment after tax (Per cent)
Current	Rs 200	Rs -	Rs -	-
A	278	78	28	35.9
B	414	136	31	22.8
C	620	206	25	12.1
D	868	248	12	4.8

[a] out-of-pocket outlay.

[b] from Table 2.

To move from the current policy to level A, Southeastern must invest an additional Rs 78,000 in finished goods inventory.

We have identified the costs that vary and those that remain fixed as sales expand due to recovery of lost sales. The validity of the analysis depends on our ability correctly to identify fixed and variable costs in the range of sales in question.

We see from Table 5.4 that the incremental of marginal E(R) declines. As finished goods inventories are increased, each successive increment recaptures less lost sales and therefore less lost contribution. At levels A and B, E(R) appears to be quite attractive. Policy D, returning only 4.8 per cent after taxes, does not seem attractive. Which policy should Southeastern adopt? The answer depends on the target or required rate of return on investment in inventories. We will return to this topic in the final section in this chapter.

An important feature of the analysis above is that it examines the incremental return on successive increments of inventory. To move from the current policy to level D would require a total investment of Rs 668,000. This investment would generate additional operating profit of Rs 9600, an E(R) of 14.4 per cent. However, the E(R) on the last increment, from level C to level D, is only 4.8 per cent. By looking at several increments, we can better determine the point at which marginal E(R) falls below the required rate within increments; the figures in Table 5.4 represent averages. The marginal E(R) on the last rupee of investment in increment B is quite a bit lower than the average E(R), 22.8 per cent, on increment B as a whole.

Inventory Policy in Seasonal Firms

Inventory policy in a firm with a pronounced seasonal sales pattern usually involves some additional complicating factors. A major policy question in manufacturing firms with seasonal sales is whether to adopt a level or a seasonal production policy.

In such situations, production and inventory policy must be considered jointly. Level production results in savings in costs of setup, hiring, training, morale, productivity and related factors. Savings in these areas must be traded off against higher carrying costs due to the higher average inventory level under production.

The return on investment approach is applicable to inventory decisions in seasonal firms, but the analysis is more complex. The general approach is to analyse production and inventory costs under each policy alternative. Annual E (R) then is computed using the average investment in inventory over the year.

Inventory Management

Establishing the appropriate overall level of inventory investment is usually the primary responsibility of the finance manager. Day-to-day management of inventory is usually the responsibility of the production manager. Included in the production manager's responsibility is the determination of economic order quantities, safety stocks, and reorder points for every individual item stocked. In the case of finished goods, the sales department is likely to take a strong interest in levels of safety stocks. The production manager is also responsible for ordering, receiving, handling, storing, protecting, and issuing inventory. In most firms, inventory management comprises an important set of responsibilities indeed and is a topic on which volumes have been written.

The term 'inventory control' is often used to describe the responsibilities of the production manager with respect to inventories. For the past two decades, the application of computers has brought major advances to inventory management; sophisticated automated inventory control systems are now available that integrate many of the necessary functions including determination of EOQ and reorder points, automatic preparation of orders, generation of accounting entries, and compilation of management information.[6]

In most firms, policy formulation and inventory management involves an iterative process that goes on in a more or less continuous manner. Close cooperation is necessary between the financial manager and the production and sales managers. The financial manager's responsibility is a continuing one to evaluate and reevaluate the firm's aggregate investment in inventory to ensure that, at the margin, expected return on investment in inventory is acceptable.

---

6. See Richard I. Levin and Charles A. Kirkpatrick, Quantitative Approaches to Management, 3rd ed. (New York: McGraw-Hill, 1975), Chaps. 7 and 8, and the references cited therein.

The Required Return on Investment in Receivables and Inventory

From the perspective of the finance manager, our approach to the management of accounts receivable and inventory has centered on calculating expected return on investment at the margin. In each case, we identified policy alternatives, determined incremental investment and operating earnings, and calculated the marginal expected rate of return.

An important feature of our analysis was that we excluded financing costs. We considered only operating cash flows; hence, our resale was the expected operating return. We found in the case of both receivables and inventory that as the level of investment increases, marginal operating E(R) declines. In each case, we were left with the question of how far to expand. We noted that the optimum, that is, the point at which the value of the firm is maximised, lies at the point where marginal operating E(R) falls below the return necessary to compensate those who supply the funds for investment. This latter rate we referred to as the required rate of return.

What is the required rate of return? Is it the rate at which the firm can borrow? It is not, for the borrowing rate does not adequately account for the risk of investment in receivables and inventory. In the case of receivables, accounts obtained by loosening credit policy become progressively more risky. As policy becomes progressively looser, accounts become subject to an increasing probability of default. By the same token, cash flows associated with expansion of inventory are also uncertain. Recapture of lost sales is not guaranteed, and as inventory is expanded, the degree of uncertainty regarding such recaptures increases. We can conclude that, at the margin, the cash flows and therefore the expected return attributable to additional investment in receivables and inventory may be subject to considerably uncertainty.

How is the required rate of return related to risk? This is a question we will examine in depth later. There, we will find that lenders and investors are risk-averse and require compensation for both time and risk. The more risky the investment opportunity, the higher the return demanded by suppliers of funds. In other words, as risk increases, the required rate of return increases.

As the investment in accounts receivable and inventory is increased, two things happen. First, marginal E (R) falls. Second, risk increases, so the required rate of return increases. Determination of the marginal E (R) and the required rate of return (RRR) must be done for accounts receivable and inventory separately. Each will have its own marginal E (R) and RRR schedules and its own optimum.

In practice, determining the required rate of return is not easy. We know that it slopes upward from the rate on riskless investment, usually taken to be the rate on treasury obligations. One workable approach to determining the required rate is to categorize investments into risk classes. In the case of receivables, accounts might be classified as low, medium, and high risk, and a different required rate established for each. Similarly, this is also applicable to estimates of investment in inventory.

Just-in-Time Inventory Control

The just-in-time inventory control system is more than just an inventory control system. It is a production and management system. Under this system, not only is inventory cut down to a minimum but the time and physical distance between the various production operations is also reduced. In addition, management is willing to sacrifice costs to develop close relationships with suppliers to ensure speedy replenishment of inventory in the event of stock-out in return for being able to carry less safety stock.

The just-in-time inventory control system was originally developed in Japan by Taiichi Okno, a vice-president of Toyota. Originally, the system was called the "Kanban" system, after the cards placed in the parts bins, and used to call for a new supply. The idea behind the just-in-time system is that the firm should keep a minimum level of inventory on hand, relying on suppliers to furnish parts "just-in-time" for them to be assembled. This is in direct contrast to the traditional inventory philosophy of U.S. firms which is sometimes referred to as a "just-in-case" system which keeps healthy levels of safety stocks to ensure that production will not be interrupted. While large inventories may not be a bad idea when interest rates are low, but when interest rates are high, they become very costly.

While the just-in-time inventory system is intuitively appealing, it has not proven an easy system to implement. Long distance from suppliers, and plants that were constructed with too much space to store inventory and not enough doors and loading docks to get inventory into the plant quickly, have limited the successful implementation of this system. In addition, the firm's relationship with its suppliers has also been forced to change. Since the firm relies on its suppliers to immediately deliver high quality parts and materials, they must have a close long-term relationship with them. But in spite of the difficulties of implementation, many U.S. firms are committed to moving toward a just-in-time inventory system. By moving toward this system General Motors, for example, cut its inventory by 17 per cent between 1981 and 1984, saving the company hundreds of millions of dollars a year.

While the just-in-time system does not at first appear to bear much of a relationship to the EOQ model, it merely alters some of the assumptions of the EOQ model with respect to delivery time and ordering costs and draws out the implications. Actually it is just a new approach to the EOQ model, which tries to produce the lowest average level of inventory possible.

The just-in-time system attacks the average level of inventory equation, discussed earlier, in two places. First, by locating inventory supplies in convenient locations, laying out plants in such a way that it is inexpensive and easy to unload new inventory shipments, and computerising the inventory order system, the cost of ordering new inventory, O is reduced. Second, by developing a strong relationship with suppliers located in the same geographical area and setting up restocking strategies that cut time, the safety stock is also reduced. Thus, the philosophy behind the just-in-time inventory system is that the benefits associated with reducing inventory and delivery time cut to a bare minimum through adjustment in the EOQ model, will more than offset the costs associated with the increased possibility of stock-out.

Summary

The finance manager should view the expansion of accounts receivable and inventories as investment decisions, using value-maximisation as the conceptual framework. Receivables and inventories should be expanded to the point where the marginal expected return on additional investment equals the return required by suppliers of funds.

As in the case of receivables, the financial manager should be concerned with the return on investment in inventories. Inventories serve as buffers to de-couple the purchasing, production, and sales activities of the firm so that all do not have to proceed at the same rate and so that unexpected events are not disruptive. Such buffers are necessary because of transaction costs (friction losses) and uncertainty. As inventories are expanded, some costs rise and others decline. Rising costs (or carrying costs) include storage costs, servicing costs, and risk of loss in value. Declining costs include costs of ordering, production, and lost sales.

Inventory theory provides a framework for analysing inventory costs. The economic order quantity (EOQ) model deals with the trade-off between carrying costs and ordering costs. The control limit model deals with the trade-off between carrying costs and the cost of being out of required stocks. Minimizing the sum of all inventory costs leads to the point of maximum operating profit. As in the case of accounts receivable, the optimal inventory policy must consider not only operating profit, but also the return on investment. The expected return on incremental investment in inventory can be calculated by identifying the various elements of cost associated with different inventory levels, calculating incremental operating profit, and dividing by the required incremental investment.

The objective of both credit policy and inventory policy is to maximise the value of the firm. In both cases, the policy that accomplishes this objective lies at the point where marginal expected operating return falls below the return necessary to compensate suppliers of funds.

Appendix: Derivation of the Economic Order Quantity

The economic order quantity (EOQ) involves a trade-off between ordering (or setup) costs and carrying costs. A larger order quantity reduces the frequency of ordering and therefore total ordering costs go down, but increases the average inventory and therefore, carrying costs go up.

Let

Q = order quantity

R = usage per period

O = order cost per order

C = carrying cost per period

Assuming usage to be constant over each period, the average inventory is Q/2. Total carrying cost per period then is the average number of units times carrying cost per unit, or (Q/2) C.

The number of orders placed per period is total usage divided by units per order, or R/Q. Total ordering cost per period then is orders placed times cost per order, or (R/Q) O.

$T = CQ/2 + RD/Q$ ....(A1)

The optimal order size, Q* (600 Units), is that which minimizes total cost, T to determine Q*, we differentiate expression (A1) with respect to Q, set the result equal to zero, and solve for Q:

$dT/dQ = C/2 - RO/Q2$ ....(A2)

Setting (A2) equal to zero and solving for Q, we get

$C/2 - RO/Q2 = 0$ ....(A3)

$Q2 = 2RO/C$ ....(A4)

$Q^* = EOQ = \text{root } 2RO/C$ ....(A5)

Questions

1. Describe the functions of the three major types of inventory.
2. What are the principal costs of holding inventories?
3. What two questions does inventory theory intend to answer?
4. On what does the optimal size of the safety stock depend?
5. The function of the safety stock is to prevent stock-outs. Explain.
6. Considering inventory and receivables separately, the optimal level of investment is the point at which the expected operating profit is maximised. True or false? Explain.

Problems

1. Delta Electric Company is considering a request from Bill's Electronics for open account credit in the amount of Rs 1,000 (figured at Delta's selling price). Delta's gross margin on the particular merchandise to be purchased by Bill's is 17 per cent. Delta's salesperson expects Bill's to purchase Rs 5,000 of merchandise annually. On all sales, Delta will incur variable expenses of 2 per cent for the salesperson commissions and 1.5 per cent for warehousing.

   a. Calculate the Economic Order Quantity for the firm.

   b. What would be the total annual Inventory costs of the firm if it orders in this quantity?

2. The management of Bland Company is concerned about the seemingly large losses it has been experiencing in lost sales due to finished goods Inventory of Rs 150,000 and has estimated lost sales at Rs 525,000 per year. Variable costs have consistently remained at 75 per cent of sales, and Carrying Costs of Inventory (excluding financing costs) are 4 per cent annually.

   Assuming a tax rate of 48 per cent, an after-tax required rate of return of 15 per cent on investment in Inventory, and the projected figures shown below, determine the optimal level of Inventory for the company.

Policy	Inventory Level	Annual Lost Sales
Current	Rs 150,000	Rs 525,000
A	200,000	375,000
B	250,000	250,000
C	300,000	150,000
D	350,000	75,000
E	400,000	25,000
F	450,000	0

CHAPTER VI

Working Capital Management and Dividend Policy

Learning Objectives

- ❑ The importance of dividend policy in the overall financing policy of a firm
- ❑ The changing patterns of working capital financing of firms
- ❑ The impact of dividend policy on the value of the firm
- ❑ Mechanics of dividend payment
- ❑ The concept of stock dividends and stock splits and their impact on the firm's value

Chapter Organization

- The chapter starts with the increasing importance of internal financing in the firm's overall financing policy. The shift in the financing of working capital requirements from the external sources to the internal sources has been highlighted in the chapter.
- The theoretical argument of relevance/ irrelevance of dividends in the firm's valuation have been discussed briefly in the next section.
- The last section of the chapter takes up the mechanics of paying dividends. The concepts of stock dividends and stock splits have been illustrated along with their impact on the firm's value.

CHAPTER 6

Working Capital Management and Dividend Policy

Dividend policy is essentially a part of financing policy, as the amount of dividend a firm pays has a direct bearing on the internal funds generated by it. Higher the payout ratio, lower would be the proportion of internal funds in the total financing of the firm. The basic issue in the dividend policy is that of determination of the payout ratio that, in turn, depends on the total financing requirements of the firm. Myers and Majuf's famous 1984 'pecking order' hypothesis attempts to describe how firms raise capital. They hypothesize that firms are driven by information asymmetries and transaction costs to use internally generated capital first before turning to more expensive sources of financing. Once their internal sources are used, then firms will use debt (where the information asymmetry problem is less severe) first and then as a last resort-equity. The internal funds are preferred over the external funds for several reasons, including that of absence of floatation costs and information asymmetry in the real world situation, besides the fact that a new issue signals bad news to the market. Also the management's control does not get diluted in case of internal financing unlike the external financing, which entails an intrusion into management.

Contrary to the pecking order of financing observed for firms in advanced countries, those in the developing countries have traditionally been dependent more on the external sources of finance, with a significant share coming from the stock markets. In the developed countries like US, UK, Japan, Canada, et al., internal funds have on an average contributed to 2/3 of the average investments, historically. Equity and bonds have been below 10% of the total investments. As compared to this, external financing in the developing countries like India has been around 50% of the total investments. However, with the corporatisation of the Indian economy, and increasing competition in the business environment, the Indian firms have started becoming more and more cost conscious and consequently, they are focusing on internal funds for financing. Also, the other benefits associated with the funds generated internally have made internal funds the preferred source for financing in the Indian business environment, as can be seen from Table 6.1. As shown in the table, the retentions as a percentage of PAT have gone up significantly in the 1988-96 period as compared to 1972-80 period.

Table 6.1: Average Profit Retention Ratio for Indian firms

Years	Retained Profits as a % of PAT
1972-80	52.6
1980-88	62.9
1988-96	70.7

Source: CMIE database

There has been a noticeable shift in the patterns of financing of Indian companies. The importance of internal finances in the overall financing has increased gradually over the period of time as indicated in Table 6.2 & 6.3. The table shows the increase in the proportion of internal financing from 30.6% in the 1992-97 period to 34% in 1997-98 for select Indian firms in the sample. As the result, the proportion of external funds has gone down from 69.4% to 66%. This increased reliance on internal funds has been more evident in the case of small firms as compared to large firms. Table 6.3 summarises the sources of funds of firms in CMIE Prowess database over the 1990s. The figures in Table 6.3 reinforce the increased significance of internal sources of financing. As can be seen in the table, the percentage of internal funds in the sources of funds has gone up from 25.6% in 1992-94 period to 35.6% in 1998-2000. Even in case of the largest firms, who should ideally have the best access to equity and debt financing from the formal financial sector, this fraction went up from 30.9% to 50.5%. These figures suggest that over the 1990s, India's financial system has not been able to decouple investment opportunities from free cash flows.

Table 6.2: Sources and Uses of Funds for Select Indian Firms (Changing Patterns)

(In percentage)

	1992-97	1997-98
Sources of Funds		
Internal	30.6	34
Depreciation	12.3	16.3
Reserves & surplus	18.3	17.7
External	69.4	66
Paid up capital	4.8	1.6
Share Premium	20.7	6.6
Long term borrowings	12.6	24.4
Debentures	5.6	8.6
Bank borrowings for working capital	7.5	6.3
Fixed Deposits	0.5	1.3
Sundry creditors	9.6	9.3
Other current liabilities	8.0	7.9
Uses of Funds		
Gross Fixed assets	51.9	62.6
Inventories	11.4	8.4
Financial Investments	9.7	7.2
Other current assets	27.0	21.8

Source: CMIE database

Table 6.3: Sources of Funds for Indian Firms in 1990s

	All Firms			Large Firms		
	1992-94	1995-97	1998-2000	1992-94	1995-97	1998-2000
Internal sources	25.6	34.0	35.6	30.9	42.8	50.5
Capital markets	26.1	21.1	17.7	24.3	17.8	12.3
Banks	7.0	11.8	13.6	5.5	10.8	10.1

Source: Rajmani Rajan & Ajay Shah, "New Directions in Indian Financial Sector Policy", October 2003.

The internal funds as a percentage of GDP have consistently gone up for Indian firms over the past two decades as can be inferred from the data given in Table 6.4, below.

Table 6.4: Funding pattern of Indian corporate sector

(Percent of GDP)

Year	Internal funds	Gross Domestic Investment
1981-86	1.72	4.50
1986-91	2.28	4.38
1991-97	3.65	7.46

Source: CSO, National accounts statistics, various issues

The equity markets in developing countries until the mid-1980s generally suffered from the classical defects of bank-dominated economies, that is, shortage of equity capital, lack of liquidity, absence of foreign institutional investors, and lack of investor's confidence in the stock market. The pecking order of financing has traditionally been defied in such economies. Also, the dividend policy has not been an important consideration in the financing policy making. Traditionally, the Indian economy has been a bank dominated economy with commercial banks being the main source of working capital financing. A clear-cut compartmentalisation between the money market and capital market segments has been observed in the Indian economy, which has led to Development Financial Institutions (DFIs) focusing on the long-term financing needs of the Indian firms and commercial banks on the working capital financing.

Beginning with the decade of the 90s, there have been two noticeable developments that have made a profound impact on the financial policy making of Indian firms:

1. Emergence of universal banking system[1] wherein the dichotomy between DFIs and commercial banks has disappeared. Commercial banks today are providing even the long-term financial assistance normally the domain of the term lending institutions, and are active

1. A system in which the financial institutions provide a basket of financial services instead of concentrating on a few services only. Under such a regime, the dichotomy between the capital market and money market segment gets eroded, the players in both the segments being the same. Also, fee based services assume equal, if not more, importance in such an arrangement.

players in the capital markets. Also, these banks are focusing equally on the fee-based services along with the traditional fund based services. On the other hand, the erstwhile DFIs like IDBI, ICICI, etc., have started entering the commercial banking and retail banking segments that were hitherto the bastions of commercial banks.

Thus, beginning with the 1990s, the banks and financial institutions in India have not only increased the number of products in their basket but also, the clear-cut dichotomy that prevailed in their areas of operations has disappeared. Now, the commercial banks are not solely concentrating on the working capital financing as their product for the corporates, in fact almost all the commercial banks have become active capital market players with their separate capital market divisions. This shift in the lending patterns of commercial banks has been both the cause and the effect of reduction in the corporate working capital financing by commercial banks. This changing pattern of financing by banks has been accompanied by the increasing margins of firms as the result of the government's policies towards liberalisation and globalisation. The increased profit margin has resulted not only in the increased pay out of dividends but also in the increased surplus at the firms' level. The productive deployment of this surplus is the major concern for different Indian firms. These firms are using more and more of their internal surplus for their working capital financing needs as this not only saves the transactions cost that firms might have to pay in raising those funds from outside but also ensures the productive deployment of their surplus.

2. The decade of the 90s has been witness to increasing activism on part of investors. Today, Indian investors are much more assertive and conscious about value creation opportunities. Shareholders have access to multiple opportunities of investments and are thus no more indifferent as to the payment/non-payment of dividends. This increased assertiveness of the shareholders has forced the company management to focus on the possible options for value creation. The dividend policy these days has become very relevant and is being reckoned as an important determinant of firms' financing strategy.

Management of Dividends

Systematic actions by companies regarding dividends imply that firms have specific dividend policies. The financial manager should be capable of answering questions regarding why a dividend policy is needed, what factors influence dividend policy, and what alternatives exist for implementing a dividend policy. These and the related topics of stock dividends, stock splits, and stock repurchases are discussed in the following sections of the chapter.

Importance of Dividend Policy

Dividends, in the normal use of the word, refer to that portion of retained earnings that is paid to stockholders. Dividend policy refers to the policy or guidelines that management uses in establishing the portion of retained earnings that is to be paid in dividends. Given the managerial objective of share price maximisation, dividend policy becomes very important, assuming, of course, that investors show a preference for dividends over capital gains. Judging the importance of dividend policy requires consideration of various hypotheses on dividend policies. Some of these hypotheses are examined in the following paragraphs.

Residual Theory of Dividends

The residual theory of dividends states that policy decisions regarding dividends do not require active managerial deliberations. A firm that has desirable investment alternatives available will finance them with some combination of equity and debt. The residual theory argues that requirements for equity financing are met by retained earnings. Retained earnings in excess of equity-financing requirements, or residual retained earnings, are paid out in dividends. The theory implies that for rapidly growing firms with substantial equity-financing requirements, the dividend payout ratio should be zero. On the other hand, zero-growth firms should pay 100 per cent of retained earnings in dividends. This theory holds that dividend policy is a passive managerial policy. Evidence indicates that for a variety of reasons, firms may choose the paying of dividends even if they have large equity-financing requirements. The behaviour of firms indicates that financial managers do act as if dividend policy has an influence on share prices.

Irrelevance of Dividends

The second hypothesis advanced by Miller and Modigliani holds that dividends are irrelevant.[2] The irrelevance of dividends hypothesis states that investors are indifferent to the choice between dividends and retained earnings. This theory is based on the following assumptions:

1. Investors are rational with access to free information.

2. No transaction costs are involved in buying or selling securities.

3. Investors pay no taxes.

4. Investors have similar perceptions about the distribution of returns from investing in any given stock.

Given these assumptions, it is hard to argue that dividends are not irrelevant. Consider an investor who owns shares in two companies A and B, identical in all respects except that A does not pay dividends and B does. Company A meets all of its equity financing requirements through retained earnings. Company B meets a portion of its equity financing requirements through retained earnings and the rest is met through issuing new common stock at the current market price. The investor, who has just received his dividends, holds stock in B because it meets his investment requirements and, therefore, proceeds to buy B's newly issued common stock with his dividend income. According to the irrelevance hypothesis, B does not incur any costs in selling the new stock and the investor does not pay any taxes on his dividends. The net result is that the dividends that B paid are recycled back to B. After this recycling process has been completed, A and B become identical in all respects. The number of shares outstanding would vary but since the total asset base is identical, net income and total shareholder wealth would be identical also.[3]

---

2. Merton H. Miller and F. Modigliani, "Dividend Policy, Growth and the Valuation of Shares," Journal of Business, Vol. 34 (October 1961), pp. 411-433.

3. In this discussion, the phrase "equity-financing requirements" is used for illustrative purposes. Consistent with the irrelevance of dividends hypothesis is the view that leverage is irrelevant. Therefore, the firm is indifferent as to the choice between using equity or any other financing alternative.

Although the irrelevance of dividends hypothesis is plausible given the assumptions, the assumptions themselves are not. For example, typical securities transactions involve costs. At the very least, it is difficult for the firm to issue new stock at the current market price. Second, investors do pay taxes. Dividend income after taxes that is recycled to the firm is going to be less than the original dividends paid by the firm. Finally, it is not at all obvious that all investors have similar risk and return perceptions about a company.

Taxes on dividends are at the investor's marginal tax rate, whereas long-term capital gains are at a lower rate. As the marginal tax rate for the investor increases, his preference for capital gains over current dividend yield should increase. Two studies seem to support this notion. One study reports that payout ratios vary inversely with capital gains preferential tax treatment. When the difference between normal and capital gains taxes increases, dividend payout ratios decline and vice versa.[4] The results of yet another study indicate that dividend payout ratios vary inversely with investors' implied marginal tax rates. When investors' marginal tax rates go up, their preference appears to be for stocks with lower dividend payout ratios.[5]

The implication of the discussion is that firms may be able to influence share prices by following appropriate dividend policies. Two determinants of a dividend policy are the investment alternatives available to a firm and the capital gains/current yield preferences of its stockholders. Firms that have relatively few investment opportunities and face a slowdown in their growth rates would be better off with a high dividend payout ratio. Similarly, firms with proportionately more tax-exempt institutional stockholders may choose higher dividend payout ratios.

The behaviour of firms appears to be very consistent with the notion that a viable dividend policy is very important and that adjustment to dividend payouts needs to be made when circumstances indicate as such. Normally, high payouts are due to lower capital expenditure requirements.[6] Companies also appear to be responding to the dividend yield requirements of stockholders.[7] Overall, dividend policy appears to be a viable managerial device for increasing share price.

---

4. John A. Britain, Corporate Dividend Policy, Washington, D.C.: Brooking Institution, 1966
5. Edwin J. Elton, and M.J. Grubber, "Marginal Stockholder Rates and the Clientele Effect," Review of Economics and Statistics, Vol. 52 (February 1970), pp. 68-74.
6. "More and More Firms Boost Dividends", op. Cit., p.1.
7. Ibid., p.1.

Spot Quiz on Importance of Dividend Policy

1. Dividend policy refers to the rupee amount of dividends paid annually. T ❑ F ❑

2. The residual theory of dividends argues that retained earnings left after meeting equity financing requirements should be paid in dividends. T ❑ F ❑

3. The irrelevance of dividends hypothesis argues that it is immaterial whether firms pay dividends. T ❑ F ❑

4. The assumptions for the irrelevance of dividends hypothesis do not appear to be in keeping with reality. T ❑ F ❑

5. The investor's marginal tax rate has no implications for a dividend policy.

Factors Influencing Dividend Policy

Investment opportunities available to the firm have an influence on dividend policy as well as stockholder's requirements for capital gains versus current yield. These and other factors that influence dividend policy are examined in this section.

Investment Opportunities

Investment opportunities are important determinants of dividend policy. A firm that has desirable investment alternatives available and has the potential for above-normal growth will find it suitable to retain a portion of net income. This action allows the firm to utilise equity funds at a lower cost than by selling new common stock. In recent years, firms in the electronics, data processing, and fast food franchising industries have grown at an above-normal rate, and have followed a practice of maintaining a low dividend payout ratio.

A firm whose investment opportunities are limited does not have high financing requirements and may choose a high dividend payout ratio. Firms in the automobile, appliance, and chemical industries service mature, saturated markets. Their investment alternatives generally tend to be limited. Consequently, many of the firms in these industries maintain relatively high dividend payout ratios.

Stockholder Requirements

Taxes and demographic characteristics influence the investor's preference between capital gains and current yield. Stockholders in higher tax brackets would prefer to postpone current income for capital gains later on, which would be taxed at a lower rate. Stockholders in lower tax brackets would have a greater preference for current income. Similarly, stockholders in lower age brackets, who are just beginning to form households, would prefer capital gains over current income. Stockholders in higher age brackets would prefer current income and stability in dividends over long-term capital gains. Obviously, a firm cannot meet all of these requirements simultaneously. To some extent, investors are attracted to a firm because of its existing dividend policy. However, stockholders have been known to make their wishes known to management.

Restrictions in Loan Agreements

Dividend policy is also affected by restrictive clauses in loan agreements. Lenders prefer to specify sufficient restrictions in loan agreements with the idea of safeguarding their financial position. Generally, these restrictions require that a firm cannot pay dividends from earnings retained in the past. A firm may find that this restriction limits its ability to pay dividends even if it has sufficient cash to continue its existing dividend policy. Similar types of restrictions are also frequently utilised in new preferred stock issues. These restrictions may prevent a company from paying dividends on common stock until dividends on preferred stock have been paid.

Liquidity Requirements

The typical firm generates cash flows on a continuous basis. A growing firm will be able to invest its profits and depreciation shielded funds quickly. Thus, despite profits, a firm may not be in a liquid enough position to justify paying anything other than nominal dividends. A firm that is growing and has to expand its assets base would like to maintain a low dividend payout ratio.

Control

Big MNCs have shareholders who number in the crores. The dominant groups in these companies are in no danger of losing their control of the corporation when new common shares are issued. Dominant groups, wishing to retain their control, seek to do all equity financing internally. Therefore, where corporate control is an important consideration, the dividend payout ratio tends to be low.

Legal Requirements

Dividend policies are also affected by the legal requirements of the state in which the firm is incorporated. In general terms, state requirements call for dividends to be paid only when the firm's balance sheet shows positive retained earnings. Normal dividends cannot exceed accumulated retained earnings. Firms that are undergoing bankruptcy proceedings are also legally prevented from paying dividends. Finally, financial institutions, such as insurance companies and pension funds, are limited to a certain list of firms in which they can invest. A firm's dividend policy may be influenced by its desire to become eligible or remain eligible for this list.

Spot Quiz on Factors Influencing Dividend Policy

1. A firm with large financing needs may choose a lower dividend payout ratio. T ❑ F ❑
2. ABC Ltd. has large financing requirements. It also maintains a high dividend payout ratio. The implication is that ABC Ltd's management is fairly responsive to stockholder requirements. T ❑ F ❑
3. A firm with constant excess liquidity should consider raising its dividend payout ratio. T ❑ F ❑
4. A bankrupt firm can declare and pay a dividend. T ❑ F ❑
5. Loan agreements cannot influence dividend policy. T ❑ F ❑

Alternative Dividend Policies

A firm can follow one of a variety of dividend policies, which include stable Rupee dividend, stable payout ratio, and stable regular dividends supplemented with extra dividends. Stock repurchase may also be viewed as an alternative dividend policy. It is treated in a later section in the chapter.

Stable Rupee Dividends

A stable rupee dividends policy means that the firm is going to pay a fixed amount of dividends per share annually. This amount will remain fixed at a certain level until the firm's management is convinced that a permanent level of higher earnings per share justifies increasing dividends per share. A firm may see a number of benefits in pursuing a stable rupee dividends policy. First, investors value stable returns more highly than fluctuating returns. A dividend stream of Rs 1 annually may be valued more than a dividend stream that averages Rs 1 annually but varies from Rs 0.50 to Rs 1.50 in any given year. Maintaining stable dividends may lead to a higher market value for the firm's stock.

Second, an increase in dividends under a stable rupee dividends policy has the potential of providing a positive signal to stockholders. By increasing dividends, management is voicing its confidence in the firm's ability to sustain this higher level of dividends.

Third, financial institutions such as insurance companies and pension funds are limited in terms of what stocks they can buy. They can maintain equity positions only in companies on the legal lists. Among other requirements, a record of dividend payments is necessary for a company to be placed on the legal list. A firm wishing to enlarge the pool of potential stockholders may pursue a stable dividends policy to remain on or become eligible for legal lists.

Stable Payout Ratio

A firm maintaining a stable payout ratio policy would change its annual rupee dividends to conform to some pre-specified payout ratio. Change in earnings per share is generally followed by corresponding changes in dividends per share. This adjustment of dividends per share to fluctuations in earnings per share implies a stable payout ratio policy. A stable payout ratio policy may be suitable for firms whose earnings tend to fluctuate from one year to the next.

Stable Regular Dividends Supplemented with Extra Dividends

Some firms may choose to follow a combination of the two policies above. They are, in spirit, committed to maintaining stable dividends, which are supported by "normal" levels of earnings. However, in years when their profits are "abnormally" high, they pay an extra dividend over and above their stable, regular dividend. Legally, of course, there is no distinction between a regular dividend and an extra dividend. However, firms use this policy to tell the stockholders, "Look, we are committed to paying our regular dividends and we shall strive to continue to do so. This year we made extra profits, therefore, we are temporarily increasing the dividends and calling the increase extra dividends. However, you should not expect any extra dividends next year if profits are not at very high levels." These days, companies with super normal profits in a particular year resort to this dividend policy; in good years, it pays year-end extra dividends. This policy is well suited for firms in certain basic industries that are capable of sustaining normal profits most years. The automobile industry is an example. The industry is mature with replacement of automobiles accounting for a majority of sales. Barring labour strikes, automobile firms can count on some minimal level of profits. When the economy expands and car buying increases, profits are temporarily increased and extra dividends become desirable.

Spot Quiz on Alternative Dividend Policies

1. An increase in dividends for a firm following a stable rupee dividends policy reflects management's confidence in the firm. T ❑ F ❑

2. A firm with long-run declining profits but a stable rupee dividend will be able to fool stockholders about the firm's prospects. T ❑ F ❑

3. A firm with volatile earnings may find a stable payout ratio suitable. T ❑ F ❑
4. Regular dividends can be legally distinguished from extra dividends. T ❑ F ❑

Mechanics of Paying Dividends

Firms typically pay dividends annually. The firm is under no legal or contractual obligation to pay dividends. Dividends, when declared by the firm's board of directors, become a liabilitv and the firm is responsible for paying them.

Declaration Date

The declaration date indicates when the board of directors meet to declare dividend per common share. It should be kept in mind that the words 'regular' and 'interim' are used to impart a message to the stockholder. In a legal sense, they have no meaning.

Amount

The dividend notice also indicates the amount that shall be paid in dividends.

Holder of Record Date

The holder of record date indicates the data that will be used in determining the list of stockholders who receive dividends. Anyone holding stock on the holder of record date receives the dividends declared.

Ex-Dividend Date

The ex-dividend date does not show up in the dividend notice. The investor who buys stock today can hardly expect to have it registered in his name immediately. In stock buying and selling, the convention is to allow four business days for the transfer of title to the stock. If August 26 is the record date, four business days prior to August 26, i.e., August 22, would be the ex-dividend date. Anyone who bought stock on or after August 22 bought the stock ex-dividend and did not receive the dividends declared on the declaration date. Anyone who purchased the stock on the business day prior to August 22, was the holder of record on August 26, and received the dividend declared.

Payment Date

The dividend cheques/divident warrants are mailed to stockholders on the payment date.

Spot Quiz on Mechanics of Paying Dividends

1. A firm, by declaring a dividend, creates a liability. T ❑ F ❑

2. For a publicly-held firm, the holder of record date and ex-dividend date can be the same. T ❑ F ❑

3. A firm that mentions "quarterly" in its dividend notice is legally obligated to declare another dividend in the coming quarter. T ❑ F ❑

Stock Dividends and Stock Splits

In the previous sections, we have covered the situation of firms paying cash dividend on its common stock. Frequently, firms will declare stock dividends and stock splits. The topics of stock dividends and stock splits are covered in this section.

A stock dividend is the payment of dividends in stock. Malta Packing Company pays a 10 per cent stock dividend. This means that a stockholder holding 100 shares on the holder of record date will receive an additional 10 shares in Malta Packing.

A stock split is very similar to a stock dividend. The primary differences are in the percentage of new stock issues and in the accounting treatment. By accepted convention, any increase of less than 25 per cent in common stock outstanding is considered a stock dividend. Any increase equal to or in excess of 25 per cent of outstanding shares is viewed as a stock split. From an accounting viewpoint, retained earnings are capitalised when a stock dividend is paid, whereas in stock splits, the par value of the common stock is adjusted for the new shares outstanding. The example that follows will illustrate the difference between stock dividends and stock splits.

Marine Industrial Corporation has 10 crores, Rs 2 per common shares outstanding. The current market value of its common stock is Rs 60 per share. Its total net worth is Rs 370 crores. The existing equity portion of the balance sheet for Marine Industrial is shown in part (a) of Table 6.5. Marine Industrial issues to its stockholders one new common share for every four shares outstanding. For purposes of illustration, we can view this distribution either as a 25 per cent stock dividend or as a 5-for-4 stock split. If this distribution is viewed as a stock dividend, (1) the par value of Marine Industrial's common stock remains the same; (2) Marine is going to issue 2.5 crores new shares (25 per cent of 10 crores) with a total market value of Rs 150 crores (2.5 crores × Rs 60); (3) Rs 150 crores is going to be transferred from the retained earnings to common stock, with capital surplus accounts with 2.5 crores × Rs 2 or Rs 5 crores being transferred to the common stock account and the remainder Rs 150 - Rs 5 or Rs 145 crores going into the capital surplus account. The new equity structure for Marine is shown in part (b) of Table 6.5.

As the example indicates, retained earnings are capitalised when stock dividends are paid. Obviously, firms with small amounts of retained earnings cannot pay stock dividends.

Table 6.5: Marine Industrial Corporation: Accounting for Stock Dividends and Splits[a]
(in crores of rupees)

(a)	Equity section before adjustment, common stock (10 crores, Rs 2 par)	Rs.20.0
	Capital surplus	10.0
	Retained earnings	340.0
	Total equity	370.0

Contd..

(b)	Equity section after 25% stock dividend common stock (12.5 crores, Rs 2 par)	Rs.25.0
	Capital surplus	155.0
	Retained earnings	190.0
	Total equity	370.0
(c)	Equity section after 5-for-4 split, common stock (12.5 crores, Rs 1.60 par)	Rs 20.0
	Capital surplus	10.0
	Retained earnings	340.0
	Total equity	370.0

[a] The current market price of the common stock is Rs 60 a share.

In a stock split, the rupee amount of all accounts remains the same. The par value of the common stock is adjusted to reflect the total number of shares outstanding after the split. For Marine Industrial, par value of a share becomes Rs 20/12.5 = Rs 1.60. The equity section is shown in part (c) of Table 6.5. It should be noted that in stock dividends and stock splits, the total equity of stockholders remains unchanged.

Effect of Stock Dividends and Splits on Earnings and Prices

Since the firm has more shares outstanding, earning per share will decline due to a stock dividend or split. Earning per share after the stock dividend or split are given by

E (after) = E (before) / F

where, F is the ratio of shares outstanding after the stock dividend or split to the shares outstanding before. Assume that Marine Industrial's EPS was Rs 5 before the distribution of new shares. The ratio of shares outstanding after and before is 12.5/10 = 1.25. The E (after) would be Rs 5/1.25 = Rs 4. In theoretical terms, the market price of the common stocks should also decline to reflect this lower E (after). The price after the distribution of new stock is given by P (after)/F. For Marine P (after) is Rs 60/1.25 = Rs 48 a share.

In theory, stock dividends and splits do not create or represent any value for the stockholders. In real life, a number of benefits may be realised. Stock dividends and splits may signal to investors management's positive expectations of the firm. Next, lowering the market price of the common stock via a split may place the price in a more "popular" price range. Finally, stock dividends or splits may result in higher dividends for stockholders. For example, a firm that pays a 5 per cent stock dividend and maintains its dividends per share has, in fact, increased its dividends by 5 per cent. All of these factors may result in a higher market price solely due to a stock dividend or split.

Spot Quiz on Stock Dividends and Stock Splits

1. From a practice viewpoint, stock dividends and stock splits are similar.
   T ❑ F ❑

2. A 100 per cent stock dividend is equivalent to a 2 for 1 stock split.
   T ❑ F ❑

3. A 4 for 1 stock split will lower earnings per share by 25 per cent.
   T ❑ F ❑

4. A 50 per cent stock dividend creates value for the stockholder, because he ends up owning one more share for every two owned previously.
   T ❑ F ❑

Stock Repurchases

From time to time, firms repurchase their own common shares. A firm may repurchase its own stock for a variety of reasons. For example, stock may be repurchased to meet stock option needs; or, repurchased stock may be used to acquire another firm. In general, though, firms repurchase stock to retire them. Retiring stocks results in fewer shares outstanding.[8] Current total net income remains unaffected by the stock repurchase, and earnings per share increase because there are fewer shares outstanding after the repurchase. If the P/E ratio remains the same before and after the repurchase, the price of common stock will increase by a certain amount. This amount will constitute capital gains for the stockholders who did not sell their stock to the company.

If the firm had not selected the stock repurchase, it would have had excess cash that could have been paid to stockholders as an extra dividend.

8. Retired stock is also called treasury stock. Treasury stock is not entitled to share in dividends or in liquidation proceeding.

Therefore, stock repurchases are similar to paying extra dividends to stockholders. The major difference is that dividends are taxed at the investors' marginal tax rate, whereas capital gains are taxed at a lower rate.[9]

Effect of Stock Repurchase on Firm's Performance

A condensed balance sheet for Taxes Electronics Inc. is given in Table 6.6. Texas Electronics has total assets of Rs 130 crores, of which cash is Rs 14 crores. The firm has approximately Rs 10 crores in excess cash that can be either paid out in dividends or used to repurchase stock. The firm's current earnings per share aie Rs 1.20. It has 11 crores shares outstanding, currently selling for Rs 9 per share.

This firm has been advised that it can either pay a dividend of 90 paise per share to liquidate its excess cash or it can repurchase 1 crore of its outstanding shares at Rs 9.90 a share. In either situation, Texas Electronics will reduce its cash and its common equity account by Rs 9.9 crores.

Table 6.6: Texas Electronics Inc.: Balance Sheet, December 31, 1999

(in crores of rupees)

Cash	Rs 14.0	Current liabilities	Rs 35.0
Other current assets	76.0	Long-term debt	17.0
Total current assets	90.0	Total debt	52.0
Net plant	40.0	Common equity	78.0
Total assets	Rs 130.0	Total debt and equity	Rs 130.0

Total current earnings are Rs 1.20 × 11 = Rs 13.2 crores and current P/E ratio is Rs 9/Rs 1.20 = 7.5. It is assumed that the P/E ratio will remain the same after the repurchase. The effect of the repurchase on earnings per share and P/E ratio is summarised in Table 6.7. Earnings per share increase to Rs 1.32 after the repurchase. If it is assumed that the P/E ratio remains constant, the price of the stock after the repurchase will increase to Rs 9.90 per share. As a result of the Rs 9.9 crores cash outflow, the current ratio will decline and the leverage ratio will increase. However, these changes would also take place with 90 paise per share cash dividend.

9. Capital gains taxes are not paid unless the investor sells his stock.

As this example illustrates, under the repurchase plan the stockholder is left with stock worth Rs 9.90 after the share repurchase. If the firm decides to pay a cash dividend, the stockholder has common stock worth Rs 9.00 a share plus 90 paise per share in cash. The rupee amounts earned as dividend is taxable in the current tax year. The capital gain, provided it is sustained over time, is taxable at a lower tax rate in the year the stock is sold.

The similarity between a stock repurchase and a cash dividend is influenced by the repurchase price of Rs 9.90. Had the repurchase price been established at a price lower than Rs 9.90, the remaining stockholders would benefit at the expense of stockholders who sell their share to the firm. A repurchase price higher than Rs 9.90 would benefit the selling stockholders more. In fact, it could be argued that Rs 9.90 is the equilibrium repurchase price. Any repurchase price below the equilibrium price would not attract any sellers. Any repurchase price above the equilibrium price would attract all stockholders.

Table 6.7: Texas Electronics Inc.: Effect of Stock Repurchase

Item	Before repurchase	After repurchase
Total current earnings	Rs 13.2 crore	Rs 13.2 crore
Shares outstanding	11.0 crore	10.3 crore
Earnings per share	Rs 1.20	Rs 1.32
Price earnings ratio	7.50	7.50
Price	Rs 9.00	Rs 9.90
Current ratio[a]	2.57	2.29
Total debt to total assets[b]	40%	43%

[a] the before ratio is 90/35 = 2.57, and the after ratio is (90-9.9)/35=2.29

[b] The before ratio is 52/130 = 40%, and the after ratio is 52/(130-9.9) = 43%

The equilibrium repurchase price is given by

Equilibrium repurchase price = current price + equivalent amount if cash dividend is paid.

For Texas Electronics, the equilibrium repurchase price is Rs 9.00 + 0.90 or Rs 9.90 per share.

Advantages of Stock Repurchases

From the stockholder's viewpoint, the repurchase produces capital gains as opposed to current income. He also has a choice of selling or keeping his stock. With a cash dividend, the investor receives a dividend whether he wants it or not.

From the firm's viewpoint, stock repurchases reduce the firm's excess liquidity. Stock repurchases also allow the firm to adjust its capital structure very quickly. Repurchased stock can be reissued later on if the need arises.

Disadvantages of Stock Repurchases

Investors may prefer the stability of cash dividends rather than occasional stock repurchases by the firm. The investor may not be sure what impact the repurchase would have on his holdings. That is, all stockholders may not agree on what the repurchase price should be. Finally, it is not possible to repurchase stock on a quarterly basis to be a perfect substitute for cash dividends.

Overall, stock repurchases appear to be useful when used on those occasions when extraordinary accumulations of cash need to be disbursed or when the firm needs to adjust its leverage ratio upward.

1. Stock repurchases increase current earnings per share. T ❑ F ❑

2. Stock repurchases have no effect on the firm's financial structure. T ❑ F ❑

3. Stock repurchases increase return on total assets and total asset turnover. T ❑ F ❑

Summary

Dividend policy is essentially a part of financing policy as the amount of dividend a firm pays has a direct bearing on the internal funds generated by it. Higher the payout ratio, the lower would be the proportion of internal funds in the total financing of the firm. Contrary to the pecking order of financing observed for firms in advanced countries, those in the developing countries have traditionally been dependent more on the external sources of finance. However, over the past few years the funds generated internally have been the preferred source for financing the working capital requirements of the firms. This has brought to light the importance of an active and stable dividend policy.

Dividend policy refers to the policy or guidelines that management uses in establishing the portion of retained earnings that is to be paid in dividends. Given the managerial objective of share price maximisation, dividend policy becomes very important. The residual theory of dividends states that policy decisions regarding dividends do not require active managerial deliberations, and retained earnings in excess of equity-financing requirements are paid out in dividends. This theory holds that dividend policy is a passive managerial policy. The irrelevance hypothesis advanced by Miller and Modigliani states that investors are indifferent to the choice between dividends and retained earnings.

Investment opportunities available to the firm have an influence on dividend policy as well as stockholder's requirements for capital gains versus current yield. The key factors that affect the dividend policy are: possible investment opportunities, stockholders' expectations, restrictive covenants, firm's liquidity requirements, control or dilution thereof and legal requirements. A firm can follow one of a variety of dividend policies, which include stable Rupee dividend, stable payout ratio, and stable regular dividends supplemented with extra dividends. Stock repurchase may also be viewed as an alternative dividend policy.

A stock dividend is the payment of dividends in stock. A stock split is very similar to a stock dividend. The primary differences are in the percentage of new stock issues and in the accounting treatment. In theory, stock dividends and splits do not create or represent any value for the stockholders. In real life, a number of benefits may be realised. Stock dividends and splits may signal to investors, management's positive expectations of the firm. Lowering the market price of the common stock via a split may place the price in a more "popular" price range. Also, stock dividends or splits may result in higher dividends for stockholders.

Questions

1. What is meant by dividend policy? Do you think that it is important for a firm to have a dividend policy? Explain.

2. Explain what is meant by the residual theory of dividends. What implications does it hold for dividend policy?

3. On what assumptions is the irrelevance of dividends hypothesis based? Do these assumptions appear to be realistic? Why?

4. Briefly explain the various factors that have an influence on dividend policy.

5. Provide a description of various alternative dividend policies.

6. Which particular dividend policy would you recommend for the following firms? (Justify your answer by considering factors influencing dividend policies).

    a. An electric utility

    b. A food processor

    c. A soft drinks bottler

    d. A recreation vehicle manufacturer

    e. A bank

    f. A defence contractor

7. Describe the following terms:

    a. Declaration date

    b. Holder of record date

    c. Ex-dividend date

    d. Payment date

8. What are the similarities and differences between stock dividends and stock splits?

9. In theory, stock dividends and splits create no value for the stockholders. Why, then, should firms go through paying stock dividends and splitting stocks?

10. What similarities and dissimilarities do you see between a cash dividend and a stock repurchase?

11. What are the potential advantages and disadvantages of stock repurchase?

12. How is the repurchase price determined?

Problems

1. Miller Corporation and Gordon Corporation are in identical lines of business. Their financial structures are very similar. Selected data on earnings per share (EPS), dividends per share (DPS), and price/earnings (P/E) ratio are provided in the following table:

	Miller Corporation			Gordon Corporation		
Year	EPS	DPS	P/E	EPS	DPS	P/E
1991	Rs 2.10	Rs 1.05	8	Rs 2.10	Rs 1.10	8
1992	2.20	1.10	8	2.20	1.10	9
1993	2.35	1.20	8	2.32	1.10	9
1994	2.20	1.10	7	2.15	1.10	8
1995	3.00	1.50	7	2.97	1.40	8
1996	2.70	1.35	8	2.80	1.40	9
1997	2.60	1.30	9	2.65	1.40	9
1998	2.98	1.50	8	2.95	1.40	9

a. Calculate the dividend payout ratios for the two firms for the years 1991-1998. How would you characterise their dividend policies?

b. Calculate the compounded growth rates in earnings per share for the two firms for the time span 1991-1998.

c. Which firm appears to be performing better in the market?

d. What factor appears to account for the apparent difference in the market acceptance of the two firms?

2. In Spring 1999, Jerry Cohen, Financial vice-president of Data Electronics, met with a financial consultant. Cohen started by saying. "I am somewhat concerned with the manner in which the price of Data Electronics varies from one year to the next. At times we have wanted to push common stock prices. Furthermore, what really irritates me is that the stock of Boston Electronics consistently sells at a higher P/E ratio than ours. Sure, over the last few years our growth rate has slowed down. But so has Boston's. In addition, both firms

are similarly financed. What I am interested in finding out is why Data's common stock does not perform as well as Boston's." Selected data on Data Electronics and Boston Electronics are given in the following table.

	Data Electronics			Boston Electronics		
Year	EPS	DPS	P/E	EPS	DPS	P/E
1989	Rs 0.50	Rs 0.10	25	Rs 0.75	Rs 0.25	27
1990	0.60	0.15	15	0.90	0.25	19
1991	0.90	0.18	10	1.32	0.50	15
1992	1.10	0.22	10	1.65	0.50	22
1993	1.30	0.26	15	1.65	0.50	16
1994	1.40	0.28	10	2.07	0.50	10
1995	1.52	0.60	8	2.30	0.80	8
1996	1.40	0.60	7	2.20	0.80	8
1997	1.60	0.60	7	2.38	0.80	7
1998	1.70	0.60	6	2.55	0.80	7

a. Calculate the dividend payout ratios for Data Electronics and Boston Electronics for the years 1989-1998.

b. Calculate the compounded growth rates in earnings per share for the two firms over the 1989-1998 span.

c. Cohen stated that the growth rates for both firms had slowed down. Can you spot the year when the slowdown began? Calculate the growth rate for both firms for the time span characterised by the slower growth rate.

d. What factors appear to influence the different P/E ratios for the two firms? What would you suggest Cohen to do to improve Data Electronics P/E ratio?

3. Portions of the balance sheet for Hampton Industries are shown as follows:

Common stock, Rs 5 par	Rs 40,000,000
Capital surplus	10,000,000
Retained earnings	110,000,000
Total equity	Rs 160,000,000

The board of directors of Hampton Industries declares a 2-for-1 stock split. Prior to announcement of the stock split, Hampton was selling for Rs 32 a share with a price to earnings ratio of 8.

a. Show the accounting treatment for the stock split.

b. Calculate earnings per share after the stock has been split.

c. What effect will the stock split have on the market price of Hampton's common stock?

4. Jersey American Corporation, which has just declared a 4-for-1 stock split, has the following accounts:

Common stock, Re.1 par	Rs 1,000,000
Retained earnings	9,000,000
Total equity	Rs 10,000,000

Most recently, Jersey earned Rs 2.40 per common share, which is currently selling for Rs 48.

a. How are accounting entries affected by the stock split?

b. Calculate earnings per share and price of common stock after the ex-dividend data.

c. What is the maximum stock dividend that Jersey American would have been able to pay?

5. American Toy Company, having successfully marketed a new toy car that responds to voice commands, has excess cash on hand. The toy industry is very competitive and except for the routine bread and butter products, it is hard to successfully market an innovative toy. The management of American Toy, after deliberation, has decided to pay the excess cash to stockholders via either an extra cash dividend or a stock repurchase. The common stock of American Toy is currently selling for Rs 20 a share at five times earnings. The past earnings performance of American Toy has been somewhat erratic. Consequently, its stock has a tendency to fluctuate widely and appears to be of interest to high tax bracket investors who are willing to speculate on potential capital gains. If American decides to pay an

extra dividend, the amount would be Rs 1.20 a share. Establish the equilibrium repurchase price. Should American Toy pay the cash dividend or repurchase some of its common stock? What factors influenced your answer?

6. Montana Land properties Inc. recently sold a large piece of grazing land to a commercial developer who intends to develop a resort centre there. Montana Land's regular business is to raise cattle prior to selling them to feed lot operations. Management feels that the land sale was a very rare transaction which was not likely to occur again over the planning horizon. Montana Land, through operation in spot and future commodities markets, has been able to maintain a steady, if non-spectacular, financial profile. Total net income from normal business operations was Rs 5 crores. Extraordinary net income after taxes due to the land sale is Rs 3 crores.

   The sale of the land will have no material impact on the normal operations of Montana Land, and its normal earnings will not be affected by the land sale. Montana Land currently has 1 crore shares outstanding. The common stock is receiving Rs 4 per share annually in dividends and is selling for Rs 50 per share.

   a. If Montana Land decides to pay an extra cash dividend to completely deplete its extraordinary income, what would this amount to on a per share basis?

   b. Calculate the equilibrium repurchase price if Montana Land decides to deplete its extraordinary income by repurchasing its common stock.

   c. How many shares will Montana Land be able to repurchase? Calculate the earnings per share after the repurchase (base your calculations on normal earnings).

   d. After repurchase, what would the new dividends per share and dividend yield be if the total rupee amount of dividends is unchanged?

   e. What should Montana Land do with respect to the extra dividend or repurchase? Why?

Answers to Spot Quizzes

Importance of Dividend Policy

1. Dividend policy refers to managerial guidelines regarding paying dividends. T ☐ F ☑
2. Definitional. T ☑ F ☐
3. Under this hypothesis, dividend policy is irrelevant. T ☑ F ☐
4. There are taxes and transaction costs. T ☑ F ☐
5. The marginal tax rate influences requirements for dividends and capital gains. T ☐ F ☑

Factors Influencing Dividend Policy

1. It may choose to retain more to finance expansion. T ☑ F ☐
2. AT&T appears to be meeting stockholders' needs for current dividends. T ☑ F ☐
3. This is a viable alternative for reducing liquidity. T ☑ F ☐
4. It is prevented from declaring and paying a dividend. T ☐ F ☑
5. Loan agreements can include clauses related to dividends. T ☐ F ☑

Alternative Dividend Policies

1. Implies a "permanent" higher level of earnings. T ☑ F ☐
2. Declining profits with ultimately impair its ability to pay dividends. T ☐ F ☑
3. Some firms follow this dividend policy. T ☑ F ☐
4. There is no legal distinction. T ☐ F ☑

Mechanics of Paying Dividends

1. A dividend declared becomes a liability for the company. T ☑ F ❑
2. The ex-dividend date comes four business days before the holder of record date. T ❑ F ☑
3. There is no legal requirement to do this. T ❑ F ☑

Stock Dividends and Stock Splits

1. The effects are the same. T ☑ F ❑
2. Both result in doubling the number of shares outstanding. T ☑ F ❑
3. It will lower EPS by 75 percent. T ❑ F ☑
4. The price is adjusted accordingly. T ❑ F ☑

Stock Repurchase

1. There are fewer shares outstanding. T ☑ F ❑
2. They increase leverage. T ❑ F ☑
3. Repurchases reduce cash and therefore, the total asset base. T ☑ F ❑

Index